IN A LIBERAL TRADITION

Also by Victor Bonham-Carter

THE ENGLISH VILLAGE

DARTINGTON HALL (*with W. B. Curry*)

FARMING THE LAND

John Bonham-Carter (1788–1838)

IN A LIBERAL TRADITION

A SOCIAL BIOGRAPHY

1700–1950

By

VICTOR BONHAM-CARTER

CONSTABLE

LONDON

LONDON
PUBLISHED BY
Constable and Company, Ltd.
10-12 ORANGE STREET, W.C.2

INDIA
Orient Longmans Private Ltd.
BOMBAY CALCUTTA MADRAS

SOUTH *and* EAST AFRICA
Longmans, Green and Company Ltd.
CAPE TOWN NAIROBI

AUSTRALIA *and* NEW ZEALAND
Thomas C. Lothian Pty. Ltd.
SYDNEY ADELAIDE MELBOURNE
PERTH BRISBANE AUCKLAND (N.Z.)

First published 1960

PRINTED IN GREAT BRITAIN
BY R. & R. CLARK, LTD., EDINBURGH

TO MY MOTHER

AND TO THE MEMORY

OF MY FATHER

CONTENTS

ILLUSTRATIONS

DIAGRAMS

APPENDICES

INTRODUCTION

This book is not intended to be an ordinary family history, although it does contain a great deal of information about my father and his forebears. I have therefore tried to eliminate so far as possible matters of purely private interest, and have simplified the narrative wherever I could. None the less there is a certain residue essential for continuity and for the general guidance of the reader. It includes, for example, family pedigrees; but even these have been reduced to the bare bones.

My aim has been to draw upon original documents dating back to the 17th century, in order to describe the growth of a middle-class Dissenting family against a wider background of social history, and to illustrate a theme. This theme concerns an attitude or characteristic, which runs like a thread through the whole fabric of the family, and may be termed liberalism (with a small 'l') or liberal-mindedness. It is a hard word to define, and it would perhaps be misleading to restrict the definition to a single sentence, like an entry in a dictionary. It has, however, expressed itself quite clearly in at least one member of each generation and in various ways: in religion as Unitarianism; in politics as Whiggism and Liberalism; in professional life as devotion to the idea of public service; in society as common-sense humanity allied to strong individualism. Thus I regard the book as a 'social biography', for the subject is not the family as such, but that section of English society to which it has belonged, and its liberal tradition.

Part Two is devoted to my father, and for several good reasons. One is that he left me a personal memoir of some 40,000 words, also a complete journal of the four years when he was Governor of Malta 1936–40, and numerous letters and papers. Another—and by far the most important one—is that he personified the ideal of liberal character in public and private life.

Much of the value of this book derives from the fact that it is based on *original* documents—letters, journals, sketches, accounts, memoranda, and other unpublished material. I have been very fortunate in the manner in which I have been given access to all these records, or have otherwise received advice, and I wish to express my sincere thanks to all who have given me help.

The foundation document of Part One is a MS. entitled *Some Account of the Carter Family*. This was compiled over sixty years ago by A. T. Everitt, secretary of Pike, Spicer and Co., the family brewery in Portsmouth, assisted by my uncle Gerard who was then working in the firm. This MS. was expanded by my grandfather and eventually came into the possession of my cousin Sibella, who kindly passed it on to me, together with the main mass of family records and all her own valuable notes. I also received a trunk of early 19th-century letters and notebooks from my uncle, Sir Edgar Bonham-Carter. I am most grateful. For further information about the Carters and their connexion with Portsmouth, I am deeply indebted to Rev. J. R. Sturges, minister of the John Pounds Memorial Church (which stands on the site of the old High Street Unitarian Chapel); F. A. Emery Wallis of the Portsmouth Museums Society; A. Corney of the Cumberland House Museum; and A. E. Wadham, secretary of Brickwoods Ltd. (which absorbed Pike, Spicer and Co. in 1911). For information about Buriton, I wish to thank Mrs. A. L. Bonham-Carter, Rear-Admiral Sir S. S. and Lady Bonham-Carter, and George Legge. For information about Adhurst St. Mary and for the loan of many valuable documents, I wish to record my thanks to Mr. and Mrs. Alan Lubbock. I was likewise given much help by the Archivists of the County Borough of Southampton, the County of Hampshire, and the City of Winchester. My uncle, Sir Maurice Bonham-Carter, was good enough to lend me three boxes of letters written by and to my great-aunt Hilary, covering the period 1830–60; these had already been indexed and analysed by Miss Charlotte Toynbee, a most useful service. In the matter of Unitarianism

I turned to Rev. J. R. Sturges, E. H. Goodland, Rev. G. Randall Jones, and above all to Rev. H. Lismer Short, Warden of Manchester College, Oxford, without whose comprehensive knowledge and scholarship I could never have mastered this part of my task. Finally I have to thank Capt. A. Evelegh, R.N., and Miss Ella Giffard for permission to refer to a family memoir by Miss Mary Giffard.

Part Two is based in its entirety upon my father's MSS. and personal correspondence. But here again I received invaluable help in checking and expanding the material and in relating it to contemporary events. As follows:

The Headmaster and the Senior Master of Clifton College. Captain B. H. Liddell Hart, the distinguished military historian; and D. W. King, War Office Librarian. Sir Harry Luke, and Sir Edward Jackson, who both served terms as Lieutenant-Governor of Malta under my father. I have drawn heavily on Sir Harry Luke's authoritative book *Malta* (Harrap) and on his article 'Towards a Maltese Constitution' published in *The Round Table* in September 1958. John Birch, formerly Taunton Borough Librarian, now in charge of the City Library of Fremantle, Western Australia, who read through the entire MS. and checked a host of details.

I would also like to thank my mother and my wife, who gave me useful advice on many points of style and fact.

Other acknowledgments will be found in the body of the text.

Finally, it is my intention to deposit the bulk of these family documents in the Hampshire Record Office (with smaller depositions at Winchester and Portsmouth) for permanent preservation, with the provision that they be made available for research.

VICTOR BONHAM-CARTER

EAST ANSTEY,
NORTH DEVON,
September 1959

PART ONE

A NEW FAMILY

CHAPTER I

THE CARTERS OF PORTSMOUTH

APRIL 15th, 1797, was a day of extreme danger, one of the most critical in English history: comparable in its consequences to March 21st, 1918, the opening of the *Kaiserschlacht Michael*; or to one of the dying days of May 1940, when the British Army was trying to escape through Dunkirk. On that April day, one hundred and sixty years ago, a mutiny exploded among the ships of the Channel fleet stationed at Spithead. The extremity of the danger lay less in the disaffection, which had a reasonable cause, than in the place and timing of the outbreak. Here were terrible possibilities.

By 1797 England had been at war with revolutionary France for four years: a miserable period of military defeats abroad, and of constant fear at home lest the social order disrupt in blood and violence, as it had done in France. One stout bulwark, however, kept the enemy from these shores, and sustained the faith of the nation—the Navy. Six fleets blockaded the continental ports from Texel to Toulon, and prevented any concentration of hostile ships, superior in strength and capable of forcing a crossing of the Channel. Once the command of the Channel was lost, there was nothing to hinder invasion by an overwhelming force of seasoned and successful troops, led by Napoleon in person. But the Navy itself was in an evil state, and had long been so. The needs of the war had expanded the Service far beyond its normal reserve of manpower, and had caused the impressment of large numbers of unwilling landsmen, some of them the scourings of the gaols, others ordinary honest men. Pay and conditions, inadequate even by contemporary standards, had continued to deteriorate; administration was corrupt; and discipline was only maintained by a mixture of extreme harshness and the force of a few enlightened men.

Such was the background of events of April 15th, when the seamen of the flagship H.M.S. *London* suddenly refused to obey orders. Rushing into the shrouds, they gave three mighty cheers, a signal instantly answered by the other ships, and the whole fleet burst into mutiny. Delegates now came aboard the *London* to present their complaints to Admiral Colpoys. Their chief demands were for an increase of pay from 10d. to 1s. a day, the settlement of long-standing arrears, proper shore leave, and the suppression of 'Pursers' tricks' and other petty tyrannies. They did not ask for the abolition of flogging or even for better food, and they promised to return to orders should the French fleet come out, though it is doubtful whether they could have controlled events to that extent. The conference was a long one. So much so that some of the sailors waiting in boats for the return of their delegates became impatient, and tried to go on board themselves. They were immediately resisted by the officers, and three of them shot dead by a party of marines. This action so infuriated the crew of the *London* that they arrested the admiral and the captain and shut them into their cabins, where they remained in fear of their lives. The mutineers then asked the commander of Portsmouth garrison to be allowed to pass through the town in procession, in order to give a public funeral to their dead comrades and bury them in Kingston Churchyard. This request was abruptly refused, and the town batteries were manned against an attack from the fleet.

At this critical point, a figure appeared without whom the day would have ended in tragedy, and perhaps worse. An appeal was made to the mayor of Portsmouth, Sir John Carter, who proceeded to exercise immense tact and perseverance as intermediary and peace-maker. In the end he declared he would be personally responsible for public order, and so persuaded both sides to come to terms. This man was my great-great-grandfather, and his place in the story and theme of this book will duly be described.

An arrangement was made for the bodies of the dead sailors to be landed at the Common Hard at Portsea. There they were met by the ships' contingents who had disembarked at a different point, and had been led through Portsmouth by Sir John himself and his friend, Mr. Godwin. At Portsea the procession took up the coffins and made its way undisturbed to Kingston Church, accompanied by the two magistrates as before. So great was Sir John's influence over the sailors that they scrupulously respected his instructions, and even went so far as to lock up in a private house two of their men, who had taken too much liquor and were showing signs of becoming quarrelsome. At the end of the day some of the managing delegates came up to Sir John to tell him that everyone had returned safely on board, and to thank him for his great kindness. Sir John then took the opportunity of enquiring after the admiral, a conversation reported in the following terms:

'Do you know him, your Honour?'

'Yes, I have a great respect for him, and I hope you will not do him any harm.'

'No, by God, your Honour, he shall not be hurt.'

The promise was faithfully kept. The admiral, expecting every minute to be hanged at the yardarm, had put his affairs in order and made a new will, by which he left an annuity of £20 to each of the widows of the three dead sailors. The next morning, however, he was secretly brought ashore, escaping another boat sent in pursuit from H.M.S. *Mars*. He was then handed over to Sir John Carter who, at the sailors' request, rendered a formal receipt for his live body.

Soon afterwards the Admiralty decided to meet the men's demands, and the whole affair came to a peaceful conclusion. At the Nore, by contrast, a similar episode had a violent outcome, and the chief delegate of the men, Richard Parker, was hanged. But it was not the end for Sir John Carter. So strong was the fear of revolution and so prejudiced his political opponents that he was virulently abused, and secretly denounced to the Government as a Jacobin and a traitor to his country. But his friends and his actions spoke for him. The Home Secretary, the Duke of Portland, to whom the anonymous letter of denunciation had been sent, returned it to Sir John, assuring him of the confidence of the Government, and proposing an offer of award for the discovery of the offender. But Sir John would have none of it. At the same time Admiral Colpoys told the King that he owed his life to Sir John Carter, whose Whig principles had been misinterpreted, and that His Majesty had no more patriotic subject in the kingdom.

All this was not mere verbiage. The Admiralty at any rate had had good reason to distrust the Carters of Portsmouth, although their true patriotism had never been doubted. But in order to understand this political quarrel, we must first look into the origins, both of the Carters and of Portsmouth itself.

* * *

The name of Carter occurs in the registers of Portsmouth and Alverstoke as far back as the reign of Queen Elizabeth I. In the late 17th century one Roger Carter was described as a 'freemason': that is, a mason who had completed his apprenticeship and was admitted to full membership of the guild on payment of the sum of 2d. This seems to have been a standard charge, for Roger was later fined the same amount by the Court Leet for allowing a window of his new house in St. Thomas' Street to encroach upon the highway. Roger Carter was married three times, his second wife Sarah Ridge belonging to one of the leading merchant families of the town. Through her he advanced his interests in society and in business, and in 1673 he set up on his own as a master mason.

Roger's eldest surviving son was John, the first of four generations to bear that name.* John Carter I was only 17 when his father died in 1689, and he did not follow the family trade. Instead he was apprenticed as a shipwright, and is believed later

* See simplified pedigree on page 8.

to have become a timber merchant, supplying oak and other hardwoods for the construction of men-of-war.

By this time Portsmouth was growing in size and importance, and could fairly claim to have become the chief port and dockyard of the Navy. Formerly it had been only one of several south coast harbours; and at least until the 16th century was overshadowed by the Cinque Ports which commanded the Channel crossing to France. As early as 1212, however, King John ordered the Sheriff of Southampton:

> to cause our Docks at Portsmouth to be enclosed with a Good and Strong Wall in such manner as our beloved and faithful William Archdeacon of Taunton will tell you for the preservation of our Ships and Galleys: and likewise to cause penthouses to be made to the same Walls as the same Archdeacon will also tell you in which all our Ships' tackle may be safely kept, and use as much dispatch as you can in order that the same may be completed this summer lest in the ensuing winter our Ships and Galleys and their Rigging should incur any damage by your default and when we know the cost it shall be accounted to you.

Three hundred years later Portsmouth was declared a Garrison Town and a Royal Dockyard, having the first dry dock known to have been built in this country, and under Henry VIII was considerably raised in importance. There then followed a long lull until 1658, when Cromwell made some small extensions; but these were the beginnings of a regular programme of development over the next two hundred and fifty years. Records show, however, that even as late as the 1650s the dockyard was still extremely small. 'There was no mast house, no dry dock,* not above one hundred shipwrights and only one team of horses.' The earliest permanent dock is believed to have been constructed in Cromwell's time, while in Charles II's reign—thanks to the efforts of Samuel Pepys—the dockyard area was more than doubled.

None the less naval business and administration were very

* The original dry dock had not been replaced.

THE CARTER PEDIGREE

Roger Carter = Sarah Ridge, his second wife
died 1689
Freemason, Burgess of
Portsmouth Corporation

John Carter I = Mary White, daughter of James White, alderman, and prominent Dissenter
1672–1732
Shipwright and
Timber Merchant
Burgess of Portsmouth
Corporation

John Carter II = (1) Susanna Pike, daughter of William Pike, brewer. Her sister Ann married John Bonham.
(2) Mary Burford, his housekeeper
1715–94
Seven times Mayor
of Portsmouth
Leader of campaign
against the Admiralty

5 children, the eldest being

Sir John Carter = Dorothy Cuthbert
1741–1808
Nine times Mayor of Portsmouth
Knighted by George III in 1773
High Sheriff of Hampshire in 1784
Manager of Pike's Brewery
Intervened in the Spithead mutiny, 1797

6 children, the only son being

John Carter IV, who added the name Bonham in 1827, on inheriting the property of his cousin, Thomas Bonham of Petersfield, and so became

John Bonham-Carter I = Joanna Maria Smith, daughter of William Smith, M.P. for Norwich
1788–1838
M.P. for Portsmouth 1816–38
High Sheriff of Hampshire in 1829.

ill conducted, and continued so well into the 18th century. Soldiers of the garrison, as well as sailors, went for weeks without pay; and tradesmen, particularly bakers, commonly went bankrupt owing to the immense debts accumulated by the Admiralty: £12,000 or more being owed at any one time for provisions supplied by a single contractor. Likewise rope-makers, sawyers, and others constantly became mutinous owing to non-payment of wages, and were forced to find other jobs without notice. In the summer too it was a common thing for craftsmen to be absent, having 'gone into the country to make hay'. Thomas Middleton, Navy Commissioner, complained of the men being very unruly, and that he was obliged 'to carry a broad axe in one hand and a plane in the other to make all smooth'. Such was the turbulent Portsmouth where Roger and John Carter carried on their business; but there were sources of trouble other than Admiralty inefficiency and corruption.

The Civil War and its aftermath were still very much a reality even in 1700. This is illustrated by an anecdote about John Carter I, which may at least have a foundation of truth.

It is related that John, happening to be in London on the day that Queen Anne died, immediately set out for Portsmouth on foot, and arrived there at the end of three days. The town was as yet unaware that the Queen was dead, for John had outdistanced the mail coach: not a difficult feat since, owing to the ruinous state of the roads, vehicles were unable to travel faster than a slow walking pace, and were often delayed by accidents. John, therefore, was the first to announce the Queen's death and, it is presumed, the accession of the Elector of Hanover as George I—an unpalatable piece of news for the supporters of the Stuarts. Now it so happened that the Governor of Portsmouth was a Colonel Gibson, a Jacobite. The Colonel was so incensed by what he considered to be a seditious report put out by a Hanoverian partisan, that he immediately clapped the unfortunate John Carter into prison. And there John stayed until the mail coach came in with the official announcement a day or two later.

There is, however, another aspect to this tale, about which there is no doubt. Shortly before Queen Anne's death, moves were in progress to revive the extreme religious intolerance of the Stuart age. The Schism Act had actually been passed in 1714 to prohibit Dissenters from keeping and teaching in schools, in an attempt to force them all back inside the Established Church. In Tiverton, Devon, for example, and elsewhere new churches were being built with the sole purpose of accommodating these unwilling converts, and nothing it seemed could arrest this reactionary development. It was as much due to this as to the general fear of a Stuart revival * that the Whigs were actively preparing to defend the Protestant cause. Fortunately a second Civil War was prevented by the sudden death of the Queen, and soon afterwards these extreme religious restrictions were abandoned.

Now these events had a direct bearing upon the fortunes of the Carters, for in 1710 John Carter had married one Mary White, daughter of James White, an alderman of Portsmouth Borough and a prominent Presbyterian. It is presumed that John, born an Anglican, was converted by his wife, and that the Carters date their Nonconformity from this time. There is little doubt that this was a social rather than a religious move, and one which occurred quite often in the early years of the 18th century when trade and society were expanding. Ambitious young men married the daughters of rich Dissenters, turned Dissenter themselves, and soon dominated the congregations. We know that John Carter was a generous supporter of the first Presbyterian chapel built in Penny Street in 1691, and that he provided all the timber and deals at prime cost for its subsequent rebuilding in the High Street in 1718. The first minister known to have served this congregation was John Hickes, who was given refuge during the Monmouth Rebellion by the aged Lady Lisle, an act of mercy for which she was condemned to death by the infamous Judge Jeffreys.

* Despite the Act of Settlement, 1701, which fixed the succession on Sophia, Electress of Hanover, and her descendants—a measure passed by the Tories.

Hickes was executed at Glastonbury. The High Street chapel became intimately associated with the Carter family, at least until the middle of the 19th century, by which time it had adopted Unitarianism as its formal creed. Unfortunately it was utterly destroyed by bombing in 1940, together with many other historic buildings in Portsmouth, and virtually all the furniture and family relics have disappeared. Recently a new building has been put up on the site, and consecrated as the John Pounds Memorial Church, incorporating the two Unitarian congregations of the neighbourhood.

Since Unitarianism was to become a force in the lives of the Carters and their friends, and of other forebears of the Bonham-Carter family, it is necessary to define this term and grasp its historical significance.

In essence the term may be applied to anyone who believes in the single personality of God, in contrast to the orthodox doctrine of the Trinity. It follows that Unitarians also believe that Jesus Christ was not God, nor the Son of God, but a mortal man, imbued after His birth with the Divine Spirit, and exercised by Him to a degree not attained by any human being before or since. Although the word Unitarian was not used in England until the late 17th century, and not adopted to describe any formal organisation or creed until the late 18th, non-Trinitarian views of one kind or another had been expressed since the earliest days of the Christian Church, and condemned as heretical. With the Reformation Unitarianism (in this sense) again became a force, although it was by no means acceptable to the majority of Protestants. In England, as well as in the rest of Europe, the chief emphasis of the Reformation lay in the rejection of the dogmas and authority of the Church of Rome, in favour of a more primitive and personal Christianity as revealed in the Bible. But the very strength of Protestantism contained the elements of its own future weakness, in that freedom to interpret the message of the Bible resulted in a crop of competing creeds and sects, some as intolerant of each other as they were of Rome. The Church of England—itself a Protestant organisation though retaining much of its former Roman Catholic character and many of its usages—succeeded in disciplining religious life for a time, following the Acts of Supremacy and Uniformity of 1559, but it had to use force to do so. However, in the 17th century the Puritans, or absolute reformers, fused with the broad opposition to autocratic government, and this led to twenty years of civil disturbance. In 1660 there was a religious and social as well as a political Restoration, and a fierce reaction set in against Puritanism in all its forms. A new Act of Uniformity passed in 1662 demanded the acceptance of the Book of Common Prayer and of the authority of the bishops, or ejection from the Established Church. It was due to this Act that some 2000 ministers were deprived of their livings, and later penalised by a series of measures respecting the practice of Nonconformity and the rights of Dissenters. And it was from this body of men that the majority of Nonconformists (other than Methodists *) date their origin in England as organised sections of society.

The Presbyterians, to whom John and Mary Carter belonged, were 'moderate Dissenters', nearest related of all the sects to the Established Church. Although they had fought against Charles I, they were unwilling opponents and deeply lamented his death. They readily joined in recalling Charles II to the throne, and although subsequent events gave them cause for regret, their connexion with orthodoxy survived. With the revival of religious toleration and the growth of evangelical thought and behaviour among all sections of churchmen, they identified themselves as 'rational Dissenters': rejecting the emotional 'enthusiasm' of Evangelicalism, and subscribing to a common-sense philosophy of the kind influenced by John Locke (1632–1704) whose treatise *The Reasonableness of Christianity* argued for a complete re-examination of the gospels. Some of them were taken with the new Newtonian Cosmogony. Among their religious friends were the Lati-

* Methodism is the generic title given to the movement founded in the 18th century by John and Charles Wesley, about 100 years after the Act of 1662.

tudinarians of the Church of England; politically, they were Whigs.

It was this rational yet most human attitude, the attachment to moral values, and the complete toleration of other men and other views, that attracted a growing number of prominent people of intellect and integrity: scientists, scholars, teachers, merchants, and some of the new manufacturers. Among these was the pioneer chemist Joseph Priestley (1733–1804), the discoverer of oxygen, who began his adult life as an Independent minister and schoolmaster. It was Priestley who, when a tutor at the famous Warrington Academy, adopted the specific title 'Unitarian'; and applied it to all those who declared that nothing in religion should be accepted that was not consistent with reason, while fully maintaining their belief in God and in the humanity and uniqueness of Jesus. Not all the Presbyterians were willing to accept this label, thinking it insufficiently moderate. But leadership was already passing out of their hands, and in 1774 the first avowedly Unitarian congregation in England was founded by Theophilus Lindsey. It was these men and their followers who were to make corporate Unitarianism such a force in English life, although it always remained a minority movement. And it explains why Unitarians were so forward in the struggle for civil and religious liberty, for education, and for the broadening of social responsibility all through the 18th and 19th centuries.

* * *

This theme is strikingly illustrated by the Carter family, and by the part they played in the municipal affairs of Portsmouth. Despite the corruption of local government and the manifest failings of some of the Carters themselves, their record is none the less a remarkable one.

It will be remembered that John Carter I had married into the White family in 1710. His father-in-law was Alderman James White, a wealthy merchant and a Dissenter, and a member of the Whig faction in the Corporation, the controlling body of the town. Now there was a close link between local and national politics. At the General Election of 1714–15 the Whigs were returned to power in the House of Commons, the beginning of a long reign—first under Walpole, then under the Pelhams—which lasted until 1762, very nearly fifty years. This pattern was closely followed at Portsmouth, with the Whigs predominating among the burgesses and the aldermen who together constituted the Corporation. Since the two Members of Parliament representing the borough were also elected by this body, it is not difficult to appreciate the intimacy of the connexion in all its aspects. The two Members maintained their position to a large extent by bribery and a system of patronage, often in the form of contracts awarded by the Admiralty, itself open to pressure provided the right party was in power.

Sir Charles Wager, for example, was one of the M.P.s elected in 1714–15, and he kept his seat until 1734. During those years he held high office, and at one time or another was Comptroller and Treasurer of the Navy, and First Lord of the Admiralty. Although the Fleet was not on active service, this was a period of dockyard expansion and of other important construction, such as the building of the Royal Naval College in 1733. All this meant, in short, a great increase in trade for the builders, merchants, brewers, victuallers, and purveyors of Portsmouth. And there is little doubt that a proper share of the prosperity was enjoyed by the Carter and White families who, a few years later, cemented their relationship by joining in business partnership together. Certainly by the time he died in 1732 John Carter I had become a comparatively wealthy man.

But the Carter ascendancy did not begin yet. Although a burgess since 1682, John I never became an alderman, and so only enjoyed the fruits of power, never power itself. It was not until his son John II, elected a burgess a few months after his father's death, became an alderman in 1744 and mayor for the first time in 1747, that the Carters clearly took the lead in

Portsmouth. John II was mayor seven times altogether, and was the chief protagonist in a thirty-year struggle with the Admiralty—but first a word about the system of local government.

Most English towns of importance were governed according to an original constitution set up in the Middle Ages, but confirmed and extended under later sovereigns. In the case of Portsmouth the system in the 18th century was based upon a charter of Charles I, which provided for a mayor and a court of 12 aldermen, and an unspecified number of burgesses—'fit persons' of no real qualification, not even of residence. These burgesses varied in number—there were as many as 332 in 1681 and as few as 44 in 1781—and were elected by the aldermen, who in turn elected each other: thus producing a 'close or closed corporation'. Although the burgesses helped to elect two Members of Parliament and also chose the mayor annually from among the aldermen, the government of the town was really in the hands of the latter. Not only did they have charge of the general administration including the grant of licences, but they elected the burgesses, nominated the M.P.s, and appointed the justices from among their own number. A dominating personality among the aldermen, therefore, might well be able to dominate Portsmouth, and that is what happened after 1750.

John Carter II was a paradoxical character. He was a man of tremendous energy and persistence, who succeeded in all sincerity in combining the highest principles with extreme shrewdness, and at times an utter disregard for the rules. The portrait of him in middle age by Nathaniel Dance shows a solid, genial but determined gentleman, who must have actively enjoyed the faction campaigns in which he was engaged for most of his life. All the more so perhaps because, although he lost some of the earlier battles, he won the last one completely.

The opening encounter took place in 1749 with the publication of a lampoon entitled *The Geese in Disgrace*, in which the Corporation was accused of toadying to the Admiralty over the nomination of the M.P.s. Reference in this case was being made to Admiral Sir Edward Hawke, who had been elected both burgess and M.P. in 1747 and alderman in 1749; in return, it was inferred, for the trade he was bringing Portsmouth as a result of his successes over the French at sea and the establishment of a trading post in Newfoundland. Now this was but the last in a long sequence of events, for ever since the appointment of Sir Charles Wager as Comptroller of the Navy in 1714–15, the Admiralty had been nominating one or both of the Portsmouth M.P.s *as of right*: a practice in which the Corporation had acquiesced, for the aldermen and burgesses sitting together had always obediently voted for the nominees. In consequence no less than eight admirals had represented Portsmouth between 1721 and 1747, including the hero of Portobello, Admiral Vernon. Also high naval officers and functionaries were being enrolled as burgesses and even as aldermen as a matter of course. And so in this and other ways, such as the placing of contracts, it did seem that the Admiralty had a predominant say in the affairs of Portsmouth, and that the substance of the charges in *The Geese in Disgrace* was justified.

Now John Carter II took it upon himself to resist what he regarded as an encroachment upon the rights and privileges of the Corporation. As a private individual and citizen, he genuinely disliked any kind of bureaucratic interference by Whitehall, while politically he was also in opposition. But here the issue is confusing, for this was no clear-cut contest between Whig and Tory but between Whig and Whig. John Carter represented, at any rate in the beginning, the young progressive group, the self-styled patriotic party, who resented the red tape and corruption of the Admiralty; and regarded the latter merely as a vested interest of the reigning Whig Government which, after years of office, was spiritually dead. The Admiralty group or 'ministerialists' composed the old Whigs and after a time the remnant of the Tories as well. But the two sides can never be distinguished by politics alone. Alliances were made and broken for purely personal reasons all during the campaign, which resolved itself in the end into a struggle between the Carter faction and the rest.

In October 1750 John Carter took the initiative by calling a meeting* at his house in Thomas Street, at which no less than sixty-two new burgesses were elected, the majority of them 'patriotics'. Eighteen out of the sixty-two were children, including John Carter's own two sons—John III aged 8 and William aged 5. The ministerialists replied to this manoeuvre by threatening to withdraw the Navy contracts, thereby ruining the town. This move appeared to have some success for another admiral—Admiral Sir William Rowley—was elected M.P. in 1754, and he and Admiral Hawke represented Portsmouth together until 1761. About 1770 the fight flared up again, and the Corporation was attacked with all sorts of legal weapons, such as *Quo Warranto*, directed against its charter, and other actions aimed at its privileges. Finally in 1774 the Government party hit upon the 1750–1 elections as a likely point of attack. Information was brought against John Carter III (now Sir John Carter), who it will be remembered had been made a burgess when only a boy. This move was successful. The case was tried before Chief Justice Ashurst, and Sir John was ousted from his burgess-ship on the grounds that at the time of the election he had been too young to perform his duties. The seventeen other former minors went with him.

During the next six years the struggle continued unabated, but the ministerialists succeeded in ousting sixty of their opponents, losing only twenty-nine of their own party. In 1775 the borough was left with only five aldermen—John Carter II and his two relatives Thomas and William White on the one side, Philip Varlo and Edward Linzee on the other. Furthermore, between 1775 and 1780 no less than three mayors were ousted by *Mandamus*, including John Carter II himself in 1780. His successor, however, resigned almost at once, and the town was left without any mayor at all for four months. But

* Confirmed by a subsequent election held at the Guildhall on May 18th, 1751.

this was the culminating point of the contest. In the General Election which took place that year, Lieut.-General Robert Monckton, the Carter nominee, was returned with a large majority, while shortly afterwards Sir John Carter was restored to his privileges and elected mayor in 1782.

From that date onwards the Carter influence was paramount. The family controlled the parliamentary nominations almost without exception until the Reform Act of 1832, and was still predominant in municipal affairs long after the Municipal Corporations Act of 1835, which swept away the old order of urban government. Between 1747 and 1835 Carters were mayors of Portsmouth thirty-two times, while the thirty-five aldermen elected between 1778 and 1832 were *all* Carter nominees; likewise the majority of new burgesses. Many of them were relatives, or were connected by business or friendship. Such names as Atherley, Bonham, Cuthbert, Goodenough, Nightingale, Scott, Smith, Spicer, White. William Nightingale was the father of Florence Nightingale, and Samuel Smith was the son of William Smith, M.P. for Norwich, who both come later into the story.

All this was of course the most shameless nepotism for which in principle there was no excuse. In the context of the age, however, it is at least understandable, for there can hardly have been a single institution in England—Church, Law, or the various services of the State—where it was not the order of the day. Nor did it follow that government by private or sectional interests was necessarily inefficient or dishonest. The remarkable thing at Portsmouth, although not unique, was that the controlling interest was in the hands of the Dissenters, who were statutorily debarred from holding public office. The fact that they were able to engage in public life at all was due to certain modifications * of the law, granted them for their loyalty to the House of Hanover, and to the practice of 'occasional con-

* A ruling was made that if an unqualified person had held office for six months, he could not be challenged. Also a prosecution could only be made by complaint before a J.P., who could easily refuse to hear it—especially if he was himself a Dissenter!

John Carter (1715–1794)

Sir John Carter (1741–1808)

formity'. This term simply meant that a Dissenter had at least once to take sacrament in a church and obtain a certificate (for which he paid) stating that he had done so. Those who did this satisfied their consciences with the thought that it was a mere formality, observed under duress. Sometimes a memorandum to this effect would be handed to the officiating clergyman after the service, and both sides would be content. But for those who felt unable to follow this course, or otherwise comply, there were many trials. The City of London, for instance, profited for many years by a well-thought-out system of blackmail, which imposed a heavy fine upon any Dissenter elected to the office of sheriff, and who refused on grounds of conscience to take the oath. Over £15,000 was collected in this way, a sum that helped finance the building of the Mansion House.

At Portsmouth, and in a few other places such as Norwich, Bristol, Bridport, and Bridgwater, the Dissenters seemed to have taken matters into their own hands. There is a tradition that Sir John Carter, who was a firm supporter of the High Street Chapel, frequently heard services there during his nine mayoralties, accompanied by members of the Corporation in full state. In the old building destroyed in 1940, there was a socket in front of the gallery which accommodated the Mace on these occasions. At a later date the process was taken even further, for in 1817 the minister of the Chapel, Rev. Russell Scott,* was himself elected a burgess—eleven years before the repeal of the restraints upon Nonconformity.

The Carters certainly cannot avoid the charge of nepotism, for that was a plain inescapable fact. Their domination of Portsmouth through family influence must have been a record of its kind. So were they, with all their fine words and high principles, hypocrites as well? It is difficult to give a fair answer. Certainly, like all Dissenters, they were placed in a hypocritical position. They had to make the law and themselves look foolish, if they were not to submit to endless frustration and, at times, to real persecution. As men of strong character, with a

* Grandfather of C. P. Scott, editor of the *Manchester Guardian*.

long tradition of independence behind them, they were not the kind to stand for that. Indeed had they not acted as they did, it is unlikely that the battle for toleration and reform, which continued well into the 19th century, would have been won so roundly or so conclusively as it was.

That even old John Carter II, the greatest campaigner of them all, was a man of integrity, cannot really be doubted. Here for example are some sentences from a simple testament addressed to his children in 1761, when he had fallen ill and was expecting to die.

> As to the various Sects at present abounding in the World, the greatest part of them proceed upon very wrong principles, and by the placing of so much Stress upon the Peculiarities of their own Sect, lose the main point. The Sum of all Religion as far as I could comprehend it, is contained in these few Words: What doth the Lord thy God require of thee O Man but to DO JUSTLY, LOVE MERCY, AND WALK HUMBLY WITH THY GOD.
>
> You must judge for yourselves when you come to the years of discretion to what Church you will join yourselves for public worship. I have found most benefit and profit by attending the most moderate Dissenters, and I think their methods most likely to promote real rational Religion. Every one has a right to judge for himself in religious matters, because these matters concern a Man in the nearest point—I mean his everlasting happiness and are carried on between God and his own Soul. Civil Society may form laws to carry on the ends of Government, but no Man or Body of Men have any right to impose in matters of Religion, and whenever they do so they encroach upon the rights of Conscience, and tho' they may make many hypocrites, they cant force the mind to assent to what it does not believe; therefore all attempts of that kind are preposterous, arbitrary and absurd and should be opposed by every one who sincerely believes that Religion is not wholly external.

It was perhaps characteristic of the man that, soon after writing this, he completely recovered in health, survived his wife who died in 1769, married his housekeeper and had a second family, finally dying in harness at the ripe age of 78!

His son, Sir John Carter, was perhaps a less dogmatic person —after all he did not have to stand up to the Admiralty for thirty years—but he was just as firm and broad in his humanity, as we have already seen from the way he handled the Spithead mutiny. There was another instance of this quality. Once when a turbulent meeting involving Dissenters was being held in Portsmouth, Sir John deliberately spent the whole evening with the minister of the High Street Chapel, sitting in his house. He did this to establish an alibi, in case the minister should be accused of having been involved. Sir John was also a modest man. In 1801, at the age of 60, during the French invasion scare, he promptly presented himself to the Volunteers for service as a private. Five years later he refused a baronetcy offered him for political services by Charles James Fox. As to public record he was even more distinguished than his father: mayor of Portsmouth nine times, High Sheriff of Hampshire in 1784, and created a knight by George III on the occasion of a royal visit during his mayoralty.

In commerce he was equally successful. At the age of 25 he had entered the distilling trade. A few years later he became manager of the brewery belonging to his maternal grandfather, William Pike, another remarkable Dissenter. Pike had begun life as a humble apprentice cooper, and then made his own way as a brewer in Portsmouth, with substantial premises between Penny Street and High Street. When he died in 1777, his landed property in Hampshire, Sussex, and the Isle of Wight amounted to over 5000 acres and was worth £100,000, a large sum in those days, and all exclusive of the value of the brewery. This fortune was equally divided between William Pike's two daughters: Ann who married into the Bonham family of East and West Meon and Petersfield, and Susanna wife of John Carter II. As manager of the brewery, Sir John Carter received a salary of £400 per annum, lived in the attached house at 19 High Street, and also had a country place at Milton in Portsea.

19 High Street was an historic building, dating at least from Elizabethan times, and had once been a tavern called *The Antilope*, and a Victualling House. Thus it was that a considerable addition was made to the Carter possessions, to be yet further increased in 1826 when John IV, Sir John Carter's only son, came into the Bonham portion of the Pike inheritance; which was the cause of his joining the name Bonham to Carter. It is of some slight interest to note that the Pike brewery, renamed Pike, Spicer and Co. in 1849, remained in the hands of the Carter and Bonham-Carter families until 1911, when it was incorporated into the well-known firm of Brickwoods Ltd.

Sir John Carter, then, was fortunate in many ways. He was wealthy, able, humane, and a man of distinction in the public eye. He belonged in more senses than one to the later years of the 18th century, when the public conscience was beginning to stir, and when there was at least a prospect of reform. But it was to be left to his son to help transform that prospect into reality.

CHAPTER 2

JOHN BONHAM-CARTER

SUCH were the antecedents of the fourth John Carter, who became the first Bonham-Carter, and whose name stands at the head of this chapter. His life coincided far more aptly than his father's with the transition in temper and time from the 18th century to the 19th. Its short span of forty-nine years, 1788–1838, covered a succession of gigantic events which transformed the map of Europe and altered the whole framework of civilised society.

Born one year before the outbreak of the French Revolution, John was brought up in an atmosphere of national unrest. Almost all his boyhood and the whole of his youth were contemporary with the long war with France, and Waterloo was not fought until three months before his 27th birthday. By that time the old order in England was passing away. The Industrial Revolution had already made its mark in the midlands and the north. The ancient wool trade had deserted the southern counties, and traditional craftsmen of all kinds were fast losing their livelihood. The Farming Revolution had also begun. More and more food was needed for the growing towns, while little could be imported from Europe owing to the blockade. The countryside was in a state of turmoil. Enclosure was being forced through in the interests of better management and private gain, no less than $5\frac{1}{2}$ million acres in George III's reign alone. This meant that nearly all the open fields and much of the common land had to be fenced in and redistributed to those who could prove ownership. But since the peasants held only customary rights, not title deeds, most of them were deprived of all they had. There thus arose a mighty force of landless labourers, dependent entirely upon a pittance for wages, and soon falling into pauperism and degradation.

By 1820, when John Bonham-Carter was starting work as a barrister on the Western Circuit, there was formidable discontent all over the country—among unemployed craftsmen, dispossessed countrymen, and the turbulent new proletariat, many of them mere children, sweating in the slums and mills of the grim industrial towns. Such feelings found an outlet, naturally enough, in violence, in a general under-current of crime and in equally savage repression: above all in the smashing of machinery by the 'Luddites', the Peterloo massacre at Manchester, the rick burning and rioting of the 1830s, and the executions and transportations that followed. It was this heavy swell of savagery and frustration that finally swept away the anomalies of the past, and forced those long-overdue reforms with which John was concerned during the last ten years of his life. All this, however, was at the apex and end of his career.

At this birth, his sister Susanna Giffard remembered, there was great rejoicing, for an elder boy had died in infancy, and John was to be the only son in the family. She wrote:

> His baby manners were particularly engaging, but he was a small, delicate child. When he was about five years old, he met with a serious accident. Having gone with our Father on a Saturday evening to the hay-loft of a stable he then had in St. Thomas Street, he fell from a step ladder on the stones beneath, and received a blow on the front of his head, which in a grown-up person must have been a fracture. He was brought home in our Father's arms, became insensible and appeared to continue so till Monday morning, except that he held out his hand when desired to do so, to be bled twice on the back of it. But at that time he jumped up suddenly, and asked what day it was. On being told, he begged to have his clothes put on, saying 'I must go to school or I shall lose my place'. He was at the top of his class at a day school for little boys kept by Miss Whishaw. So great was his anxiety that he could not be pacified, till she had promised this

general rule should in his case be dispensed with. He was kept very low, and consequently much weakened by this accident. On another occasion he was so dejected at having lost his place that he hid himself behind the door in his Father's dressing-room, where he remained so long that the family were quite in alarm. His fondness for reading was extreme from the earliest age. He was more indulged by his Parents and every one about him than any child I can remember, yet it did not appear to spoil him. After he left Miss Whishaw, he used to go daily with some of his cousins to a Mr. Forester who kept the Grammar School in the town. They would go to the door of Dr. Walters' house, said to be haunted, and John was the one who dared to invoke the ghost with a 'come to me!'

In 1800, when John was 12 years old, he was sent to a boarding school at Cheshunt in Hertfordshire, kept by Rev. Eliezer Cogan, a Unitarian minister and a scholar of renown. This school was removed to Higham Hill, Walthamstow, in the following year, and was one of the best and most popular of all the Nonconformist academies, having more than sixty pupils. Several descriptions * have been published from which this account is mainly derived.

As regards the curriculum, the pupils 'read the best classical authors in both prose and poetry, whilst Latin and Greek composition always formed a part of the duties of the school'. Other subjects, however, were comparatively neglected. 'Feeble though conscientious attempts were made to teach a little geography and French; Goldsmith's *History of England* was read over regularly, from beginning to end, two or three times a year; and there was a drawing- and dancing- as well as music-master provided, as extras for those boys ordained to benefit thereby.' There was no provision for Military Exercises and Cold Bathing, items offered by rival schools, but games were encouraged, although not football.

* (1) *Those Eighty Years,* by Henry Solly. London, 1893. (2) 'Eliezer Cogan', by Alexander Gordon in the *Dictionary of National Biography*. (3) *Samuel Sharpe,* by P. W. Clayden. London, 1883. (4) *Life of Benjamin Disraeli,* by Moneypenny and Buckle. London, 1929.

But the best thing about Higham Hill was Dr. Cogan himself, who was an excellent teacher, and a wise and humane man. Extremely learned, he 'took a world of pains to keep his pupils abreast of the scholarship of the day'; and he saw to it that the school library had the latest publications. Methodical, punctual, conscientious, he was said 'never to have been absent from his duties in pursuit of pleasure'. Surprisingly enough, he was not a severe disciplinarian. 'He looked on the flogging system as equally useless and inhuman, arguing "You can never whip brains into a dull boy, and a clever boy will do better without, than with the whip".' Compare this with contemporary practice at Winchester College, the foremost Public School of England. A commoner who came to Winchester in 1800 said that on the day of his arrival there were 198 boys in the school, and 275 names reported for flogging! And Dr. Moberly, the famous Victorian headmaster, said that in his boyhood there might be twenty floggings a day, and all for slight offences.

The school was by no means restricted to Dissenters, but took in Anglicans and members of other creeds as well. This accounts no doubt for the presence of the most eminent of all its old boys, Benjamin Disraeli, who entered at 13 and stayed three or four years. As might be expected, young Disraeli was unorthodox in several senses, and Cogan said of him once, 'I dont like him. I never could get him to understand the subjunctive.' None the less he was popular with his companions, and entranced them at night with marvellous stories 'long after the one candle had been put out'. One other anecdote about Disraeli is worth recording, because it is so in character. 'The boys who were members of the Church of England had to walk some distance on Sundays to attend morning service, and it resulted from this that they fared rather badly at the midday dinner, which was usually half over by the time they got back. Disraeli himself was among the victims, so he solemnly threw out the suggestion that it might be as well if they all became Unitarians for the term of their life at school!'

John did not enjoy good health. In 1801 he caught a fever

at school, and had to be removed to his aunt's house at Shooter's Hill in Kent, in order to recuperate. The surprising thing is that he recovered as quickly as he did, in spite of the doctors. According to his father, the fever left him 'much reduced and very low, little appetite, neither Bark nor Asses milk forward him'; but he picked up in the end in his native air and surroundings at Portsmouth. He often visited his relations. Once he spent the Easter holiday at Woolwich with his eldest sister Ann, and her husband, Captain Henry Evelegh, who later rose to the rank of General. Ann related how she tried to make him acquainted with her neighbour, General Walton's son of the same age, and laughed at the uselessness of her effort when she saw them mute in the drawing-room. But after a time she perceived them mounted on two trees in their respective gardens, eyeing each other like birds, till at last John broke the ice with 'Do you ever fish?' 'Yes', was the reply, and down they both stepped and were off the whole day after trout, which was the beginning of a frequent companionship.

In October 1806, at the age of 18, he went up to Trinity College, Cambridge, the first of his family to do so. At that date Nonconformists were debarred from taking degrees at either university * although there was nothing to prevent John from pursuing his studies at Cambridge without graduating. In the event he decided to 'conform', and took first-class Honours with distinction, but this may not have been his original intention. At all events he came up against the religious difficulty soon after his arrival. In a letter to his old school friend, Frederick Pollock, later Attorney-General and Chief Baron of the Exchequer, he wrote:

> For my non-attendance at Sacrament I was shut out from Sizings † for the short time of fourteen days. With a premeditated speech I waited on the Master, who however was not visible. He was dressing, but he sent me a message begging I would trust my business to the Servant if not very particular.

* Until 1870. Oxford would not admit them, even for study.
† The right to order extra food from the College buttery.

I returned for answer and his gracious Mastership immediately expressed himself perfectly satisfied with my reasons (tho' none I had given) and reinstated me in my former rights.

Pollock was four years older than John, and Senior Wrangler in 1806. He seems, however, to have retained rooms in College until 1808 when they were taken over by John, who had previously been living in lodgings outside. A lively correspondence between the two men survives, and in returning some thirty letters to the Bonham-Carter family in the 1860s, Pollock said of John that 'he was more generally beloved than anyone I ever knew, and again he was the best school boy and the most popular man I ever met'.

Although they cover the whole of his time at Cambridge, these letters do not unfortunately reveal very much. Most of them are taken up with gossip about the dons, College 'shop', and familiar chatter between friends. John was also reading for the mathematical tripos, and there appears to have been a good deal of rivalry between Trinity and St. John's in this field. One plain fact does emerge. John had no Dissenting scruples whatever about liquor or ale or tobacco or cards or dancing or blood sports. As the son of a brewer, this is perhaps not so very surprising, but since Nonconformity is usually associated with temperance and similar things, it is of some interest. In one letter he wrote:

> I went to a ball at Hertford where I was introduced to Malthus, and was very happy at the introduction. Batten was there, but his wife on account of her increasing rotundity did not make her appearance. My time was spent in shooting, billiards, chess, backgammon and talking. Nor was it without improvement since by billiards I saw a little practical mechanics. When Saturday, the day I had fixed, arrived I silently passed it over, having determined in myself to stay till Monday—but on that day an engagement had been made for me to shoot pheasants and my resolution with not much difficulty gave way. Tuesday however I broke my bonds,

resisted the pressing invitations of my host and hostess and was deaf to the entreaties of many a fair one—and, O glorious victory, I returned to Cambridge.

In another letter to Pollock he was looking forward to a rubber of whist, and at Michaelmas 1808 he agreed to take over his stock of wines: '3 dozen and 1 bottles of Port, besides 4 bottles which I owe you, and 17 bottles of Sherry'.

John's career at Cambridge suffered only one serious interruption, when he had to return home to see to family affairs after the death of his father in May 1808. Sir John Carter had been ailing for some time, and in March of that year he made an expedition to Bath for a cure. From there he wrote the only surviving letter to his son, and it shows him to be as genial and kindly as ever.

Bath, 21 March 1808
7 The Grove

My dear Boy

I wrote you I was coming to this place where I arrived on Friday, should have been Thursday, but the weather was so severe that I brought up at Warminster. I bore the journey with very little fatigue and found a comfortable lodging provided by Mr. Temple—this place is remarkable full for the time of year. I could not bear a boarding house and therefore scarce can procure *means* to get little enough for myself and Richard,* who is everything but cook. I have not a Physician as they always make your bowels little more than an Apothecary's shop.

I took a gentle purge and began the waters this day with a small glass that sits easy on my stomach. I hope through the Almighty may be enabled to return in perfect health.

I wish to hear you got over your declamation to your satisfaction, as I know that if you do not succeed to your wishes it makes you uneasy (remember when you was at Miss Whishaw's and ran behind the door when you lost your place). Various reasons may prevent your always succeeding—our abilities may not be the same at all times. I am sure it will not be for want of application.

* Presumably his servant.

Therefore pray let me hear. Your welfare and happiness is next my heart and ever trust me. I have not a wish but that you should feel every confidence in me and believe me your best of friends. I found it in my Father most truely and be without reserve.

I am,
My dear John
Your affectionate father
JOHN CARTER

too late for the post
the 21st

* * *

Sir John Carter died at 19 High Street, Portsmouth, in May 1808. His death and all the business relating to his estate caused his son to miss the College examination that year, but John returned to Trinity for part of the Long Vacation and took over Pollock's rooms in Great Court. Two years later he obtained his degree and with distinction, finding himself listed—to his genuine surprise—as Fourth Wrangler. Trinity did well that year, having eight Wranglers, four in the first six, and all rejoiced that there was 'not a Johnian within the nine first'. Many of those who did well in the mathematical tripos in 1810 and in other years were close friends of John, and remained so afterwards: Pollock (already mentioned), Maule and Alderson who both became judges, Blomfield and Musgrave who became Bishop of London and Archbishop of York respectively, and Dicey, father of Albert Venn Dicey, Q.C., author of notable works on constitutional law, and who was to marry John's youngest daughter, Elinor, in 1872. The taking of his degree and his election as a Fellow of Trinity in 1811 involved John, as we have seen, in 'occasional conformity'; but this did not hinder him in his ambitions nor invalidate a perfectly reasonable attitude of conscientious compromise.

After leaving Cambridge, John decided to read for the Law, and entered at the Inner Temple. In 1812 he became a pupil of Bradley, a well-known Special Pleader, and in the following year was attached to Abbott, later Lord Tenterden, Chief Justice of the Common Pleas. Here he remained until 1816, by which time he had begun work as a Special Pleader on his own account. He went the Home Circuit with Abbott, now a judge, and in the spring of 1816 accompanied Mr. Justice Bayley as his marshal.

1816 was a memorable year for John Bonham-Carter, for two reasons. In September Sir Thomas Miller, one of the two M.P.s for Portsmouth, died, and John was elected unopposed in his place. On the following Christmas Day he was married in Little Parndon church, Essex, to Joanna Maria, fourth daughter of William Smith, City merchant and M.P. for Norwich.

John's election was, of course, a foregone conclusion. Family influence was still at its height, and the opposition candidate John Wilson Croker, then Secretary to the Admiralty, withdrew at an early stage when he realised how negligible his chances were. The election took place on October 9th in the Sessions Room, Portsmouth, under the presidency of the mayor, Edward Carter, John's cousin and brother-in-law. The candidate was proposed by Sir Henry White and seconded by Samuel Spicer, both aldermen of the borough and close family connexions. After a formal delay of one hour to allow any other candidate to be proposed, the mayor declared John to be duly elected.

So began John's twenty-one years representation of Portsmouth. And it might well have been thought on that October day by both friends and opponents that, however worthy his character, here once again was a safe party man. He would be of the same mould as his father and grandfather, opposed alike to autocracy and bureaucracy, and antagonistic to all privilege except (as some would cynically say) his own. He was in fact another Carter. How far John fulfilled these expectations will be described, but even in his formal speech of acceptance—reported in some detail in the *Hampshire Chronicle*—he gave strong hints of independence. Among the polished phrases, *de rigueur* on such occasions, we find some pretty straight statements.

What must we think of these men who

> Palter with us in a double sense,
> That keep the word of promise to our ear,
> And break it to our hope?

I mean, by putting into the mouth of a Sovreign in his opening address to Parliament, promises, faithful promises of economy and retrenchment, and who afterwards come down to the House of Commons with the proposal of I don't know how many millions to be lavished on sinecure placemen and useless pensioners, and I know not how many more to be appropriated to the keeping up of an unheard of and unneeded military establishment. (*Loud applause*). I must then lend my support, however feeble that support may be, to compel a different line of conduct, and to oppose measures fraught with mischief and certain calamity.

Apart from the reference to military expenditure, always a debatable issue after a war, this criticism was well aimed. Indeed it could hardly miss. On the one side were the brutal realities of dire poverty and starvation among the masses, who gained no profit from industrial wealth and few other benefits from the peace for which the country had waited so long. With wages down to a shilling a day, and bread costing a shilling a loaf, it was hardly a time for rejoicing. In some parishes, the poor rate exceeded 20s. in the pound, and literally everyone was drawing assistance except the squire who—since the entire rate had to come out of his pocket—often ended in bankruptcy as well. On the other side was the spectacle of the Prince Regent and his royal brothers, who between them cost the country not less than half a million pounds a year; quite apart from their fantastic accumulation of debts. On a slightly lower level was the example of Admiral Sir George Cockburn, a later Tory opponent of John Bonham-Carter, who blandly drew three salaries for his single post as a Lord of the Admiralty, and justified his action in the highest moral terms. And he was one among many.

Altogether John had to fight nine elections during his lifetime: in 1816, 1818, 1820, 1826, 1830, 1831, 1832, 1835, and 1837. In 1816 and 1820 he was partnered at Portsmouth by Admiral Markham, a Whig who like several others owed his start in politics to John's father, Sir John Carter. In 1818, however, Markham was surprisingly defeated by the Admiral Cockburn referred to, a strong supporter of the Government. The fact that Cockburn was able to detach a portion of the Whig majority in the Corporation was possibly due to the feeling that continued Opposition politics were doing harm to the town. At any rate this was the view protested by Rev. George Cuthbert, John's uncle, although none of the loyal Carters believed him for a moment, and bitter feelings were aroused. There were, however, other more substantial inducements, as reported by John in a letter to Joanna dated June 14th, 1818:

> I cannot yet tell what particular bribes have been offered, but I will give you one example. Cockburn sent a Captain in the Navy to Southampton to Capt. Thomas to say that if he could prevail on Mr. Atherley [a Carter relative] to stay away, he should have the command of a frigate now ready to be commissioned.

No other Tory candidate coming forward, John and Admiral Cockburn were elected together on June 17th. In reality it was a defeat, although only a temporary one, for the Carters, and they acknowledged it as such. It was said that Cockburn had assured the electors that although a Lord of the Admiralty he would be found an honest man! He courted popularity by giving several sums to charity and 20s. to each debtor confined in gaol. He also invited 700 guests to a supper and a ball. In Portsmouth little boys ran after him, and mobs drew his carriage round the town. John wrote:

> We however walk about with most undaunted parts and have carried off our defeat with the best possible grace. We were quite the great men at the dinner, and the Cuthberts and their set looked quite in the dumps. Old Bonham [his

cousin, Thomas Bonham] was quite satisfied with what I said, called me a good boy, said I could not have done better, and therefore he would pay all my expenses.

Thomas Bonham seems to have been a fairy godfather, not only to John but to the Whig cause at large. In the election which followed the death of George III in 1820, Markham turned the tables on Cockburn who thereupon petitioned against the result. The ruling committee, however, declared that the election had been valid. This led to litigation and eventually a case was brought in the King's Bench; but the final decision remained unaltered. Much of the legal work involved in this case was performed gratis by John himself, while the solicitors, Messrs. Adlington and Gregory of Bedford Row, also charged no fees. None the less costs amounted to more than £500, and these were almost certainly met by 'old Bonham'.

From 1826 onwards John was partnered by Francis Thornhill Baring who later rose to eminence as Joint Secretary of the Treasury, Chancellor of the Exchequer, and First Lord of the Admiralty; and was raised to the peerage as the first Lord Northbrook. The association of these two men in the great fight for the Reform Act of 1832, and for all the other reforming legislation of the 1830s, will be described later in these pages.

For the first ten years or so of his parliamentary career, there is but a very meagre record of John's activities. He was known to be diffident about speaking in the House, although he was an excellent committee man and was tireless in furthering the interests of his supporters, particularly Nonconformists and others who were still suffering minor persecutions. But there is a more fundamental explanation of his behaviour. The Whigs were still in opposition. With the exception of the Fox-Grenville Cabinet of 1806–7, they had been in the political wilderness since William Pitt first took office in 1783, and they would so remain until 1831. As yet there was no prospect whatever of their returning to power, and so there was little

High Street, Portsmouth (No. 19 is the house with the railings)

Copyright Country Li

Buriton Manor House

urgency or incentive for prolonged attendance at Westminster. Again, John was not a rich man. Although his father had been well off and had been paid a salary for looking after the Pike brewery, the management of this business was now in the hands of John's cousin, Edward. Likewise the Pike fortune and other inherited money had had to support his mother until her death in 1814, and was thereafter distributed between John and his five sisters. At the time of his marriage in 1816, his private income was little more than £600 a year, while his fees as a Special Pleader that year amounted to only £192: not a very large total with which to begin family life. It was essential therefore that he should make his way in his profession, and give it all the time and effort that he could afford. Happily he made an extremely successful marriage, and his wife Joanna was of the utmost assistance and comfort to him all during his life. Moreover the match received the approval of all parties from the outset.

John first made the acquaintance of the Smith family at Dr. Cogan's, where three of Joanna's brothers were educated. Walthamstow was not far from the Smiths' country home at Little Parndon, near Harlow, and for the same reason John was able to continue to go over there, when he was an undergraduate at Cambridge. Later, when reading for the Bar, he frequented their town house at Park Street, Westminster. By this date Joanna's father, William Smith, was generally acknowledged as the leading advocate for Dissenters of all denominations, and a man of republican views. He had been a Member of Parliament almost without break since 1784, most of the time for Norwich, and was now at long last beginning to reap the rewards of years of campaigning for seemingly hopeless causes. His amazing perseverance and his disregard of unpopularity were due to resources both of character and of material wealth. The Smiths had been Dissenters since the 17th century, and young William was reared on the principles of the Glorious Revolution of 1688. The family also owned a wholesale grocery business in Cannon Street and St. Swithin's Lane in the

City of London, which dated from before the Great Fire of 1666. It was the prosperity of this business that enabled William to spend so much of his life in public work, and helped him overcome the civil disabilities of his beliefs. Perhaps the most formative years were those spent in his father's house at Clapham, 'hitherto a quiet country village, but now beginning to attract a large population. Round the Common near which the Smiths lived, was a fringe of comfortable houses with large gardens of their own. To business men, Clapham offered a convenient country retreat, as it was only about five miles by road from the Common to the City, through the villages of Stockwell and Kennington, and over London Bridge.' * Prominent among the Smiths' neighbours was a group of families of Evangelical views, 'drawn together by ties of blood and friendship and a common outlook upon life'.* This was the so-called Clapham Sect, and included such men as Henry Thornton, the banker, Charles Grant, chairman of the East India Company, Zachary Macaulay, Granville Sharp, James Stephen, and William Wilberforce, who was the acknowledged leader of them all. William Smith was on intimate terms with several members of the Sect, particularly Thornton and Wilberforce, despite dogmatic differences; and it was to Wilberforce that he gave unfailing support all during the long campaign against slavery, and which ended in complete success. On other political questions they were often at variance, for Wilberforce supported Pitt while William inevitably was a friend of Fox.

In Parliament William spoke frequently and eloquently, and courageously too. In a speech made in 1790 in defence of Dr. Priestley,† when fear of the French Revolution caused a violent reaction against all kinds of religious and liberal opinion, he roundly declared that he too was a Unitarian Dissenter. In another debate in 1792 he said that as long as his name was

* Quoted from the unpublished biography of William Smith by Barbara Lady Stephen.

† See page 13. Priestley had his house and possessions destroyed by the mob for supporting the principles of the French Revolution.

William, he would stand up for his principles. Later he incurred the hostility of Robert Southey and Sir Walter Scott who hated all Whigs. But usually his opponents did not actively dislike him. They preferred rather to pour ridicule on him and his long speeches, as they did on most reformers.

> At length, when the candles burn low in their sockets,
> Up gets William Smith with both hands in his pockets,
> On a course of morality fearlessly enters,
> With all the opinions of all the Dissenters.

In private life William Smith was equally remarkable. He displayed none of that severity which we usually associate with paternal behaviour a hundred and fifty years ago. He had a fine family of thirteen, of whom five sons and five daughters survived into old age. In matters of health and learning they were all treated with exceptional good sense, affection, and even vision. For example, all the children were vaccinated against smallpox at a time when it was common to lose eight or nine out of a family of a dozen to this disease. The boys went to the best academies, while the girls received an education far in advance of the time. They were all encouraged to enlarge their minds in serious subjects and in gay, especially in the arts—painting, opera, ballet, theatre, and plenty of dancing. William Smith himself was passionately fond of pictures, and soon had a notable collection, making many purchases from French emigrés. He bought Rembrandt's *Mill* from the Duke of Orleans, and Reynolds' *Mrs. Siddons as the Tragic Muse* and Metsu's *The Sportsman's Visit* from Calonne, formerly Finance Minister to Louis XVI.

Besides these he had two other Rembrandts, several fine Cuyps, two Ruysdaels, landscapes by Claude and Nicholas Poussin, three subjects each by Vandyck and Rubens, and a representative selection by contemporary English painters such as Gainsborough, Stubbs, Wilson, and others.*

* Some of these pictures were sold later to meet election expenses, others after his death in 1835, when they fetched very low prices. One Rubens went for £25.

William also delighted in travelling, took his family all through the wilder parts of the British Isles, and to the Continent whenever the international situation permitted. He and his wife visited Paris in 1788, and saw the last Fête de St. Louis at Versailles that was ever held. He went back again after peace had been declared in 1802, taking some of the girls with him. They were piloted round the Louvre by Samuel Rogers, the poet and collector, and duly admired all the Italian loot. They saw Bonaparte review his troops before the Tuileries, and enjoyed all the entertainments they could until forced to leave in the following January, when war threatened again.

* When invasion seemed likely, Mrs. Smith retired to Ullswater with all her daughters and one of her sons, leaving London on a hot dusty day in August 1803. The main party travelled in the sociable; the groom and the maid in the gig, which must have been much more comfortable. 'At Elstree', noted Mrs. Smith, 'we met a little army of recruits to whom we gave some of Mr. Smith's addresses relative to invasion.' Joanna, now a lively girl of 12, sat on the box and handed them out. At Tapton near Sheffield, they paid a visit to the William Shores, whose son William had just inherited £100,000 from a Mr. Nightingale, an eccentric Derbyshire squire who had made a fortune in lead mining and other enterprises. This young William Shore later changed his name to Nightingale, and married Mrs. Smith's third daughter Frances (Fanny), to become the father of Florence Nightingale, a name that will recur later in this book. When the invasion scare was over, the family settled down at their country house at Little Parndon, and it is then that we begin to hear of Joanna more often. Although only 13 years old, she made a great impression at a ball given in the neighbourhood. 'Everybody admired Joey and her dancing', wrote one of her sisters. 'She looked uncommonly pretty and skipped away with so much life and spirit that the dullest caught new animation and imitated her capers.' Her partners on that occasion, however, were not

* The following paragraph is largely a quotation from the Stephen MS.

very exciting—a Miss Johnson (*sic*) described as being 'too much like a hop pole—a Mr. Towers, a sort of dasher—and Mr. Petre, a pretty little Boy about 6 years old.'

At this date—1803—John was still a schoolboy at Dr. Cogan's, paying his first visits to Little Parndon with Joanna's brothers. He and Joanna therefore got to know each other at a young age, and their acquaintance ripened all during John's youth at Cambridge and early manhood in London. They had to wait a long time to get married, however, until John was 28 and Joanna 25, and no doubt it was John's impecuniousness that prevented an earlier wedding. Certainly his father-in-law is unlikely to have made any difficulties, although he did sound a friendly warning when John accepted the invitation to stand for Portsmouth. To this John replied:

> Your kind letter has given me very great pleasure, although it begins with a query which has been to me the subject of much anxious consideration; and I cannot refrain from confessing to you that I still feel an occasional heartsinking when I look forward to the probable effect which an introduction to Parliament at this early period of my professional career will have on my future progress. In this place and to my friends here such a confession must never pass my lips—the present opportunity cannot be rejected.

He never regretted taking this step, and his success at Portsmouth may well have decided him to get married without further delay. In fact the wedding took place two months after the election, and was warmly welcomed by both families and their friends. Congratulatory letters came in from such minor celebrities as old Mrs. Barbauld, the poetess, and Mrs. Opie, the popular novelist and wife of John Opie, R.A. A tone of gruff humour was introduced by old Thomas Bonham who wrote:

> Petersfield
> Dec 22nd 1816
>
> MADAM,
>
> I had great pleasure in learning from *Him* that you are not fond of trinkets.

I hope you will not learn from *Him* that when we meet there is any cause why we may not shake hands as old friends.

I have the Honour to be,
Your most obedient humble Servant
THO. BONHAM

Addressed to
Miss Johanna Smith
or Mrs. Carter *as the case may be.*

The best surprise of all came from Joanna's eldest brother Ben, who was to succeed his father as M.P. for Norwich. Ben was then living as a bachelor at No. 16 Duke Street, Westminster, a charming house facing St. James Park, which was demolished later in the century to make way for the India Office. Ben gave the newly married couple both his house and furniture, and promptly sought a new house for himself elsewhere. It was a most generous gesture, and John and Joanna made No. 16 their home for several years, before moving a few doors up the street to No. 21.

For the next decade it was a tale of hard work and hard-earned fees, balancing the budget of a steadily increasing family. Of ten children born between 1817 and 1837, eight survived childhood—four boys (John, Alfred, Henry, Hugh) and four girls (Hilary, Frances, Alice, Elinor).* Four of these and another boy Thomas, who died young, were born before 1826 when the whole outlook was transformed by the inheritance from Thomas Bonham. John was perfectly aware of his expectations, but publicly declared he would make himself independent of 'old Bonham's' intentions before he should be 40, and this he certainly succeeded in doing. None the less it was hard going. In a letter dated November 19th, 1816, the day of Prince Charlotte's funeral, he wrote: 'I have been all day working in my Chambers alone—not a Client on this day of mourning'. And that was not the only occasion. When Hopkins, the family solicitor, dined with him in London at

* See simplified pedigree on page 131.

this period, he was accorded with: 'I don't know what you do with yourself in the evenings, but I always work'.

As a Special Pleader, whose job it was to draft the pleadings, he never earned as much as £300 a year, but in January 1819 he was finally called to the Bar and began practising as a fully qualified barrister. In that year his earnings jumped to over £750, and thereafter they rose almost without a break until 1826 when they totalled just under £1850. In the following year he retired from active legal work. There is no doubt that he was an exceptionally able advocate, and would have earned large sums had he continued in his profession. A complete table of his income is set out in Appendix A.

In March 1819 he went on circuit for the first time as a barrister. He travelled down to the Assizes at Winchester, and reported to Joanna:

> I have briefs for all kinds of crimes. One, stealing in a house. Two, burglary. Three, manslaughter. Four, stealing a lamb. Five, a most horrible murder. Besides that, five causes on the civil side, and George Atherley's* forgery not yet reckoned. I have got through two of my causes and one of my prosecutions, and they tell me that I managed my prosecution well. Of my causes, one went off in nothing. In the other I had the misery of seeing my client, a poor man, lose the day and so I have returned him his fee.

He added later:

> I then prosecuted George Atherley's prisoner for uttering the forged note. The man was convicted, and will I believe be executed. Then came on the prosecution against a woman for burning her house at Milford. It was a bad case and she ought to have been tried for a capital offence—but for some reason, she was only tried for a lesser offence. Old Missing and Mr. Wickham defended her and she got off from an insufficiency in the indictment, which was not drawn by me, or under my inspection. It was said that her house was *adjoining to* other houses whereas it was only *near* others. . . .

* His first cousin, a banker at Southampton: see page 33.

He earned 32 guineas at Winchester and felt he had made a promising start. He admitted to being nervous and had hardly slept at all the night before the murder trial. But he took the utmost care with his briefs, and was supported by two particular colleagues—Blomfield, who read over his cases for him, and Tyndale who was full of wit and information. All three, it seemed, travelled together; either riding their own horses or, more likely on this occasion, in a post-chaise with one of them sitting outside on the box. Nor was entertainment lacking:

> In the course of our travels we are constantly exposed to the visits and goodfellowship of any of our brother pilgrims, who may chance to come to the same caravanserai—Tyndale and I were very anxious to keep ourselves to ourselves—but the veteran Blomfield would not suffer us to run counter to the established practices of the circuit, and so at each resting place we have always had a party. There is one gentleman who is accompanied by his wife, Mr. Wilde of Guildford Street, but it does not do. It is not considered in good taste, and, as I set up for a man of the purest taste, you may easily draw the proper conclusion.

In this fashion they travelled the Western Circuit together, John sending to Joanna regular accounts of their progress, with illuminating comments on the principal towns, the society, and the business.

Lyme Regis he described as a 'beautiful place, but lodgings are extremely dear during the season—far above our price, and it is represented to me as a dressy, tittle tattling, scandalising watering place; so I think your summer thoughts must not turn this way'. At Launceston he found no briefs and saw no prospect of any. At Bodmin, however, there was a great deal of business arising out of the prosecution of the Grampound voters for taking bribes, and of Sir Manasseh Lopes for giving them. Soon afterwards John went on to Bath, and then returned home by coach. So ended his first circuit.

Although John went the circuit every year until 1827, his personal records are intermittent, and there is a complete gap during the years 1824–5–6. Much of the matter that has survived is trivial and repetitive, as it often is in private correspondence. None the less there are flashes here and there that reveal the kind of man he was—his conscientiousness, industry, and toughness—and also throw light on the manners and customs of the day. In July 1820, for example, he wrote again from Winchester, where he had a large number of briefs in both the civil and criminal courts. The journey down had not been a great success. He had started by coach from Piccadilly, sitting on an outside seat, and had been completely soaked by rain by the time he arrived at Guildford. So he left the coach and posted on to Winchester by Farnham and Alton, arriving at 7 p.m. There he found an important letter waiting for him on which he had to pay 2s. 8d. surcharge, even though it was addressed to a M.P. who normally had the privilege of free postage. At Exeter he reported: 'One Cause I was in began yesterday at 11, lasted till 8 last night, began at 8 this morning and did not finish till half past 5. Fagging work I can assure you.' From Bodmin he made the whole journey to Wells (over 120 miles) by gig, and it took him three and a half days. Two years later he made an identical trip on horseback with a friend. The horses were sent to Ashburton, and from there the two men rode together via Exeter to Cullompton. The next day they did the remainder of the journey to Wells, 46 miles, without any difficulty. 'My mare', he said, 'has performed her part very satisfactorily. We rode 19 miles to Taunton to breakfast, then 16 to Pipers Inn to dinner, and in the evening did the remaining 11 miles. I found three briefs on my arrival which put me in excellent spirits and I played whist till 12 o'clock, and am now in high feather with no feeling of fatigue, ready for anything this morning.'

In August 1821 Joanna brought the family down to the West Country for their holidays, and John joined them after circuit business was over. Joanna was delighted with the cathedral at Wells. 'I never was so pleased with anything before of that description. It was the large market day and the town looked so gay and agreeable and picturesque, that we have taken notes of the rents of different houses in the Close.' She did not like Bridgwater. 'The "George" though comfortable inside was very gloomy so we gladly left it soon after 9, with four horses for Minehead. One stage of 26 miles. As this was supposed to be our adieu to civilisation, we bought a little provision for mind and body, Devon and Somerset Guides and Map, Chocolate and Rice. I had a very conversible stroll with a young lady on Sunday evening. From her account I should guess that the politics of Bridgwater were strongly Whiggish. The Coronation gentry ball was only attended by six couples. There was a gentlemen's dinner but it seemed that by the wine they drank they were made rather unfit to appear in the ball room.'

A final entry of interest is taken from the summer circuit of 1823, when John prosecuted the men who had committed a great robbery of all Lady Caroline Damer's plate at Milton Abbey in Dorset. The men tried were an uncle, two brothers, and an accomplice. One of the brothers had lived sixteen years with the family as footman. John said: 'We were of course very anxious to convict the footman, and all were found guilty. The Judge seems anxious to hang them all.'

* * *

We now come to John's great change of fortune—his inheritance from Thomas Bonham, and the foundation of the Bonham-Carter family proper.

Thomas Bonham died peacefully at the Castle House, Petersfield, on December 15th, 1826. He was 72, not a very great age, but his gruff stilted manner and old-fashioned bachelor habits had earned him the epithet of 'old', at least since middle age. His gruffness too was deceptive. Although he often barked and occasionally bit hard, he had a warm heart, and his generosity has already been remarked. The Bonhams were an ancient family originating in Wiltshire, where they were known to be lords of the manor of Great Wishford in the

13th century. A farm and a chapel still bear their name adjoining what is now the National Trust estate at Stourhead. Later the family established itself in other counties, in Essex for example, and Hampshire. The Hampshire Bonhams settled at Warnford in the early 17th century in the person of an earlier Thomas Bonham, who was steward to the lord of the manor. In due course this Thomas purchased 1000 acres for himself at Warnford and, through his wife, acquired other property at the Meons and near Petersfield, becoming a substantial proprietor in his own right. The landed interest continued, and was strengthened by his grandson John, the husband of Ann Pike, whose sister Susanna married John Carter II, the girls inheriting a large fortune in cash and real estate from their father, William Pike.* John and Ann Bonham had a modest family, two daughters and two sons, Henry and Thomas, neither of whom ever married. The line thus came to an end with the death of Thomas in 1826.

Henry Bonham died in his fifties in 1800, but before then he and Thomas lived together for many years at the Castle House, Petersfield, which their father had acquired from the Jolliffe family in 1749. Several stories have been handed down about the old brothers, and a few facts. Both were members of the renowned Hambledon Cricket Club, and served terms as secretary and joint steward. Henry filled the latter position for five seasons between 1774 and 1795, always with Rev. Charles 'Squire' Powlett, the leading patron and supporter of the game. Henry also played in one match in 1778 against Surrey at Laleham Burway, scoring 4 and 9; there is no evidence that Thomas ever played. Possibly it was they who arranged the boys' match, Hambledon versus Petersfield and Buriton, which took place on a rainy day in August 1781. But the club served several purposes besides cricket. Practice day was usually on Tuesday, when the members also met for convivial purposes. Songs were sung, and large quantities of port, sherry, claret, and punch were drunk—the wine being bought by the hogs-head

* See pages 21-22.

from Winchester. Bets were also arranged—£500 a side on the best of three matches. Unhappily, membership fell away in the 1790s owing to the discouragement of the French war and to the rival attractions of the Marylebone Cricket Club in London. The club minutes closed on September 21st, 1796, with the entry 'No Gentlemen'.

These convivial habits were of course current among gentlemen at that time. At home the Bonhams had a strict routine, dining every day at 5 and sitting over their port till 10, at which hour the old butler convoyed them up the broad shallow staircase to bed, walking close behind with outspread hands lest they should lurch too far out of course. They were a hospitable pair and had two regular guests, a Colonel King and Rev. Whicher, rector of Petersfield. Parson Whicher used to shoot over the Bonham lands and dined with the other three every day except Sunday. But they thought him rather mean because, although he would send them some of the bag, he always kept the woodcock (of which they were all very fond) for his own Sunday dinner. The Bonham cook took particular umbrage at this and at his behaviour generally, expressing her feelings in an ode which began:

> You be Prince of Hells,
> 'Tis here you lives and dwells,
> You goes about and finds things out,
> And then comes here and tells.

Both Henry and Thomas did their duties as citizens, as magistrates and in other ways. Surprisingly enough—for they were pacifically minded and loathed the French war—they both served in the local Volunteer unit, the Petersfield Infantry, of which Thomas was Captain and Commander. Since most of the Volunteers were friends and neighbours, this post placed him occasionally in a quandary. For instance, he was inclined to be a martinet, as amateur soldiers often are, and it hurt his notions of discipline that people should blow their noses on parade, a thing that frequently happened in damp weather.

On the other hand he did not quite know how to put a stop to this practice without giving offence, for clearly a man could not swear violently at his neighbours if he wished to retain their goodwill. So he made a little plot with his brother. Henry was to blow his nose ostentatiously at the next muster and receive the outpourings of the Captain's wrath. The plot took effect. Harry Bonham blew his nose like a trumpet, and the Captain reacted to this impropriety with such variety and energy of language that the whole company took it to heart, and observed perfect decorum on that important point throughout the rest of their training.

A military connexion of a rather different kind was the presence in Petersfield of a number of French officers, who were out on parole from Porchester Castle. These gentlemen had been taken prisoner in the early part of the war, which had opened in February 1793, and some of them were entertained at Castle House where there was an excellent library containing many French volumes. Henry was himself a fair scholar, and judging by the letters he received from some of his guests after repatriation, his gesture was much appreciated. He also made them small loans from time to time, and may well have persuaded Parson Whicher to relinquish a woodcock or two when the Frenchmen came to dinner. More important he wrote a letter to the French Commissioner in London attesting the good behaviour of the prisoners, and this it seems was used to good effect in negotiating their exchange with the British authorities.

Not all the Frenchmen were well behaved, however, for the records contain two small hand-written cards, presented no doubt by the local constable, and which bear the following message:

> Pardonnez moi C'est de mon devoir de vous dire qu'il ne faut pas promener par ici C'est de mon devoir d'arrêter quique soit qui a sur lui quelque instrument dont on se sert pour attraper des Poissons des Phaisans des Perdrix ou des Lièvres.

> La Loi ordonne que la Personne qui sera arrêté ou il payera sur le champ cinq livres Sterling ou il sera mis dans quelque prison.

The Castle House was a large imposing mansion * of historic interest in the market square at Petersfield. It had extensive gardens and stables, and is thought originally to have been an inn, perhaps the chief hostelry in the town. It may therefore have been the subject of an entry by Samuel Pepys in his Diary of May 1st, 1661, which reads:

> Up early, and bated at Petersfield, in the room which the King lay in lately at his being there. Here very merry, and played us and our wives at bowls.

An indication that both Pepys and Charles II stopped there on the way to Portsmouth. The most striking feature of the house was not its architecture but its magnificent panelling and chimney-pieces, and decorative ironwork outside. The house was lived in by the Bonham-Carter family until 1858 and remained in their possession until the present century. Unhappily it was torn down about forty years ago, when the panelling and ironwork were sold off by speculators for a larger sum (it was said) than that obtained for the whole property. The site is now occupied by the Post Office and the Midland Bank and other buildings, but part of the grounds is still cultivated as a market garden.

But there was another property of even greater consequence at Buriton, a small village three miles south of Petersfield. The Buriton estate had been bought independently by Henry Bonham in 1798 from his friend Lord Stawell, but Henry never lived there, nor did Thomas who inherited it from his brother. Neither was it occupied by John Bonham-Carter, to whom it passed in 1826, nor by any of his descendants until comparatively recently. Since Buriton only left the hands of the Bonham-Carters in 1958 after a connexion of 160 years, it

* Some of the French prisoners addressed their letters to Henry Bonham '*dans son hôtel*', in the sense of a large town house.

is a property of more than ordinary family interest—but there are other associations too of wider appeal.

Buriton lies close under the South Downs in the Rother valley, along the Sussex boundary. It has an intimate beauty, entirely English, deriving from that miraculous partnership between man and Nature, which came about when the land was enclosed and improved in the 18th century. All along the south horizon run the high backs of the chalk hills, thickly clothed with woods and hangers that fall down to the village below. The cottages and farms seem to grow right out of the ground, as if they had taken root there long ago. Their brick and cob walls, with roofs of thatch and tile, belong as naturally to the landscape as the oaks that flourish in the heavy soil. The church, an unpretentious building with a simple square tower which once had Petersfield in its parish, stands against a background of sombre green, with graceful trees overlooking the village pond.

It is here in this corner that you find the manor house which Henry Bonham bought. Outwardly little has altered. On one side of the manor yard stands the original farmhouse—a modest timber-framed cottage, with an 18th century front of clunch blocks and red-brick quoins, and an Elizabethan chimney. Next to it rises a three-storeyed Georgian wing in plain brick, built about the year 1745. Facing the house is a magnificent barn, over 130 feet long, with ten bays, and pedimented in the classic manner with Breton blue doors. Both buildings are flanked on the west side by stables of similar magnificence.

The family responsible for all this grandiosity was the Gibbons, father and grandfather of the author of *The Decline and Fall of the Roman Empire*. The grandfather had made a fortune as an Army contractor, lost most of it in the South Sea Bubble, but managed to save the property at Buriton which he had purchased in 1719. The father, a poor dilettante sort of fellow, who buried himself in country pursuits, rebuilt the farmstead as we see it now. Edward Gibbon himself did not care for the country, and had few good words for his father's house or household. He left this description in his Autobiography*:

My father's residence in Hampshire, where I have passed many light, and some heavy hours, was at Buriton, near Petersfield, one mile from the Portsmouth road, and at the easy distance of fifty-eight miles from London. An old mansion, in a state of decay, had been converted into the fashion and convenience of a modern house; and if strangers had nothing to see, the inhabitants had little to desire. The spot was not happily chosen, at the end of the village and the bottom of the hill: but the aspect of the adjacent grounds was various and cheerful; the downs commanded a noble prospect, and the long hanging woods in sight of the house could not perhaps have been improved by art or expense. My father kept in his own hands the whole of the estate, and even rented some additional land; and whatsoever might be the balance of profit and loss, the farm supplied him with amusement and plenty. The produce maintained a number of men and horses, which were multiplied by the intermixture of domestic and rural servants; and in the intervals of labour the favourite team, a handsome set of bays or greys, was harnessed to the coach. The economy of the house was regulated by the taste and prudence of Mrs. Gibbon [his stepmother]. She prided herself in the elegance of her occasional dinners; and from the uncleanly avarice of Madame Pavilliard, I was suddenly transported to the daily neatness and luxury of an English table. Our immediate neighbourhood was rare and rustic; but from the verge of our hills, as far as Chichester and Goodwood, the western district of Sussex was interspersed with noble seats and hospitable families, with whom we cultivated a friendly, and might have enjoyed a very frequent, intercourse. As my stay at Buriton was always voluntary, I was received and dismissed with smiles; but the comforts of my retirement did not depend on the ordinary pleasures of the country. My father could never inspire me with his love and knowledge of farming. I never handled a gun, I seldom mounted a horse; and my philosophic walks were soon terminated by

* Taken from the *Everyman* edition of 1948.

a shady bench, where I was long detained by the sedentary amusement of reading or meditation. At home I occupied a pleasant and spacious apartment; the library on the same floor was soon considered as my favourite domain; and I might say with truth I was never less alone than when by myself.

My sole complaint, which I piously suppressed, arose from the kind restraint imposed on the freedom of my time. By the habit of early rising I always secured a sacred portion of the day, and many scattered moments were stolen and employed by my studious industry. But the family hours of breakfast, of dinner, of tea, and of supper, were regular and long: after breakfast Mrs. Gibbon expected my company in her dressing-room; after tea my father claimed my conversation and the perusal of the newspapers; and in the midst of an interesting work I was often called down to receive the visit of some idle neighbours. Their dinners and visits required, in due course, a similar return; and I dreaded the period of the full moon, which was usually reserved for our more distant excursions.

Even from this account it is clear that Gibbon found life at Buriton less disagreeable than he pretended; especially when it afforded him respite from a long spell of service in the South Hampshire Regiment of the Militia between 1760 and 1762. Moreover, he did manage to do some writing there; for example the *Essay on the Study of Literature* which he composed in French in six weeks after his return from Switzerland in 1758; two other minor works; and some drafts of *The Decline and Fall*. In time he must have grown fond of the place, even though he did not always live there, for after his father's death in 1770 he kept Buriton nineteen more years until 1789, when pressed by debts he finally disposed of it to Lord Stawell. Nine years after that Stawell sold it to Henry Bonham.

* * *

Buriton, the Castle House, and all other property at Petersfield, the Meons, and in the Isle of Wight, amounting to several thousand acres, together with investments which included a majority shareholding in the Pike brewery at Portsmouth, were all left by Thomas Bonham to John Bonham-Carter. Apart from a number of small legacies amounting to some £12,000, the only other bequest of importance was an estate at Hardham in Sussex which passed to John's first cousin and brother-in-law, Edward Carter. The provisions of the will caused disappointment, even indignation, among other members of the family who had had expectations. John dealt with the situation firmly but tactfully. He told Joanna:

> I have had a letter from Mr. Goodenough [his uncle] with the same matter as you write. I have sent him a proper answer, saying (as is the truth) that I am annoyed at the thought of the disappointment of others—but I have not said and I really cannot say that I have much regret about them in particular. Mr. B. never liked the Goodenoughs, and tho' it was his doctrine that a man shd not give away his property from his relations, it was also part of the same doctrine that amongst his relations he might choose whom he liked best as the object of his bounty. This is enough to acct for his consideration of Ned [Edward Carter]; but his connection with him as manager of the brewery and still more as the person to whom he looked to maintain the family interest in the Corporation made it (I shd have thought) a matter to be expected that he shd stand above the rest in Mr. B's estimation. I am sure too that Mr. B. gave me the brewery property with a view to my interest in the Borough. I wrote yesty to Capt. T. W. Carter to inform him of the situation in which I stood . . . and Ned wrote to the two Atherleys [cousins]. I thought this course the most proper considering that they were all as nearly related to Mr. Bonham as I and Ned, and by those means I shall at once put an end to speculation. I took care to inform him that the will was made in 1817 and that Mr. B. had told me what he had done for Ned and me within a few months after he had made it.

Thomas Bonham was buried at East Meon 'in a decent but not expensive manner', as directed in his will. His funeral was attended by John, Edward Carter, the family solicitor, his old friends Colonel King and Rev. Whicher, and half a dozen of his tenants and servants. Not long afterwards Joanna took the children to stay at Castle House. John warned her: 'I think it not improbable that when your ladyship arrives at Petersfield you will be welcomed with a peal on the bells. If so, mind that you refuse not your guinea, and if you pay Buriton a visit I think you may expect the same compliment at the same expense.' In February 1827 John received the royal licence and authority that 'he and his issue may (in order to testify his esteem and regard for his said kinsman, Thomas Bonham Esq.) assume and use the surname of Bonham, in addition to and before the present surname of Carter'. A few weeks later he was addressing Joanna as 'Dear Queen of Petersfield' and admitting that he was tripping on the use of the new name.*

By this time he was away again in the west on professional business. He was harassed at not being at Petersfield when so many family matters claimed his attention, and by the ironical fact that now, when he had as much private income as he needed (nearly £4000 p.a. from land and investments), he was securing more briefs than ever—27 out of 36 at Launceston in March, and 17 out of 26 at Bodmin in August during his last circuit. But he had firmly made up his mind to give up active advocacy. 'The mode of my retirement from the Sessions by not taking any criminal briefs has given great satisfaction to my friends at the Bar. Numbers of briefs were offered and a pretty good haul I should have had, but even the sight of the fees on the briefs did not tempt me.'

By the autumn of 1827 John was free at last to settle the family in the country, and devote almost all his working time to Parliament. Curiously enough neither he nor Joanna seem to have considered moving into Buriton, which was left in the occupation of the tenant. This was a surprising arrangement in

* I have referred to John as John Bonham-Carter since the beginning of this chapter, when he was still John Carter, simply to avoid confusion with his relations.

view of the beauty and associations of the manor, which had been modernised by the Gibbons and was quite large enough for the family. Possibly Joanna did not like living beside a farmyard. Less surprising was the decision against living permanently at Petersfield which was a town, though a small one, for they had been living a town life ever since their marriage, and John would continue to use Duke Street, Westminster, as a *pied-à-terre* while attending Parliament. In the end they rented a large country house in the Petersfield district: first, Fairoak near Rogate, and then in 1832 they took a ten-year lease of Ditcham Grove from Mr. Cowper Coles. This was a pleasant Palladian mansion high up on the downs above Buriton, surrounded by magnificent woods, with views deep into Hampshire and Sussex.

* * *

John Bonham-Carter's change of fortune happened at a most propitious moment for his political career, since the long years of Whig opposition were at last coming to an end. Freed from the necessity of earning his living, he could now play a full part in all the preparations for the Reform Bill and the other reforming legislation of the 1830s—one of the most exciting and significant periods in English political history.

It will be remembered that when John was first elected for Portsmouth in 1816, the Whigs had been out of office —with one short break—for more than thirty years, and their prospects of returning to power were then as remote as ever. Although the country was deep in distress and discontent, the Government remained firmly in the hands of a Tory administration, which depended for its existence upon a corrupt electoral system and a pervading sense of fear among the governing classes. Liberalism was still regarded as a form of Jacobinism, while monstrous repressive laws merely served to inflame a highly dangerous and revolutionary situation. The climax came with the Six Acts of 1819 which savagely penalised any idea or action, however mild, directed against the State, and it is not unlikely that a revolution would indeed have broken out had not the mad old king, George III, died in 1820. Shortly afterwards a more enlightened Tory administration took office, and a policy of moderation began to have an effect. In 1823 Peel started the reform of the criminal law, and put an end to capital punishment for minor offences. Huskisson laid the foundations of Free Trade at a time when the national economy was showing signs of revival; and Canning, later Prime Minister for a few months before his death in 1827, encouraged moderate proposals for constitutional reform.

It looked almost as if the Tories were going to steal the Whigs' thunder—but both parties were divided. While Canning had the support of many of the Whigs, he was distrusted by the right wing Tories, who appeared to regain their ascendancy with the appointment of the Duke of Wellington as Prime Minister in the autumn of 1827. But the Duke surprised his opponents and disappointed his followers by permitting two notable pieces of reforming legislation: the repeal of the Test and Corporation Acts in 1828, by which Dissenters were at last openly and formally permitted to hold public office; and the Catholic Emancipation Act in 1829 which awarded the same rights to Roman Catholics and brought Daniel O'Connell and the Irish representatives into the House of Commons on the side of the Whigs. Like all else that is unpopular but necessary, these two Acts—passed into law with the help of the Opposition—lost the Duke his traditional support and prepared the way for the return of the Whigs, after nearly fifty years * in the political wilderness.

By the summer of 1830 the reform of the House of Commons had become a national issue, and it remained so until the Reform Act was finally passed in June 1832. Inevitable as it may seem now, the process was far from inevitable at the time, for the Bill was hindered all along by personal and party disagreements and by passionate feeling. Neither side was sure of the outcome until the very end, and for two years after the

* Since 1783.

death of George IV on June 26th, 1830, the nation lived in an atmosphere of tense emergency.

As a young man George had favoured the Whigs, largely out of antipathy to his father, and formed a close friendship with Charles James Fox. His character, however, was so egoistic and unstable that he surprised nobody when, after assuming the Regency in 1811, he threw in his lot with the Tories. Thereafter he became increasingly intransigent towards social and political change, and his death in 1830 released a flood of hope and speculation about the future. Moreover, much was expected of the new king, William IV, a breezy and eccentric sailor, and quite the most popular of the royal brothers.

Events then moved apace. In July the nation was electrified by the abdication of Charles X of France, the direct outcome of his efforts to destroy the constitutional Charter of 1814, which had been accepted by the Bourbons as a condition of their restoration. At the same moment came the resignation of the Duke of Wellington's Government which, though long anticipated, did much to excite the hopes of the reformers. The autumn election that followed brought striking successes to the Whigs. They gained not only most of the free seats, but also many of the pocket principalities whose electors usually voted as paid and directed, but now showed a remarkable independence.

The House of Commons reassembled on November 2nd, and the Whigs at once raised the question of parliamentary reform. To this the Duke replied that he had no plan prepared or contemplated, nor would he ever consider one, declaring that: 'the system of representation possesses the full and entire confidence of the country'. A fortnight later the Government was defeated on another issue, and the Duke resigned. The king then called upon Lord Grey to form a new administration.

The moment for which the Whigs had waited so long had now arrived. But although they had been swept into office by a powerful and popular movement, their position was neither so strong nor so clearcut as appeared. Like the Tories, they were a medley of factions and personalities, bound by no tight party organisation and constantly shifting in composition. In the main they were an aristocratic party—the first 'reformed' administration contained no less than a dozen peers. Such men held liberal principles for philosophical or family reasons, but socially they differed hardly at all from their Tory counterparts. At the same time, even before 1832, there was a strong leaven of middle class—squires, merchants, manufacturers, and professional men, many of them Dissenters like John Bonham-Carter—backed outside Parliament by a few Radicals, notably Joseph Hume and Francis Place, who had no fixed political loyalties but followed a policy of 'radical reform' that resembled socialism.

Although most Whigs held together on matters of broad principle, the party as a whole suffered from disunity and the extreme individualism of some of its members. An outstanding example was Henry Brougham, later Lord Chancellor, a brilliant lawyer and a sincere educationist who took the lead in founding London University: but a volatile intemperate man who terrified both friends and enemies by his violent opinions and unpredictable actions. On a more moderate plane, the same attitude of indiscipline was displayed even by John Bonham-Carter who once wrote to Francis Baring*: 'I am sure I should be very uneasy under the idea of *service* and a positive engagement to support my superiors thro' thick and thin'. So long as the Whigs were in Opposition, these weaknesses were relatively unimportant. In an administration, however, they were intolerable, and for some months before the autumn elections of 1830 serious attempts were being made to resolve differences, and instil a sense of party unity.

And there was another serious handicap. The Whigs had been so long out of office, that they lacked leaders who knew how to govern. Lord Grey himself, the new Prime Minister, though a wise man and adroit in handling Parliament (as he was soon to show), was worn down by many years in opposition and had to be persuaded to remain in politics. He was well

* His colleague at Portsmouth since 1826. See page 34.

supported by the Chancellor of the Exchequer and Leader of the House, Lord Althorp, whose financial skill and patent honesty gained him deep respect—but was not an inspiring speaker. Most of the younger Whig ministers were inexperienced; and so Grey felt it necessary to offer two of the most important posts to Canningite Tories—Lord Melbourne who became Home Secretary, and Lord Palmerston Foreign Secretary, neither of whom showed much enthusiasm for reform. However, the most pressing issue—the drafting of the Reform Bill—was placed in the hands of a 'ginger group' under the chairmanship of Grey's son-in-law, the future Lord Durham, and included Lord John Russell, who was to help pilot the Bill so successfully through all its phases in Parliament.

Few Governments, however, have had a more distasteful beginning—particularly as the Whigs claimed to be the party of freedom—for there was an immediate call to suppress the agricultural riots in the southern counties. The trouble had started in Kent during the previous summer over the question of wages, although the causes were far older and deeper than that. In 1830 an agricultural labourer received a miserable wage of between 1s. and 2s. a day, supplemented if he had a family by an allowance from the parish: a degrading and inefficient system which kept wages low and debased employment, while putting an enormous burden on the rates. Encouraged by union activities in the towns and by the partial repeal of the Combination Laws, groups of labourers took matters into their own hands, met the farmers in a body and demanded a basic wage of up to 2s. 6d. a day. These early meetings were orderly, and in many cases the farmers were agreeable. In return they asked the labourers for support in obtaining reductions in rents and tithes.

But there were other grievances. Many men, or their fathers before them, had lost their own holdings through Enclosure, and had come to depend solely upon wages for their living. They now found that employment was decreasing owing to the new machinery, particularly threshing machines, which performed in a week what had previously given several men work all during the winter, flailing the grain from the sheaves as they lay upon the barn floor. They therefore demanded the destruction of these engines, and when refused destroyed them themselves.

This was the thin edge of violence. It soon led to the burning of barns and ricks, threats to stubborn masters, and in Hampshire to the pulling down of the hated poor houses at Headley and Selborne. The whole movement gathered momentum and spread quickly to the west; partly because it had an element of organisation, partly due to the power of rumour and the mythology of vengeance in the guise of 'Capt. Swing'. For a time the authorities were overawed. In November farmers and landowners, now thoroughly frightened, appealed to the Government for help; and so it became the first act of Lord Melbourne as Home Secretary to deal with the situation.

Melbourne did not hesitate. He upbraided the magistrates for allowing themselves to be intimidated, and for attempting to mediate in the matter of wages or the destruction of machinery. He ordered them to restore order at once with the aid of the Special Constabulary, and if necessary to call upon detachments of troops which were then being sent to the disaffected areas. These measures had an immediate effect, and hundreds of men were herded into the gaols at Winchester, Reading, Salisbury, and other provincial towns.

John Bonham-Carter was at Petersfield at this time, close to the centre of the disturbances. Some letters that he sent and received give a vivid impression of these events.

From Henry Budd

It is true that the mob destroyed the Poor House at Headley this day and insisted on Mr. Dickinson signing a letter to reduce his tithe to £350 a year. They then left Headley and proceeded to Kingsley with intent to destroy the threshing machines of Sir T. Miller. Yesterday they burnt the Poor House at Selborne with all poor Harrison's furniture and wearing apparel, and threaten to murder his family, which Mrs. Dowling at the Anchor at Liphook has informed me are in her house, and it is said that the people mean to come over tomorrow and have them or destroy the house. I have therefore stationed the soldiers there for their protection, and beg you to forward me a reinforcement as speedily as possible.

I have taken the evidence of a man to whom the fellows taken away from home by Dr. Quarrier yesterday said 'If they do not give you all you want let us go in and kill them and destroy the house.'

From J. V. Hugonin, Alton

As you may probably like to know how we are going on, I am happy to inform you that the determined threats of the mob to pull down our Poor House have not been attempted, I believe entirely owing to the good conduct of the labourers of the parish of Alton not joining them. I have been in no apprehension of my own Parish doing anything, but the mob from the lawless districts of Selborne, Kingsley, Hawkley, etc is of a more formidable description than the common run of mobs at present and in numbers consisted of certainly not less than Six Hundred (report magnified them to 2000 which of course I did not believe)—a force I could not in common prudence attempt to resist with a few Special Constables, altho' the town of Alton has come forward in a very spirited and consolidated way. Mr. Edward Knight has been with me today to say his house is threatened to be pulled down and he appears to be in expectation of a visit of some kind. I have however got 30 soldiers with which I can undertake to prevent any violence by *any number* of the mob. You will probably think this smacks too much of the old Soldier.

I was sorry to send Mrs. H. to Nursted yesterday, but it was to calm her agitation, not from any fear of violence to my house, as I thought it probable I might be in search of Military the whole night.

From W. Mitchell, Anchor Inn, Liphook

Mr. Budd has opened your letter and requested me to say that Robert Holdaway is taken—with Aaron Harding and

John Cobb—all of Selborne. Matthew Triggs of Headley is also in Custody—a very bad Case—and one Harding of Kingsley. We expect that George Dedman will be taken tonight. We are just returned having been out since 9 o'clock. Mr. Coles and his Party who were to go to Empshott and Greatham are not returned. Mr. Coles has sent in seven, viz. Henry Bone, H. Heather (?), Thomas Blanchard, Thomas Greentrees (?), William Bicknell, Thomas Lemon and Thomas Marshall, and I suppose he is gone to Empshott to take Thomas Robinson.

Mr. Budd requests me to apologise for his not writing which he would have done but his Hands were too cold to write and I need not say that mine are no better. We do not want any reinforcement, and as you have more Life Guards sent to Petersfield Mr. Budd does not see any necessity for detaining the Infantry at Petersfield any longer.

From John Bonham-Carter to his wife

Having got my letter telling me of the capture of one of the rioters, I was obliged to dispatch an express to Winton to inform the General and place some of the troops at his disposal and I received the answer at 4 this morning, and the infantry are now gone back to Portsmouth except a small detachment at Liphook. I went early this morning with Richard and my working (?) friend who is now our inmate to Liphook to confront him with the prisoners, and assist thereby in making out the commitments and I returned with him in the rear of 12 prisoners chained together in a fish cart with soldiers in another cart. I forwarded them from this place under *the civil power* of 6 Constables only—Mr. Coles riding with them as far as Horndean.

I cant come. There is always some advice wanted and the moment I stepped out of the chaise I had to take an examination. Send me shirts and some of my check (?) worsted stockings and one pair of drawers to last over *Tuesday*.

From J. Beckett, County Gaol, Winchester

I shall feel obliged if you will not send any Men to the Gaol, there being already 53 in custody and in the Course of an hour I expect 50 more. They are sending prisoners from all quarters.

Special Commissioners were sent round to try the prisoners, and by early 1831 all was over. Although only one man lost his life in the riots, and he a rioter, 450 men and boys were transported to Australia, 9 executed, and 400 others imprisoned. It was not a creditable episode and highly embarrassing to the Whig Government, while William Cobbett's triumphant acquittal in July on a charge of incitement embarrassed it still further. John Bonham-Carter completed his duties by serving on the committee appointed by the Hampshire Quarter Sessions to investigate claims arising out of the disturbances. In the same issue of the *Hampshire Chronicle* in which this announcement appeared, there was a small significant paragraph, which needs no comment:

> Of a population amounting to upwards of 1200 in the parish of East Meon, not more than 50 attended the church on Sunday last.

* * *

Once the rioters had been sentenced, the Government lost no time in promoting the business for which it had been elected, and in March 1831 Lord John Russell introduced the Reform Bill to the House of Commons. It was far more drastic than any of the Tories and many of the Whigs thought possible, and caused a sensation. Briefly, it proposed to disfranchise some sixty rotten boroughs and distribute the seats among the growing towns and the more populous counties. The life of Parliament was to be limited to five years. The right to vote was to be given to all householders paying an annual rent of £10 and upwards, but the system of voting was to remain open and public as before, no secret ballot being proposed. These were the basic clauses, and with one exception they remained unaltered when the Bill finally became law. But much was to happen before then, and John Bonham-Carter was intimately concerned with the progress of the Bill at all its stages and in all its hazards.

His own position under the Bill was a delicate one. Although Portsmouth would retain two members, being a large and important town, the number of voters would increase tenfold and thereby seem to endanger the Carter monopoly. As an active reformer, then, he stood in danger of being 'hoist with his own petard'. He was of course aware of this but welcomed it on principle,* and as it turned out the risk was more than justified. The fact that he and Baring were elected together twice before the Reform Act and three times after showed that they were accepted on a basis of merit, not monopoly. At the same time, active reformer though he was, John was far from being a Radical. In December 1830 he attended a public meeting at Portsmouth to pass a number of resolutions in favour of reform, and these were presented to Parliament in the form of a petition—John and Baring placing it before the Commons, Lord Brougham acting on their behalf in the Lords. It was one among many similar petitions which served as an outlet to public opinion, and greatly strengthened the hands of the ministers. John was careful at that meeting, however, to control the extremists who wanted to talk about tithes, church rates, pluralities of livings, and bishops—subjects which he managed to pass off as being irrelevant, '*tho' very palatable* to the majority of the audience'.

On January 21st he had a letter from Lord Althorp asking him to be sure of attending the House—a polite message, not a whip—when the Reform Bill came forward, and he duly supported it at the First and Second Reading, which it survived by a majority of 1. The Bill then foundered in Committee and Parliament was dissolved. The Whigs now went to the country on the sole issue of reform, and returned on a wave of popular enthusiasm with a clear majority of 136. Vast sums of

* When Sir Robert Peel taxed him in a reform debate with the state of the Borough of Portsmouth (still a 'close corporation'), John replied with disarming agreement 'Hear! Hear!' On another similar occasion John is quoted as saying: 'We keep the Borough of Portsmouth *close* for the purpose of making sure of two members to vote for throwing *open* all boroughs in the kingdom'.

money were spent on the election by both sides, in an effort to capture or retain even the most unlikely seats.

In mid-April John was busy canvassing both for himself and Baring, and for the county candidates. On 27th he wrote to Joanna from Winchester:

> Nothing can surpass the enthusiastic spirit of the people. No money, not the whole £100,000 said to be subscribed by the Boromongers could beat us—if all spent in the County. Last night I went to Southampton and returned here to sleep—attended a Committee, talked incessantly—and retired with a lot of cheers—Coaches, waggons, Steam Boats offered to carry voters free of expense. The gentry (aye and many of the Clergy too) coming forward.

In May he wrote twice to Baring about election expenses. The letters show how necessary it still was to have private money, or to know people who had it, whichever side you were on. In this case apparently, after the local committees had met all their outgoings, there was still a bill outstanding for printing, advertising, the chairing, the under-sheriff's charges, secretarial and sundry expenses, amounting to £425. John proposed, and it was agreed, that this sum should be shared equally between himself, a Mr. Jervoise, Baring, and Baring's father, Sir Thomas. He also obtained substantial help from his brother-in-law, William Nightingale, who had a large house at Embley Park near Romsey.

In his second letter he could not refrain, as a lawyer, from adding a critical note about the Reform Bill. His comments may partly explain why the Bill in its original form failed to gain acceptance even by some of the Whigs.

> The framees do not seem to have referred enough to the existing Election Statutes for their choice of terms and phrases—nor have they taken care to use the same language in different clauses relating to the same subject matter. This is a great fault in the composition of Acts of Parliament, because no argument is more common on the construction

of a Statute than that by which it is inferred that the legislature meant something different when it used different language, or rather when it did not use *precisely the same language*. . . . I confess I am somewhat anxious that this Great Act should be drawn with all that precision which to some persons may appear over ridiculous.

In June 1831 the Bill was presented for the second time and passed all its Readings, thanks mainly to the firmness and patience of Althorp and Russell. But they were unable to prevent one important modification—the limitation of the rural franchise to those paying an annual rent of £50, not £10. The Bill then went before the Lords where it was rejected at the Second Reading by a majority of 41, largely due to the generalship of the Duke of Wellington. This move had been foreseen and Grey let it be known that he would now ask the king to create sufficient peers to ensure the Bill's success. But the reaction in the country was one of extreme excitement and violence, and everywhere there were public protests and demonstrations. Rioting broke out in several towns, and at Bristol the mob got completely out of hand, destroying the Mansion and Custom Houses, the Bishop's Palace, and the principal gaols.

Under this pressure Grey wasted no time in re-introducing the Bill once more, but he was prepared to modify it in order to overcome some of the peers' objections, providing there was no sacrifice of principle. It was at this point that John's advice was solicited, as a lawyer and experienced Parliamentarian; and he was in constant touch with Althorp, Russell, and Brougham from the moment the Bill was presented to the Commons for the third time in December 1831 to its final enactment in June 1832.

According to Le Marchant, private secretary to Brougham and Althorp's biographer, John stood behind Althorp and Russell all through the committee stage, which lasted six weeks from January 29th to March 16th, revising and improving the clauses—Wednesdays and Saturdays generally being given up to the work. This is of great interest in view of John's earlier criticisms of the terminology of the Bill. He concentrated particularly on the 36th clause—the establishment of a system of registration of voters—and afterwards made this his main contribution to Parliament and the Whig party. It is likely that he drafted the manuals for county and borough electors, of which proof copies survive with corrections in his own handwriting, and which were published under the auspices of the Reform Association. It is known that he did a great deal for the local registration committees; and that he and Daniel Howard, his political agent at Portsmouth and an alderman of the Corporation, worked unceasingly to make sure that all Liberal sympathisers were properly registered through south and east Hampshire, and that they exercised their vote. He often personally attended the courts held by the Revising Barristers, who were appointed to check the lists of voters once a year—behaviour that was criticised as being contrary, it was said, to parliamentary etiquette. However that may be, he fought the issues impartially, wishing to make the franchise as broad and effective as possible. He once wrote to Baring:

> Tomorrow the Barristers sit at Portsmouth and it is thought right that I should attend and help anyone whether friend or foe to acquire the franchise. . . . At Botley I had the great satisfaction of protecting the vote of the Dissenting Minister against the *personal* objection of Mr. Baker, the Tory clergyman. Then I must go to Lymington to throw my broad shield over a Radical Dissenting Minister there.

In April 1832 the Bill was ready for the Lords again. Grey was optimistic and considered that the threat of peer-making would ensure a majority in its favour this time. The other Whig leaders were equally hopeful. In a conversation with Francis Baring, Althorp expressed firm confidence. When asked what he would do if the Bill failed, he replied that he would be only too happy to retire, being heartily sick of politics and longing to return home. And the Bill did fail. An amendment was passed postponing the disfranchisement of the rotten boroughs, one of the basic aims and clauses of the whole Bill. This produced an impossible situation and Grey went straight to the king. John wrote to Joanna on May 8th:

> The crisis has arrived sooner than I had expected, but it could not have come at a better time or under a better shape. You will see that the Govt were beaten last night in the Lords by a majority of 35. Lord Grey is now with the king and tomorrow it will be known what course is to be taken. I anticipate the making of 40 or 50 peers.

Followed on May 9th by:

> The Whigs are out. Lords Grey and Brougham saw the king yesterday. Peers or Resignation their communication to him, and this morning he has answd. Resignation and it is done.
>
> Under the present uncertain position of affairs I think it will be absurd to take a house and you must remain where you are till I can advise you further.

Affairs were indeed uncertain. The whole country was once more in an uproar, and for eleven days ordinary business practically came to a standstill. Newspapers appeared with black borders, and placards were displayed with notices of refusal to pay taxes until the Reform Bill was passed. There was again some rioting, although nothing approaching the scale of Bristol the previous year, and evidence that plans were being made to distribute arms. Much, however, was done by the Political Unions, founded by Thomas Attwood, the Birmingham Radical, and others, to canalise and control the tremendous upsurge of popular anger.

In the face of all this, the Tories were quite unable to form a Government, and the Whigs resumed office with the knowledge that they would no longer be opposed. Towards the end of May the Bill was sent up to the Lords for the third time and, many Opposition peers abstaining, passed into law. On June 7th it was given the Royal Assent with the usual words 'Le

Roi le veult'. Its enemies preferred to say 'La Canaille le veult'.

* * *

The Reform Act of 1832 is rightly regarded as the foundation stone of modern government in England, and a great event in political history. By comparison with today, however, it seems a mild and conservative Act, and we wonder perhaps why it caused such an upheaval. The fact is that it was *not* a truly revolutionary measure, and merely transferred the reins of power from the aristocracy to the middle class—to the merchants and manufacturers in the towns, and to the farmers in the country. The labourers and mechanics had to wait until Disraeli's Act of 1867 and Gladstone's of 1884 before they too were given the vote. None the less an almost painless 'revolution' was a great step forward, and it set off a train of social legislation consonant with the reforming temper of the time: the Emancipation Act (1833), the Poor Law Amendment Act (1834), the Municipal Corporations Act (1835), the Tithe Commutation Act (1836), the Births and Deaths Registration Act (1836), and the Marriage Act (1836). Each measure was a definite extension of liberty, or a correction of an old abuse.

John Bonham-Carter was involved in one way or another in all this legislation. The Municipal Corporations Act 1835 put an end to the 'close corporation' of Portsmouth, an anomaly that had embarrassed him as a reformer, but it made small difference to the position of the Carters. His cousin, Edward Carter, was re-elected mayor under the new dispensation, and the family continued to exert influence on the affairs of Portsmouth until late in the century. John's interest in the franchise led to his appointment as Chairman of the Select Committee whose enquiries resulted in Lord John Russell's Registration and Marriage Acts of 1836. These Acts caused little or no controversy, because church registers (hitherto the sole records) had long been inaccurate and ill-preserved, and in any event were evidence only of baptisms, not births; and of burials, not deaths.

The transfer of registration and the licensing of civil marriages was a sensible non-partisan step, typical of John's work and attitude to public affairs. He was at heart a modest man who disliked publicity, preferring to work behind the scenes, and let others take the name and the credit. Edward Hopkins, the family solicitor who practised at Alresford and who did a great deal of business with John, left this revealing note about him:

> He scarcely spoke in the House, and when speaking on the Hustings, at meetings and elsewhere, he spoke tersely and to the point, without hesitation, but in rather a curt and severe style and without any attempt at oratory. His opinion on law questions was much looked up to and often asked in the House, where he was sure to give a straightforward decided answer which could be relied upon as to the correctness of the law and to the impartiality of the judgment. He frequently also during a debate would cross to the other side of the House and by quiet conversation and reasoning with individual members, tend to bring the question in hand to a settlement much more than could have been done by an eloquent speech.
>
> Being such a thorough man of business, both by habit and taste and therewithall with a mind of so active a tenour, he required some constant object, and that of a larger scope upon which to exercise his energies: and this after retiring from his profession, in which no doubt he would have attained the highest honours, some other equally engrossing pursuit was equally necessary to him. He could, they say, have been made Solicitor General had he not retired.
>
> His conversation was always manly, sound, and to the point. No one presided so well at table. There was never anything of a frivolous or loose nature in the conversation there; his being, although, often playful and jocose—and he would always point the friendly joke at anyone present in the best manner—and was always replete with sound information. No consideration for what the world would think of him or any the slightest undue deference to the opinion of others, did he allow to influence either his

judgment or his actions, when once his decision was taken as to the conscientious and right course to pursue.

John's modesty was a part of his nature, but he may also have kept himself in the background for a less lofty reason, wanting a little freedom to enjoy life with his growing family at Ditcham. It is possible too that he may have preferred to remain free in order to criticise his own party, as a member of the reformist group of the Liberals. It is hard, otherwise, to understand why he refused no less than four major appointments offered him by ministers, who knew his value and wished to reward him for all he had done.

These appointments, as revealed in his correspondence, were:

1832: A Lord of the Admiralty under Sir James Graham.
1833: Under-Secretary of State for the Colonies, in place of Lord Goderich.
Before 1836: Chief Secretary for Ireland.
Also, at some unspecified date, he was asked by Lord Brougham if he would agree to become a Privy Councillor.

'Last night', he wrote once, 'I had a note from one of the Cabinet offering me in the most flattering terms an office under the Government of great responsibility and high pay. It was tempting, very tempting, but I have resisted the temptation.'

His refusals, voluntary at first, later became compulsory. By 1836 he was in the early stages of diabetes, then an incurable disease; indeed his doctors never really knew what was wrong with him. He never gave up work, but tried to regain health by long visits to the Nightingales at Lea Hurst in Derbyshire, to Liverpool to see William Rathbone, the philanthropist, and to Ireland. He spent more and more time at Ditcham, where he still managed to shoot and entertain his friends. He was elected again with Baring at the General Election of 1837, but he could no longer tour the Hampshire constituencies as he used to—as when he helped Palmerston win South Hants in 1832. In fact, he had become so weak that Baring had to make all the speeches at Portsmouth and generally bear the burden of the election.

The end came suddenly in February 1838. Hopkins, the solicitor, was with him in London at the time—they were busy working on the Petersfield Election Petition together—and saw him just after the doctors had told him to expect the worst. He was walking up and down the room in his dressing-gown, much moved, as if the news had taken him by surprise. He still refused to admit it to Joanna when he wrote to her on February 11th:

> DEAR LOVE,
>
> Chambers and Prout have just been with me. I am terribly out of condition, but they hope to bring me round. Chambers says he is sure the mind has been too much excited, and I must be quite quiet, but that if you can leave the children and be with me a few hours every day—not allowing me to talk or see people and having the carriage at my command, it will be the best thing for me.

But he admitted it to Baring:

> Do I ask too much in begging you if possible to come to me for a few minutes. I am quivering on the balance of life and death.

Baring came, and so did Joanna, but John died six days later. He was 49.

CHAPTER 3

JACK, HILARY, AND HARRY

WHEN John Bonham-Carter died in February 1838, Joanna did not immediately alter her way of life. A good wife and mother, she was much loved by her children and well supported by her eldest son Jack * then aged 20, and by her eldest daughter Hilary aged 17. That she was usually addressed as 'Dearest Mum' not 'Dear Mama' reveals a degree of affectionate informality uncommon in an early Victorian family. Yet, though practical in small matters, sociable and at times remarkably adventurous, Joanna was not so competent as to manage everything on her own. There was really no need. She was not poor. Her business affairs were well looked after by Edward Hopkins, the Alresford solicitor. She had the constant companionship of her spinster sister Julia; the strong arm of her eldest brother Ben, who had now succeeded their father William Smith as M.P. for Norwich; the gay and homely society of countless cousins and other close relations, but especially the Nightingales with their two large houses at Embley near Romsey and Lea Hurst in Derbyshire, and the Nicholsons at Waverley Abbey near Farnham. Furthermore the lease of Ditcham—first rented after the passing of the Reform Act—did not run out until 1842. She had therefore ample time in which to make plans and let her family grow up in sense and years.

The spirit of freedom, reason and tolerance, so remarkable in John, was now disseminated among his seven surviving children, who cultivated it in different and characteristic ways, but best of all by three: by Jack in politics and in all the activi-

* John Bonham-Carter II—see simplified pedigree on page 131.

ties of country life; by Hilary in society, especially in her friendship with some of the leading women of her day; by Harry in business in London, and in his work with Florence Nightingale for the establishment of nursing. These three were true symbols and samples of their age; and their story is representative of a mass of middle-class families who came into privilege and power in mid-Victorian England.

* * *

At Ditcham much devolved upon Hilary, even while a young girl, for she was only 11 when the family first moved in. Quite soon her letters (of which a great number survive) altered in tone from a carefree childishness to a precocious sense of responsibility. It was a trait that never left her. The fact was that her parents were often absent in London—her father on business and her mother with him, or perhaps confined with a new baby—and after her elder brother Jack had gone up to Cambridge in 1835, Ditcham was left for long periods in her charge. Besides this John came to depend on his daughter more and more as his illness grew worse. It therefore fell to Hilary, notwithstanding a large domestic staff, two governesses and various visiting tutors, to run the house, keep an eye on her younger brothers and sisters, and to see to their education as well as her own.

To the children she was indeed a second mother. Hugh was her favourite.

> Hugh and I had a little war yesterday, that is we fell out about *Haw*—he insisting it was *how* tho' he knew what *law*, *caw*, etc spelt. So he sat upon a chair till he was quite tired of doing nothing but watching us and began to cry, beginning afresh every time I glanced that way hoping to excite my pity. In the end it became quite pathetic for he added '*When* shall I be happy and have a nice smiling face?' This I managed to explain. The word soon followed. We finished our reading and went out quite bright to dig up wild hyacinth roots for the little garden.

The two other boys, Alfred and Harry, were soon sent to a small boarding school at Hove, kept by a Unitarian minister, Rev. J. P. Malleson. It was a 'School for Young Gentlemen. Terms, Seventy Guineas per annum. Each Pupil has a separate bed, and is expected to bring with him a Silver Fork and Spoon.' Their letters had an eternal schoolboy flavour. One from Alfred, for instance:

> Harry wrote to you and said did not he that he wanted a cake and some jam for his birthday, but I told you that M. said we were not to have cakes, so I say will you send us three pots of Raspberry, 1 of currant and 1 of honey.

Harry was a gentle easy-going boy, not over fond of work —at any rate during the holidays:

> Last night, after he had finished a little bit of lesson after supper, he spent a quarter of an hour before bed-time rolling on the sofa and saying he liked to be idle and wished to be idle always, Hillie! I said he would not think so in the morning when he was not tired. 'Well—but I shall try to think so!'

Among these vivid and affectionate flashes were dry references to the cost of Cocoa candles, Windsor soap, medicaments, and a village charity.

> A bad Charity—nothing but green faggots to be had—coals much better—Buriton people like coals very much—manage very well without grates. Papa wrote a little plan of a coal concern—giving £5. 8s. to make 6 ton, if the farmers will give the carriage from Emsworth.

By this time Papa was giving them all much anxiety. He was so obviously getting worse. One day he would take a vapour bath. Another time he would go down to the Isle of Wight to see his properties and seek refreshment in the sea air. More often he would just sit and read, visibly weakening. As to lessons, they never stopped, but it was Hilary who set the pace and kept the governesses up to the mark.

> Miss Whicher came yesterday and dined at ½ past 4. Worked at your Continentals which I had saved until now, and with much pleasure, and then at the Book of Gems, whilst I practised.

Yet all this diligence and self-improvement induced fits of depression and loss of confidence.

> I have not been doing very well lately. I have not finished my lessons till quite late in the evening, and I have been talking when I ought to have been doing them, and I am only doing a very little better now. I generally dawdle or only go to the piano and sing not very steadily or play a duet.

Poor Hilary!

This rather sombre routine was broken occasionally by visits to the Nightingales at Embley. There time passed much more pleasantly, even though Uncle Night (of whom they were all very fond) demanded an historical essay now and then, while classes in Latin, French, chemistry, and English grammar continued almost as before. Hilary's cousins Parthe (Parthenope) and Flo (Florence) were high-spirited gregarious creatures, attractive and popular, inclined to quarrel and turn to Hilary as their confidant. But all three were genuinely attached. Flo always regarded Hilary as her favourite cousin and their life-long intimacy sprang out of these early family gatherings. In the evenings they would make music, or sit round the table to listen to the latest instalment of *Oliver Twist*. Once they went over to the Palmerston's to see a travelling Irish actor perform his repertory of monologues and ballads. On Sundays they attended Wellow church, where a relative, Rev. Jervis Trigge Giffard, had been installed as vicar. Jervis was married and his first child, a son, had lately arrived. It was a puny baby, and the story went that when the proud young father showed it to a venerable neighbour, Farmer Moody, the old man put on his spectacles and said: 'Lor' sir, why he aint wuth savin'!' Jervis' sermons were plain and palatable and he was a good man. As a student he had learned medicine in Paris under the great surgeon Dupuytren, with the intention of applying his knowledge to parish work. And so it proved. He impressed Florence, and when she finally turned towards nursing, he taught her all he knew. Dupuytren's treatment of gunshot wounds proved highly relevant in the Crimea.

Although Florence came to abhor the polite and decorative existence of the kind followed at Embley and Ditcham, it did at least give Hilary an outlet for her own individual talent. She was a born artist, had a gift for drawing, a keen sense of form and colour, and she was an apt pupil. Her sketch-books abound with landscapes, portraits, and conversation-pieces, which are both aesthetic and highly personal. Her master at Ditcham was William White, a minor artist not mentioned in the reference books, who executed beautiful if a trifle idealised portraits of members of the family; some of them are illustrated here. His son also gave lessons, and it is thought that Hilary may have learned most of her technique from him. Her talent ripened during the next fifteen years, but alas she never fulfilled her promise as an artist because of social and personal inhibitions, which will be described.

Not long after her father's death in February 1838, Hilary travelled up to Liverpool to spend six months in a finishing school in Upper Parliament Street. This was a small boarding establishment for young ladies, of families holding liberal opinions in religion and politics; and in various other ways it was in advance of its time. The headmistress was Miss Rachel Martineau, sister of Harriet the popular author, and of James the renowned Unitarian divine. With this remarkable trio Hilary soon formed a lasting connexion. Rachel was a broad-minded and percipient teacher, giving her pupils full rein to develop themselves in their own way, and encouraging them to take interest in new ideas and current events. The young ladies paid regular visits to the Mechanics Institution where a Mr. Phillips was giving a course in Pneumatics. Phillips was a sensitive soul. 'At a chemical lecture not long since, at which all the experiments failed, he took it so much to heart that when

Miss M. asked him to a party, he said he could not yet enter into society!' Another time it was the theatre. 'Last week Miss M. took seven of us to see Charles Kean in *Hamlet* I had no *ardent* desire to see him and was neither more nor less disappointed than I expected. The rest of the troop was horrid bad.'

But the great attraction was Dr. James Martineau who held classes in astronomy, and whose sermons filled the Unitarian chapel in Paradise Street, of which he was minister. He was engaged at the time in a public controversy with the Anglicans, led by Rev. Fielding Ould. Ould had taken a very high line; accused the Unitarians of ignorance of the Scriptures, defective scholarship, and blasphemy; and misrepresented them as polytheists. That he was prepared to enter into discussion at all was, he inferred, an act of condescension, for the two parties were not on the same religious level. Martineau's reply was devastating. If Ould was reluctant to enter into discussion, then he could not be very sure of his ground, and arrogance merely served to mask weakness. No one had the monopoly of truth which could only be sought by continuous thought and rational intercourse. Moreover, dogma was of human not divine origin, nor was the Bible an infallible book. Unitarians believed in God, not three manifestations of Him. They revered Jesus, but refuted mystical pretensions, and applied the acid test of reason and conscience to all religious concepts.

There was no doubt that Martineau created a powerful impression. He is now acknowledged as one of the profoundest religious thinkers of the 19th century, and his influence upon ethics was very great. In 1839 he was at the beginning of a theological development which led him eventually to regard morality as the keystone of all religion, springing from an inner consciousness which is the Divine Spirit in man. This was in contrast to the older, predominantly rational creed which caused a number of Dissenters to abandon religion proper for political economy and mere secularism. Ironically enough this is what happened to James' elder sister, Harriet.

Hilary's connexion with Harriet Martineau in 1838–9 was a

brief one. After a penurious and painful youth, at odds with her mother, deaf and constantly ill, Harriet first seized public interest with her *Illustrations of Political Economy*, published in 1832. This book fed the popular appetite for 'knowledge without pain', and explained in fictional form such things as parliamentary representation and the structure of society to thousands of middle-class readers, lately agitated by the Reform Act and hungering for further reforms. Her success induced Harriet to move to London where she became a literary lion, and was welcomed above all by Liberal ministers who provided her with data for further *Illustrations* on Taxation, the Poor Laws, and similar subjects of current political interest. Harriet's industry was colossal. She published no less than thirty-six volumes of digested facts in two and a half years, and thereafter toured America where she lent her support to the abolition of slavery, a very hardy thing for a foreigner and a woman to do. On her return she produced *Deerbrook*, an indifferent but emotionally provocative novel, which entranced Hilary, who read it at Liverpool and met the author on one of her fleeting visits to Miss Rachel. Harriet was now at the height of her early successes, tirelessly writing, talking, travelling, and over-working beyond all reason. Finally she collapsed, took lodgings at Tynemouth, and remained there an invalid for four years.

It was at Tynemouth that Hilary paid her a prolonged visit in 1841, recording her impressions in a miniature journal, addressed to her mother. Although prostrate and often in pain, Harriet was mentally as alive as ever.

> Did I tell you that Dr. Greenhow [Harriet's physician and brother-in-law] has had a couch made for her on which she lies on her face. She sleeps on it with much comfort, and it is so contrived that she can write and read without inconvenience. . . . Another pursuit that Miss M. has planned for herself is reading Euclid and going on regularly to Mathematics. She has never studied Mathematics, as she had the clear reasoning mind and had not found it necessary or

advisable in her very busy days, but she has a great taste for them, and rejoices in having the leisure to attend to them now.

Harriet expatiated to Hilary on America and many other subjects, but when she gave her a 'curious account of Animal Magnetism', she presaged her own extraordinary recovery three years later. In June 1844 a Mr. Spencer Hall came to Newcastle to lecture upon mesmerism. Dr. Greenhow was a member of the audience, and recommended Harriet to give it a trial. A séance was arranged in the most respectable circumstances, and Harriet sustained immediate relief. She forthwith dispensed with all Dr. Greenhow's drugs, and entered upon a prolonged course of treatment, at the end of which time she pronounced herself completely cured. Soon afterwards she retired to the Lake District, whence she poured out a spate of books and articles for the remaining thirty years of her life. It is doubtful whether her output has often been equalled. It included more than 1600 articles for the *Daily News*, on subjects ranging from Drainage to the Death of Prince Albert and, at the behest of Florence Nightingale, a plea for medical reform in the Army; also *A Complete Guide to the English Lakes*, a formidable *Autobiography*, and some frank correspondence with a Mr. Atkinson, described as a 'phreno-physiologist', which made it quite clear that Miss Martineau no longer believed in God.

All this happened of course long after Hilary had left Tynemouth. But her meeting with Harriet was not an isolated event, for the Bonham-Carters and the Martineaus continued their acquaintance. Apart from correspondence, Hilary's two younger sisters, Alice and Elinor, duly attended Miss Rachel's school, while James Martineau's children also kept in touch. The main link was the fact that both families belonged to similar social and religious circles, liberal in outlook, and reformers at heart.

* * *

In 1842 the lease of Ditcham Grove finally came to an end, and the Bonham-Carter family was faced with the prospect of finding a new home. At this point Hilary's mother, Joanna, showed extraordinary initiative. She decided, ostensibly for health reasons, to take all the younger members of the family abroad for two years on a latter-day Grand Tour. Now such a venture belonged properly to the previous century, but doubtless Joanna recalled that exciting time when she had accompanied her father, William Smith, to Paris in the winter of 1802–3—indeed an unforgettable experience. She therefore made up her mind that her children should see something of the civilised world before committing themselves to the ties and tasks of a new home.

There was an 18th-century air to this journey in more than one respect. For one thing, Joanna borrowed an immense travelling carriage which Uncle Nightingale had had specially constructed for a similar enterprise five years previously. 'The inside was fitted with devices of his own invention for eating, resting, reading, and writing in comfort. On the roof were seats for servants and for the family to enjoy the air and admire the scenery in fine weather. Six horses drew the carriage, ridden by postillions.'* Thus equipped they took the steamer from Portsmouth where, Hilary noted:

> We had a most picturesque departure. Waiting under the old stone archway of the Sally Port at 12 o'clock, until a man with a lantern came flickering down the steps, and between starlight and lantern dimly burning we found our way over the strip of beach . . . and rowed quietly to the steamer, exalting our lantern to prevent a concussion.

The crossing to Le Havre was tolerable, but they thoroughly enjoyed the trip up the Seine to Rouen. Here they hired a second vehicle, for the entire party consisted of Joanna, Hilary aged 21, Fanny 19, Harry 15, Alice 13, Hugh 9, Elinor 5, Eliza Carter (a cousin about the same age as Hugh), Miss Rankin (the girls' governess), another nursery governess, Mr.

* Quoted from *Florence Nightingale*, by Cecil Woodham-Smith, page 19. (Constable.)

Hutton (Hugh's tutor), and a courier: twelve people altogether. Jack and Alfred came on later.

It soon transpired that abroad, as at home, many of the day-to-day responsibilities were to be placed upon Hilary's young shoulders; but it did not prevent her from enjoying all the new sights and experiences to the full. She was keenly alive to everything of interest and beauty, and busily recorded her impressions almost daily. Her sketch-books teem with little drawings of delicacy and acute observation—a peasant mother with her baby, the corner of an old street, a Gothic façade, or a broad view of the Rouen waterside—all these testify to her sensitivity and skill. Moreover, she and all the children, as they grew up, became keen linguists. They were very far removed from the type of English tourists then beginning to appear—rich, haughty, and thoroughly proud of their inability to talk the language and treat on equal terms with the 'natives'.

In due course the family convoy arrived at St. Germain, where they settled down for two months in a pleasant country surrounding, yet sufficiently close to the capital to enjoy its life and entertainments. At the end of June they moved into an apartment in the Champs-Élysées for the last six weeks of their stay. Fortunately for Hilary the person they knew best in Paris—Mary Clarke—was the one compatriot who was able to introduce her to the most stimulating and civilised company. The two women—though twenty-eight years apart—had first met in 1839 at the Nightingales', and had taken to each other with warmth. Now they happily renewed their acquaintance at Clarkey's home at No. 120 rue du Bac.

Mary Clarke was an extraordinary creature. Of Scottish-Irish origin, she had lived in France since the age of 8, and was a complete cosmopolitan. In appearance she was small, plain, with large bright eyes and masses of curls (then out of fashion), having all the fascination of a *belle laide*, bursting with charm and vitality. She talked brilliantly and inspired others, whether gifted or not, to do likewise. But of course there were many brilliant men and women at that time in Paris: Guizot, Thiers, de Tocqueville, Elie de Beaumont, the geologist, Roulin, the traveller and naturalist, the great Chateaubriand who lived in the rooms below Clarkey's, and Madame Récamier who had first launched her into society; all these and many others frequented the Clarke salon. But the two most intimate friends were Claude Fauriel, the medievalist and Provençal scholar, and Julius Mohl, the German-born orientalist, whom Clarkey married in 1847. These two men were to be seen nearly every evening at the rue du Bac, and helped to do the honours of the house. Mohl, incidentally, lived in a classical bachelor establishment with Jean-Jacques Ampère, the son of the scientist. Their rooms were piled with dust and books, and the story went that Clarkey finally agreed to marry Julius to save him from asphyxiation. Also that at the wedding Ampère was told to blow his nose loudly when the moment came for the bride to declare her age. According to Hilary, Julius Mohl had 'something of the droll half-sulky expression of a lion. What an idea of power he gives one, with his head as round as the world. He very often talks English and likes it exceedingly as a language, because it lends itself to the droll. . . . "Miss 'Illee, take this chair, it is the only decent chair in the room."'

Her description of a visit to Madame Récamier at Neuilly is equally vivid:

> Saturday. Behold Miss Clarkey had been invited to a matinée at Madame Récamier's . . . and thither we went straight from our atelier, trimming up our toilettes en route, and arriving at 4 o'clock. The salon de réception was exceedingly pretty, lofty, cool, with a red moulding on the walls, and the mosaic-looking inlaid floor that had a very Pompeian effect in the light of the closed blinds. Monsieur de Chateaubriand was there—but slipped away before half a dozen people had met. Poor old man, he dislikes company, and is ennuyé like all waning heroes. Madame R. was herself very amiable and graceful and elegant too (in blue muslin and black lace and white bonnet tho' this may not sound exactly like 60 years of age in dress).

YOUTHFUL STUDIES OF THREE OF JOHN BONHAM-CARTER'S CHILDREN: HARRY (top); JACK (*left*); AND HILARY (*right*)

Harry and his wife Sibella in old age; with their daughter Joan, and a grandson

But the great bond between Hilary and Clarkey was their passion for painting and drawing, and their enjoyment of pictures. They visited the Louvre together, where they settled down to draw in a 'deep and wide silence'; and discussed the merits of the Spanish school, which Hilary criticised for its gloom—'the mysterious, sombre, religious subjects of Spain, with its endless martyrs and saints'. She far preferred the Italians with their 'entrainé joyousness', or the Dutch with their 'conscientious, broad daylight imitation of Nature'. 'Miss Clarkey goes to the Louvre 5 days out of 7 from 9 till 11½, and to an atelier for 4 or 5 hours more, about as often, for her drawing is meat and drink to her.'

This atelier was Steuben's Life School. They went there because 'his drawing is so grammatical and good, and he is said to teach well; but this signifies less than it seems, for he comes only every alternate day and gives about 5 minutes to each person. He has 2 ladies' ateliers and 1 or 2 for men.'

At the beginning of August 1842 the entire Bonham-Carter family, now larger than ever with the arrival from England of Jack, Alfred, and Aunt Julia Smith, moved on to Switzerland. This was the second, and perhaps the true start of the Tour, which was to last until August 1844. We must, however, resist the temptation to delve too deeply into the neat packets of letters and the thick pink journals which so faithfully record this time. In general it may be said that the family 'did' parts of Switzerland and northern Italy with the utmost conscientiousness, at least in the summer months. Sometimes they kept together in a body. More often they split into divisions—the older boys, for example, making off with their knapsacks on a long march to Interlaken, Lauterbrunnen, over the Kleiner Scheidegg to Grindelwald, St. Gothard, and down to Hospenthal, where they met the main party; thence proceeding all together to Como, Pallanza, and the Italian Lakes.

For Hilary Italy was the next inevitable step in her career, as it has always been for amateur painters—but especially young females, armed with rolls of cartridge paper and canvas, and with exaltation in their hearts. Hilary was inspired by everything she saw, tearing off long ecstatic essays to the Nightingales and to Clarkey in Paris, missing nothing and yearning for the unattainable. She dreamed of living in Italy for ever, among the mountains and the monuments, giving up her whole life to her art, painting the purple and cypress landscapes, the classical ochre villas, the extravagant tones and traceries, and the dark dramatic Latins themselves: all beneath a pure sky as deeply blue as the depths of Lake Maggiore.

But such moods did not last. There was always the family: their plans and needs, and her deep abiding affection for them all. Nor could she entirely subdue her Puritan streak (uncharacteristically intolerant for a Unitarian). From Genoa, where they spent the winter of 1842–3, she complained:

> Did you ever go to Midnight Mass, as we have done? Detestable affair that it is. In a Theatre it would have been bad. In a Cathedral and calling itself a religious ceremony it is quite shocking. . . . In some of the churches they have what is called a 'Presepio', a model of the manger with little figures, some in yellow shorts, others en grande toilette à la mode—the stable, and the town of Bethlehem behind—and the puerilities throughout are miserable.

In March 1843 the expeditions began again, this time without Harry who, with his head shaved, was recovering from fever in Lausanne and being tutored by a Protestant pasteur. At Florence Hilary disappeared into the Uffizi and all the chapels, while at Rome she was naturally overwhelmed—by the unimaginable riches of the city, and by the heat. And so the summer passed slowly and idyllically until they all reassembled in the early autumn in Lausanne. In October Aunt Julia took Harry off to complete his studies in Berlin, while Joanna returned to England, leaving Hilary in charge of the children and the staff. Soon the cortège moved on again, not to Genoa as in the previous winter but to Nice, after an improving circulation through southern France by way of Orange and Avignon.

Hilary was disappointed in Nice, though the time passed well enough—in French lessons and dancing (not waltzes, which were considered indecorous), in drawing as always, and in excursions to the hills. The chief excitement was an accident to Miss Rankin, who was miraculously cured by Animal Magnetism. Joanna returned to her family in April 1844, and then allowed herself to be conducted by easy stages through all the old haunts into southern Germany, and so on to England at last at the end of August. Most of the children had been away for two and a quarter years.

* * *

For Hilary the return to full domesticity was hard. It was harder still having to traipse round after Mama, who seemed incapable of finding a permanent home. For years ahead life was to consist of a series of seasons in rented houses, punctuated by visits and family gatherings, seeing the same faces, hearing the same remarks. In December 1844, however, Hilary managed to escape the annual assembly summoned by the Nicholsons at Waverley Abbey, and spent Christmas quietly with Flo Nightingale. At 25 and 24 they both felt very old. 'Flo and I say there is not anybody so ancient as our 2 selves—centuries are nothing to us.' Later they recovered their spirits reading Miss Elizabeth Barrett's new poems.

In January 1846 Hilary wrote to Clarkey that she had been dining with

> another great lantern of these days. Mr. Macaulay is rather wonderful to hear, for he talks a great deal and has a most *extraordinary* memory: of course the critical world and folks with no memories at all think that he is conceitedly showing it off, but his intimates say it is perfectly natural and that the same tokens of it come in all his little everday talk or story-telling to the children of his sister, which one willingly and gladly believes, altho' his voice is *so* loud and he *does* address us altogether as tho' we were a crowd assembled before his hustings. I could not help thinking the while that Mr. Mohl

probably 'knows everything' more than he does by far, and has a marvellously more pleasant way of telling, without any trumpets intentional or otherwise.

More compelling than even Macaulay's loud voice was the news of Sir Robert Peel's conversion to Free Trade and his proposed repeal of the Corn Laws.

> It is generally expected that Sir Robert will carry his Bill and retire like a scapegoat into the Desert. . . . The Poor little Queen behaved in the most perfect manner thro'out her ministerial crisis. She was more earnest, simple and straightforward in her behaviour and in her letters than any sovereign with his royal etiquette has been for a long time past.

That summer the frightful news of the failure of the Irish potato crop and of starving peasants exploded into even the politest of English households. Hilary wrote with irony.

> People are very willing to give help *now*. There are fewer dishes at the fine dinner parties, and ladies manufacture rough garments to send over, and leave off buying little presents for themselves and their friends. Of course the shops begin to complain, and our own poor say they are set aside, so that the thing presses indirectly and will do so more and more until next harvest—it must be an unusually good harvest to do any *real* good. One wonders whether the animosity against England will be quite wiped out in the next year or two.

But the Irish Question and the Free Trade Question and other pressing questions of the day soon found their proper place with the advent of a new political excitement, for Jack was going to stand for Parliament.

Now Jack had followed his father at Trinity College, Cambridge, but he had not inherited John's brilliance. As an undergraduate he was diffident and dull, and had to be heavily coached to secure third-class Honours in 1839. But he took to politics like a duck to water. He spoke at his father's last election, and stood for Petersfield in 1842, though without success. Then in 1846 he was adopted in the Liberal interest at Winchester,* and in the following year was triumphantly returned at the head of the poll. He was greatly helped by his relations who turned out in force, and by the good name of his father—as related by Hilary to her friends in Paris:

> What a beautiful thing is a good man's memory!—for Papa's career was not a brilliant one—he was not eloquent—nor much admired nor followed after, but he was valued and trusted, consulted and trusted, and never found wanting, with a confidence that lives longer than a loud admiration.
>
> Jack did it very nicely, and looked so upright and young and honourable—neither diffident nor confident, that the comparison with the prosing Protectionising old Tory 'noodle' and the snarling declamatory wolf of a Radical, was greatly in his favour, tho' the latter is a well-known and clever orator. He came in at the head of the Poll too, tho' both of these were previously the members—the 4th candidate retreated silently the day before the Election, so that it was a complete triumph, and the enthusiastic 'masses' of Winchester gave him a tremendous *chairing* after it. They carried him round the town for 3 hours until he had perambulated nearly every street, with a band playing 'See the Conquering Hero comes', and shouting *à discrétion*.
>
> One zealous voter appeared at his window bearing a portrait of Charles James Fox, and a cry immediately arose 'That's Mr. Carter's grandfather', whilst one of the musicians turned round to gaze on the Honourable member himself saying 'He's quite a picter! Isnt he a nice little feller?' Another boasted that he had gone in the night and changed the 2 Tory names that were placarded about the town (from East and Portal) into *Beast and Bobtail*. One cunning old voter told my brother he was sorry the Government had made a new Bishop 'for there's too many of they *paarsons*, a-skrimbling about the old house like black rats behind the wainscot. Now and then one puts his head out of a hole and

* Winchester then returned two M.P.s.

gets worretted, but they're so numerous that we want a few good ferrets to send in after them and rout 'em out. If we send you to Parliament you must be one of they *Ferrets*!'

Jack had a long life in Parliament. He fought seven elections and kept his seat for nearly twenty-seven years—five more than his father—until 1874, when Gladstone lost to Disraeli in a landslide. Although Jack was less gifted and forceful than John, there was a striking resemblance between the two men, for both were modest and hard-working, avoiding the limelight and speaking but rarely in the House. They also had a common interest in the institution and processes of Parliament. In 1853 Jack introduced without success a Bill for secret voting at elections. Although included in an early draft, this clause had been struck out of the Reform Bill, and voters continued to declare themselves publicly at the hustings. It was not until 1872 that the system of the secret ballot was adopted, in which year also Jack became chairman of the Committee of Ways and Means and Deputy Speaker. The Press agreed that he was the best man for the job. 'No one has a more ample and minute knowledge of private business and the forms of the House; and no member more completely unites the recommendations of high character, conciliatory temper, and unfailing tact.' Earlier he had helped sponsor the Friendly Societies Bill, part of the campaign to establish the legal basis of the co-operative movement; and in 1866 he had been appointed a Junior Lord of the Treasury, but held the post only a few weeks before the dismissal of the Russell ministry.

This concern with the constitution and machinery of government was a family characteristic traceable to the Carters. The seed had first been sown by old John Carter II in his thirty-year wrangle with the Admiralty. The plant was fostered by his son, and then by his grandson, John Bonham-Carter I, notably in the scheme for the registration of voters incorporated in the Reform Act. It now flowered under Jack, and under Jack's younger brother Alfred, who was Referee for Private Bills in the House of Commons for nearly forty years, and worked intimately with Sir Thomas Erskine May on the famous compendium of parliamentary procedure.

Jack, then, was neither a leader nor a partisan, but a sound and reliable Liberal, and a broad-minded man. He gave himself no airs and was immensely liked. In his constituency he accumulated so much goodwill that he managed to survive the most unpromising elections, when the tide was running strongly against the Liberals elsewhere in the country. Electioneering in those days was both more personal and more good-humoured than now. Squibs and rhymes were the order of the day, with puns, local allusions and jokes of a schoolboy variety. Although these effusions have long lost their sting, the verses must at the best of times have been very feeble. Yet they do exude a faint savour of the age. Here is a tolerable example from the election of 1859, a close contest when Jack only scraped the second seat by six votes.

> Naughty Jem East
> Ask'd to a feast
> Call'd in Tom Fleming to cook it.
> Quiet Jack Carter
> Came shortly arter
> With Georgey Lefevre, and took it.

As it turned out East came in first, Jack just beat Fleming, and Lefevre was a long way at the bottom. Another rhyme with the chorus:

> Cheer, boys, cheer! for honest Bonham-Carter
> Cheer, boys, cheer! united heart and hand;
> Cheer, boys, cheer! your freedom do not barter;
> Cheer, boys, cheer! we're a tried and faithful band!

The best thing that can be said about that is that Jack was lucky to have a name that rhymed with *something*!

After Jack lost his seat at Winchester in 1874, there was an interval of eighty-four years before another member of the family entered Parliament, when his great-nephew Mark won Torrington for the Liberals in 1958. However, 1874 was not the immediate end of the family connexion with politics. Jack's eldest son, Johnny,* stood for East Hants (the old Petersfield division) as a Liberal Home Ruler in 1892 and 1897, but lost on both occasions (although only by a few hundreds in 1897) to a Unionist and a Conservative respectively. Thereafter the old Gladstonian loyalty petered out and, with one important exception,† the entire family drifted into a mild Conservatism.

After Jack had won Winchester in 1847, and married his first cousin Laura Nicholson in 1848, he stepped naturally into the social position left empty by his father ten years before. But one important thing was missing. The family was now 'county' and therefore required a 'seat'—but where? Ditcham had long been given up, Buriton was occupied by a tenant and the historic manor of the Gibbons used as an ordinary farmhouse, while the Meons were also unsuitable. But the real reason for rejecting these properties was geological and sanitary rather than social. For his health a Victorian gentleman felt it necessary to live on *sand*. The dry porous soil was an acknowledged antidote to rheumatism, and it did not foul the ladies' skirts in wet weather. Since clay and chalk were the predominant soils on the existing estate, this meant looking for a new site altogether—meanwhile Jack and Laura made their home in the old Castle House at Petersfield. Within a few years, however, they purchased some heath land at Adhurst St. Mary in the parish of Sheet, in the triangle between the Farnham and Guildford roads; and there in 1858 they erected a massive Gothic mansion, with all the appropriate outbuildings, gardens, and appointments. In later years Adhurst was duly added to until at one time the Bonham-Carter territory exceeded 6000 acres. All of it has now gone, for although Adhurst itself remains mostly intact, it has long since passed by marriage into a branch of the Lubbock family.

The Bonham-Carters were landed gentry, in the strict sense

* John Bonham-Carter III—see simplified pedigree on page 131.

† Maurice, who married Violet Asquith, parents of Mark—see page 129.

of the term, for not more than four generations. But only Jack enjoyed landownership as a fully economic enterprise, or could have done had he chosen, since the twenty years between the mid-1850s and the mid-1870s were an era of prosperity for British agriculture. This prosperity encouraged great technical interest as well as investment, and rapid progress was made in most aspects of farm practice. The crude prototypes of the early inventors were replaced by practical machinery, much of it hardly altered in principle today. The use of steam, though cumbrous and expensive, already anticipated the tractor and all the ramifications of power farming in the 20th century. Similar progress was made in crop husbandry and livestock. Although a great deal of pioneer work in evolving new or improved strains had long been completed, the lead was not widely followed—despite the efforts of the breed and show societies—until farming became generally profitable at this time. Jack and his tenants did not lag behind. At Buriton, for example, much wheat and oats were grown on the bottom lands, and 50 acres of the best hops. A flock of 500 pedigree Southdown breeding ewes were folded over the Downs in summer, and over massive fields of roots in winter; tended by four shepherds and an odd-job carter who moved the hurdles. In the autumn large numbers of heavy Devon stores were driven up from the West Country, on hoof all the way. On arrival they were sorted and sold against Buriton churchyard wall; the best of them then yarded until the spring when they were fattened off on the young grass. Likewise at East Meon it was all corn and sheep, but cow-keeping at Ramsdean. At Adhurst Jack had a fine herd of pedigree Jerseys, and milking cattle were later introduced to Buriton as well. Adhurst house, an interesting example in Gothic of balance in domestic architecture achieved *without* formal symmetry, was a symptom of confidence in English business and English farming; and everywhere about the countryside, similar houses, cottages and farmsteads were going up—monuments of Victorian solidity and unfortunate taste.

However, Jack was not a typical squire of the old sort, that is a resident landowner who lived off his rents, for he had considerable resources outside the Petersfield estates. He was chairman and majority shareholder of the Pike, Spicer brewery at Portsmouth. The income from this and other industrial holdings made it possible to maintain the landed estates at far above the rate of agricultural profits, and to enjoy all the rewards of country life—a large and comfortable home with beautiful grounds (whose upkeep demanded a dozen indoor and another dozen outdoor servants), shooting, fishing, and the generous entertainment of friends. None the less he never lost sight of the obligations of landownership: to give employment, husband the land, and take an active interest in the welfare of all those who worked for him, or who lived in the neighbourhood. Besides this, he lived a busy public life, unpaid of course. He was a M.P., a J.P., Deputy Lieutenant of Hampshire and High Sheriff in 1879, governor of two large schools, and prominent in many other ways in Petersfield and Portsmouth.

All this was of course the accepted pattern of country society, in which Jack had taken his place as an amiable and enlightened member. Yet it was to be undermined by the very principles—the basic concepts of Liberal economic policy—for which he stood. It happened in this manner.

Farming first felt the wind through a series of bad harvests. The summer of 1879 was catastrophic, the wettest season on record, and any rise in the price of grain was forestalled by a flood of cheap American corn, grown in a favourable climate upon the virgin soils of the prairies of the Middle West. Arable farming in England, hampered by the lack of landspace, the uncertainties of the weather, and the disabilities of tradition, never recovered and the bottom fell out of corn production. The home market, increasingly open to foreign competition through quickening communications, was able less and less to absorb the produce of British farms. Ten years later—thanks to refrigeration—the prices of stock also began to fall, and dead meat from America, Argentina, New Zealand, and Australia poured into the country. Cheese, butter, and wool were also heavily imported. There were now no more reserves with which to face the bad times. In any event the depression was no temporary phase, but the inevitable though delayed outcome of *laisser-faire* and Free Trade. Industry in Britain had developed to such a degree that it now depended for its existence upon the export of vast quantities of manufactured goods and services. In terms of simple economics, these had to be paid for by the import of raw materials and of cheap food emanating from the customer countries. In this way foreign food helped to keep the export trade alive, and industry had an interest in the depression of home agriculture.

The consequences for the English countryside were fundamental and far-reaching, for once the economy had been undermined, then the social superstructure slowly but surely collapsed. Many farmers went bankrupt, and most landlords were simply unable to maintain buildings and equipment out of rents, let alone obtain a reasonable return on their investment. This hastened the process which led to the virtual disappearance of the squire, and to the migration of over half a million agricultural labourers in the thirty years before 1914: an exodus encouraged by the gradual extinction of rural industries and crafts, and many of the ancillary employments of the countryside. Village life, though remarkably tenacious, slowly lost its homogeneity and force. One sign was the languishing of custom and peasant culture; another, the fact that most young country people of intelligence and enterprise left home as a matter of course.

Jack died in 1884, and so he lived long enough to see the beginning of the decline. But it was left to his son Johnny to stand up to the full force of the wind. That he was able to do so and keep the estate together was due almost entirely to his industrial possessions, and to the skill with which he reorganised the family brewery, and made it more profitable. Some of the outlying property was sold, and dairying was extended on the main farms—indeed this proved to be the means by which farming as a whole achieved a partial recovery in the early 1900s. Otherwise at Adhurst few apparent changes took place. Indeed, if anything, the social establishment was increased. Johnny was as generous and genial and just as popular as his father, though perhaps less devoted to sport. But he was fond of cricket and ran a country house festival, captaining a family XI called *The Old Caravan*. On one memorable occasion this XI, entirely composed of Bonham-Carters, defeated the town club of Petersfield.

Although twice beaten at the polls, Johnny was an indefatigable public servant. He built the village institute at Sheet, served on innumerable committees, and was a champion of 'higher' education. In fact his work in Hampshire contributed positively to the framing of the Education Act of 1902, which linked elementary and secondary schools, extended technical and other specialised forms of instruction, and made counties and county boroughs responsible for the training of older children.

With Johnny's death in 1905 the spirit of old Liberalism that had animated this branch of the family came to an end. His death also signalled the division of the estate, the preliminary to its final dissolution fifty years later. Adhurst was left to his daughter Helen, then a girl, and after her marriage in 1918 it passed out of the family altogether. Her husband, Alan Lubbock, has since emulated Johnny in distinguished services for local education, and is now (1959) chairman of Hampshire County Council. Buriton was taken over by Johnny's younger brother Lothian, who had lately been managing the brewery and living in the old house at 19 High Street, Portsmouth. Lothian was a fine sportsman, and a charming irascible man of pronounced Tory views, who did what he could to maintain the old standards of husbandry, and of paternalism in the village of Buriton. Likewise his son, Algernon, who succeeded him and who died in 1957. The history of Buriton between 1905 and 1958, when the final sales took place, was one of retreat under economic pressure. Portions of the property had to be sold off piecemeal—the Downs to the Forestry Commission, single or groups of fields to this neighbour and that, until at the end the whole estate barely exceeded 300 acres: hardly enough for the predominantly arable type of farming for which it was suited. A happy circumstance was the excellent restoration of the old manor house, and its proper use as the home of the owner. For the first time for over a century were revealed the full beauty of the panelling, and the spacious architecture of the Georgian rooms and embellishments. It was a fitting and fruitful Indian summer, coming at the end of so many years of family ownership, ever since Buriton was first bought by Henry Bonham in 1798.

The end of an old family property is naturally an occasion for sadness. Having shed tears, one must take the broad historical view, for family properties have been starting and ending since feudal days. It is better to look back with pleasure upon the stewardship of the land—the good crops grown, the stock raised, the prizes won, the hundreds of lives who derived their sustenance from the place, and whose descendants look back upon the family with affection and pride. That is a fine legacy. Buriton is now the home of another family, and the cycle of life will doubtless be repeated.

* * *

In August 1847—the year in which Jack began his political career—Mary Clarke and Julius Mohl delighted their friends by getting married. Hilary was particularly pleased, and from then on Julius became her chief correspondent. His eminence was increasing. Recently he had taken out French nationality and had also been appointed Professor of Persian at the Collège de France; but he never lost a broad European interest in public affairs, and his comments upon the growing tensions that led up to the 1848 revolutions were keen, wise, and restrained. He was a conscientious citizen too, and belonged to the National Guard; but found that before 1848 at any rate it was difficult to take his duties very seriously.

A few days ago [he wrote], I was on guard at the Tuileries. They put me as a sentinel before the great entrance from 12–2 o'clock at night. The corporal told me that I had nothing to do, and it was useless to tell me the watchword, as the soldier on the other side of the door would speak to the patrols. It was a clear and bitterly cold night, and as I was to do nothing I sat down in the sentry box meditating on the new planet. Many patrols passed me, but as I said nothing they went on peaceably. At last came a captain of the staff, who stopped a few paces from me, and we had the following dialogue:

Capt.: 'Factionnaire, dormez-vous?'
I: 'Non, mon capitaine.'
Capt.: 'Est-ce que vous n'avez rien à me dire?'
I: 'Non, mon capitaine.'
Capt.: 'Et pourquoi pas?'
I: 'Parce que mon caporal l'a défendu.'
Capt.: 'Comment!! Il vous a défendu de parler?'
I: 'Exactement.'
Capt.: 'Où est votre corps de garde?'
I: 'Au drapeau. Allez-y leur donner un savon, vous me ferez plaisir [please give them a wigging].'
Capt.: 'Quelle sacrée boutique!'

Then he went off in a fume, but I dont know what came of it. It is a wonderful institution!

Early in 1848, however, the situation was such that Julius Mohl had to take his guard duties very seriously indeed. Louis Philippe, who had long given up any pretensions to constitutional government, was forced by insurrection to abdicate; and fled to England with Guizot, his chief minister. A provisional Government then took charge, of moderate republicans under Lamartine and Ledru-Rollin, with the uncertain backing of certain socialists led by Louis Blanc. The passage of events resembled 1917 in Russia, but with a very different outcome. Under pressure, tremendous liberties were conceded —universal suffrage, freedom of the Press and public meeting, and 'national workshops' to combat unemployment. When a freshly elected Assembly attempted to modify some of these concessions, the Parisian workers rose in arms, only to be beaten down by the Army and the National Guard under General Cavaignac. A new constitution was then composed on the American model, with a legislative house and a President endowed with executive powers. In December 1848 Louis Napoleon, nephew of the great Bonaparte, became the first President of France with a clear majority of four million votes. Four years later he founded the Second Empire.

Hilary was able to follow what took place almost at first-hand, for the Mohls kept her regularly advised. Although she disapproved of Louis Philippe, Clarkey was an Orleanist at heart; while Julius was a moderate, prepared to accept any democratic régime capable of preserving order and the rights of property. Living as they did in the thick of events, their letters conveyed a vivid impression of the fears and troubles of the year. Clarkey tried to make things clear, by describing the situation as if it had happened in England:

> Imagine L. Philippe [she wrote in March], with the strength of 200,000 men, getting as drunk as a swine every night, and you will see a republic in your mind's eye, and yet a goodish sort of body in the daytime. Burning a few bridges, destroying a few rails, breaking all the windows, cutting Lord Robert's pictures to pieces, but not pillaging everybody, as he might do, not going into every man's house to set it on fire and even occasionally having some very good feelings, offering you his bottle which it is true he has taken [from] somewhere. At the same time so dangerous for the uncertainty of his movements, that all people who wish to preserve their property must be up 3 nights out of 5 to look after them. M. Mohl returned this morn at 5. It is the 4th night since Thursday last that he has spent patrolling streets in the rain—of course he cant do much in the day after. We may calculate that there are at least 80,000 gardes nationales in Paris, at this time, whose nights are thus spent; whose days consequently are diminished to one half of their value; that these 80,000 are taken from the most

industrious, enlightened morale of the nation, for as the service is voluntary it is the best who go.

I dined with Louis Blanc a fortnight ago, never thinking what he was to become. He is quite a dwarf with rather a pretty face. I took him for a little boy come to play with the Child of the House and was quite astounded he wanted to poke in his oar, but he was not much attended to. I thought he talked nonsense and did not listen.

In September, by which time the worst was over, the Mohls left Paris for a tour of Holland and Germany. Here too was the aftermath of revolution. In Frankfurt-am-Main a 'Professors' Parliament' had been sitting since May to devise a federal constitution for Germany, but it was already being undermined by both Prussia and Austria in their different ways. Over twenty years were to pass before Germany was to be welded by Bismarck into a single state, and then with only a semblance of democracy.

When Julius returned to Paris, he found things even less to his liking than before. Since his letter to Hilary is such an extraordinarily able appreciation of events, bearing the most prophetic presentiments, it is reproduced here at length:

> When we went away Cavaignac was all in all the most popular man ever seen. When we came back he was done for, and Napoleon (whom everybody laughed at a few weeks before) the great man and the inevitable President of a republic without republicans. The fact is that the republic never had any influence in the provinces except in a few towns as Lyons, Limoges, Rouen etc where the workmen are communists. The rest of the country would not hear of it, and the stupidity of the government did all it could to make a republic impossible. Therefore the peasants took hold of the name of Bonaparte, because some took him for his uncle, and the knowing ones hoped he would at least deliver them from the Republic; and when the politicals saw there was an army without chiefs, they went over to it, and so it came [about] that Thiers, Molé, Bugeaud, Montalembert and a heap of other ambitious and ambiguous men

became Bonapartists. It is a great shame, the moderate party had in a long and courageous struggle during 3 months effectually put down the red republicans, the communists, and even the party of the Nationals. The moderate people would have elected Cavaignac and forced him to get rid of the rest of the coterie du National and take reasonable ministers; we were sure to get out of the Slough of Despond by the mere force of public opinion, but now the inconceivable intrigue has disorganised the moderate party and given power to a man who is known for nothing but his foolhardiness, and who has shown himself during these last months to be as cunning as he is inefficient, and we are thrown back in a world of accidents and the most unforeseen enterprises.

One thing is certain that the red republic is killed, but it was not Bonaparte nor Thiers who killed them, but we moderate burghers who fought them in June and resisted them in everything—if anything can revive them it is the faults and imperial designs of this fellow B. The corruption of the Louis Philippe government has given us over to the republicans, their incapacity has delivered us in the hands of a pretender, and what his folly will do we shall see, but nobody can divine it. The great majority which he has got, is at any rate of great advantage to the country because it produces confidence in commercial transactions and will facilitate the re-opening of the workshops.

Lamartine is quite done for. . . . People say he is mad, I mean medically speaking, I dont know if it is true, he has been mad from vanity for many years, but this is rather an advantage in public life. I am heartily sick of all this and the eternal repetition of the same thing by everybody makes me half-crazy; we are lost in a mist of unreal follies and senseless words, and everything is neglected.

Quite soon conditions in Paris returned to comparative normality. On his marriage Julius had forsaken his bachelor flat in the rue de Grenelle, and went to live in his wife's home at 120 rue du Bac. Their apartments took up the third and fourth storeys. 'They had the fourth for their kitchen, servants' and spare room. . . . M. and Madame Mohl lived on the third, which consisted of two drawing-rooms divided from each other by a glass door, a large library, a dining-room, and bedroom. The drawing-rooms had two large windows looking into the garden of the foreign missionaries, which was full of trees and flowering shrubs, and gave a feeling of country although it was in the midst of Paris, which formed a background to the picture, with the dome of the Invalides and spire of St. Clotilde rising in the distance.' *

In a very short time the receptions regained all their former brilliance, being held on Friday instead of Saturday evenings, as in the past. 'Nothing,' we are told, 'gave dear Madame Mohl so much pleasure as to see the young people amusing themselves. The dining-room was given up to dancing, and tea was made in the small salon. The inner salon . . . was more than ever kept sacred to the more serious and distinguished guests. Sooner or later *every* distinguished person in Paris, French or foreign, passed through Madame Mohl's salon. . . . Mr. Mohl brought all the savants of the Académie and the Asiatic Society.' †

It was to this vital and renewed circle that Hilary had the good fortune to return in November 1849, and to live as an integral part of the Mohl ménage for a whole year. It was the pinnacle of her life. She was free at last of domestic responsibilities, and to devote herself entirely to art. Her master on this occasion was a man of substance in the artistic world, and moreover he recognised her ability. Philippe-Auguste Jeanron belonged to the Barbizon School, although he was not, one must admit, of the order of Millet. But he was a competent painter, a respected critic, and—when Hilary was in Paris—a man with an official position. Soon after the setting-up of the republic in the spring of 1848, he had been appointed by Ledru-Rollin to be director of the national museums, a post which he held until the end of 1850. Within a very short time he was able to repay this favour, by sheltering his patron in the

* Quoted from *Letters and Recollections of Julius and Mary Mohl*, by M. C. M. Simpson. (Kegan Paul.)

† Quoted from Simpson.

Louvre for twelve days during the June disturbances. He also prevented the mob from entering the museums, and from doing damage to the pictures and *objets d'art*.

Hilary, then, was very well placed. Unfortunately her letters make scant reference to her work—a darkly significant point—but it is not difficult to understand what happened, from the later remarks of her friends. We know that by January 1850 she had settled down to a routine, was happy in it, and had begun work in oils. Then—silence. Jeanron, it appears, was not a particularly good teacher, at any rate not for her. He was a landscape painter—a *paysagist*—while her forte was figure drawing, especially portraiture, and she was an adept at getting a likeness. Although, it was said, her drawing improved, she never mastered the handling of colour—Jeanron was himself weak in this respect—nor did she achieve finish or strong composition. Above all she never gained self-confidence, nor even the need for really hard work.

Of course a genuine artist—whatever the medium—is not only born but made. He has an inner compulsion by which he will overcome the obstacles of technique; and then, having become technically skilled, he is able to exploit his natural gift and impress his individuality upon the medium. There is nothing sadder than talent without technique. It is like frustrated love, or rather love that has allowed itself to be frustrated; and that is the explanation of Hilary.

Whereas at first she had been no more than irked by claims of family and friends, these had in time become a compulsive habit. So that, when finally freed from interference, she voluntarily created it anew. In Paris, for example, she characteristically allowed herself to become interested in Jeanron and his family, and devoted much thought to helping them in their various predicaments. This was not entirely weakness, it was due to the sense of altruism inherited from her forebears, and which ran right through the family. In public affairs and personal relationships it was a strength; in art it was fatal.

Clarkey saw it all too clearly, and it drove her nearly

demented, for she was convinced that Hilary had it in her to become a painter. Jeanron himself told her: How could he teach Miss Hilly who knew as much as himself? 'Drawing portraits! *Sketches* of her acquaintances—bah! An amateur? Non, un véritable peintre; un jour elle vendrera ses tableaux.' To Hilary, whom she loved, she became vehement: 'Draw, draw, draw', and reduced her to tears. And long after the year in Paris was over, Clarkey would write to Joanna: 'Pray exhort Hilly to work when you see her dragged about by everyone. I assure you she is too good-natured; that is her radical defect.'

But it was all to no avail. The time slipped pleasantly and all too quickly away. In July they all went to Vichy for the cure; and then in the autumn Clarkey took Hilary for a six weeks' visit to Madame Arconati at Pallanza, where they met Manzoni, the author of *I Promessi Sposi*, and some of Mazzini's friends. By December 1850 Hilary had returned to England. In after years she paid several more visits to the Mohls, and they to her, and they always maintained a loquacious and lively correspondence. But Hilary's chance had come, and irretrievably gone.

* * *

Whereas Clarkey would scold Hilary for allowing her life to deteriorate into 'one long faddle', Florence Nightingale—Hilary's first cousin—was even more outspoken, contemptuous even; but that was in character. The circumstances of the two women were remarkably alike in that both belonged to comfortable Liberal families, well educated, cultured, and socially responsible. None the less the daughters had no real future before them other than marriage; or if unmarried to look after mother. Florence, however, had set herself a far harder task than Hilary, for about the year 1844 she had decided that 'her vocation lay among the sick in hospitals'.* Now for women, hospital work and nursing were currently regarded with horror; for a refined young lady of good breeding, it was entirely out of the question. Nurses were thought to be sluts—

* Quoted from *Florence Nightingale*, by Cecil Woodham-Smith. (Constable.)

drunken, dirty, immoral creatures—and no doubt many of them were. To overcome this prejudice, therefore, was far more difficult than devoting one's life to art, which after all was concerned with the highest human instincts, and with beauty. True, many artists were supposed to be immoral, but not all of them were; and provided a young lady drew and painted what was suitable—not indelicate nudes, or nudes at all for that matter—there was nothing really wrong. Thus, when Florence Nightingale first made her wishes known to her family, they reacted with violence: mother, amazed and in floods of tears; her sister, Parthe, indignant and hysterical; only her father (Hilary's Uncle Night) seemed able to take the situation more calmly. He was distressed of course, but not really hostile, and preferred to retire into a limbo of his own where he could forget such unpleasant realities, and get away from family rows. But Florence held firmly to her course and in July 1850, when Hilary was at Vichy, she paid a visit to the Institution of Deaconesses at Kaiserswerth in Germany. This was a remarkable establishment, founded by a Protestant pastor, Fliedner, and his wife. It contained 'a hospital with a hundred beds, an infant school, a penitentiary, an orphan asylum and a normal school for training school mistresses'.* It was staffed by a hundred and sixteen deaconesses, and rigorously conducted on the most Spartan lines. A year later Florence spent a short apprenticeship there. It was the Rubicon of her life. In 1853 she was appointed superintendent of a small nursing home in Harley Street, and from there she set out for the Crimea in 1854.

This is not the place to retell the story of Florence Nightingale and the British Army in the Crimea; nor to research at any length into the remainder of her life. It is a subject that has already been treated with great thoroughness and critical brilliance by Cecil Woodham-Smith in her biography, a book to which I am deeply indebted for much of the information in this part of the chapter. The only point that needs to be

* Quoted from *Florence Nightingale*, by Cecil Woodham-Smith. (Constable.)

made—and it cannot be repeated too often—is that the Crimean adventure was but a short dynamic episode in Florence's long life, lasting less than two years. It was not the start and certainly not the end of her professional career, although it was the mainspring of all she did. After her return to England in 1856, at the age of 36, she survived fifty-six more years, most of which she devoted with demoniac energy to the reform of the medical services of the British Army, the training of nurses, and ancillary matters connected with hospitals, infirmaries, and workhouses. The source of this energy was of course her extraordinary will-power and sense of mission, but also the conviction that time was short. When she first came back, she had barely recovered from a bad bout of fever, and was both mentally and physically depleted. None the less she had to cope with a flood of publicity (which she hated), a summons to the Queen at Balmoral, and all the plaudits and presumptions of her family and friends. At the same time she threw herself into the compaign against the War Office. It was too much, even for her powers of resistance, and she collapsed. She felt certain she was going to die, and the doctors counselled absolute rest. But how could she rest when her real work was just beginning? Mountains of prejudice and red tape had to be removed, if the disasters of Scutari were not to be repeated.

Therefore she took deliberate steps, not to avoid death which was almost upon her, but to preserve her life as long as possible—by going to bed. She became an invalid, and filled her bedroom with faithful helpers whom she drove inexorably on. Some of them—those that survived—gave her years of devoted service, taking down her letters, running her errands, and enabling her to conduct an endless stream of business by which she did, in the end, accomplish the seemingly impossible. For she did not die. Her illness declined, and she slowly but surely recovered her strength. But her régime did not alter. The habit of invalidism had become too strong, and so she continued to write reports, belabour Ministers, and influence public affairs—all from her bed.

It was as Florence's chief companion that Hilary returns to this story for a brief interlude of two years. When Florence first took to her bed, she relied for her main support upon Aunt Mai (her father's sister, Mrs. Samuel Smith). Aunt Mai was a noble unselfish character, who had played an important part at Scutari, but she possessed a will of her own. In 1857 she agreed to abandon husband and family to give Florence all the help possible before she died. However, by 1860 Florence was still alive, and that summer Aunt Mai decided to go home—and go home she did. Florence was flabbergasted, then furious, and refused to speak to Aunt Mai for twenty years. It was at this juncture that Hilary reappeared. She had not radically changed since her long stay in Paris, but had been unashamedly 'faddling' for the past ten years. Her art remained much where it did, full of promise that was never fulfilled. None the less, she now took it on herself to model a statuette of Florence which was exhibited at the Royal Academy of 1862. The Nightingales did not like it. Characteristically it was a sketch rather than a finished work of art; but it was a better likeness, in purely realistic terms, than any of the other portraits of this period, and conveyed something of Florence's bitter strength as well as her compassion.

It might seem that Hilary had found her true vocation at last. She had always had great affection for Florence, a feeling that could now be united with her craving to 'do good'. Unfortunately it was Florence who was not satisfied. Although as fond of Hilary as ever and now dependent upon her, she could not bear to see good talent wasted, even if it was upon herself. She, Florence, had merely taken the place of Hilary's family, and she seemed to see in Hilary a reflection of herself, but as a failure. She therefore dismissed her in 1862 as kindly as she could, but with absolute firmness. When Clarkey came to hear of it, she implored Florence to take her back. 'If she is as useful to you as a limb, why should you amputate her? . . . She loves you better than anyone else, and it would be a balm to her poor worn out spirit if she thought she was useful to you. I say worn out because she is so.' But Florence was adamant for, as she thought, the best reasons. But it was not so. Hilary could not be changed now, and she only returned to 'faddle' her time away at home. Moreover she *was* worn out. She was in the early stages of cancer, and three years later—on September 9th, 1865—she died.

Hilary's slow illness and agonising death provoked a storm of rage and resentment in Florence. She railed against the stupidity and waste of it all. To Clarkey: 'There is *not a single person*, except yourself, who does not think that Hilary's family were quite right in the most monstrous of slow murders—and all for what? . . . I shall never cease to think as long as I live of you and M. Mohl as of Hilary's *only* friends. The golden bowl is broken—and it was the purest gold—*and the most unworked gold*—I have ever known. I shall never speak of her more, I have done. . . . How I hate well meaning people.'

* * *

But Florence had not finished with the Bonham-Carters. She had already begun to rely upon another member of the family, Hilary's younger brother Harry, now a married man and head of a large insurance company in the City. He was of quite a different stamp.

Harry had spent his childhood at Ditcham and gone to boarding school at Dr. Malleson's at Hove, where he stayed until the age of 15. He joined in the Grand Tour and continued his studies, first under pasteur Espèrendieu in Lausanne, and afterwards in Berlin where he arrived with Aunt Julia Smith in October 1843. There he found another excellent tutor, Herr Barthelmann, who also arranged for him to attend lectures at the University. Harry was fortunate in his timing since he was able to study history under von Ranke and philosophy under von Schelling. In any event he was so grounded in German thoroughness and application that it had a lasting effect upon a naturally serious character. In after life he not only displayed a keen incisive brain, but also the ability to work long hours—in effect to do two jobs at once, as Florence Nightingale found to her advantage.

Harry came back from Germany in the summer of 1845, and went up to Trinity College, Cambridge, to read mathematics, exactly as his father had done. Three years later he completed the final examinations as 5th Senior Optime, equal with William Waddington, who later became French Ambassador to the Court of St. James. At this point he parted company from his father who, it will be remembered, had 'conformed'. Since religious sanctions* were still in force at Cambridge, it was necessary to make a declaration of orthodoxy before graduating. This Harry, then a young die-hard Unitarian, refused to do, and so he never received his B.A. In other respects his early career exactly followed his father's, for he began to read law and was called to the Bar at Lincoln's Inn in 1853. For several years he practised as a conveyancer and equity draftsman, and also went the Western Circuit. Early on he had acted on one occasion as judge's marshal to Baron Martin, and was entertained at Strathfieldsaye by the old Duke of Wellington shortly before the latter's death in 1852.

Harry was probably too modest and retiring ever to make a fortune at the Bar. His fee-book (which survives) though an imposing vellum volume filled up but slowly. It had, however, a direct bearing upon both his marriage and his career. In 1853 his mother Joanna at last succeeded in finding a permanent home at Keston in Kent. Ravensbourne was a largish mid-Victorian house, built of flint, with a pretentious tower. But it had a charm of its own, standing in thirty acres of grounds, with a garden sloping south to the Ravensbourne stream in a little valley, about 200 yards below the house. Joanna had been persuaded to buy the place by a neighbouring landowner, George Warde Norman, who lived at the Rookery, Bromley Common, about a mile away. It was all open country then, and only fourteen miles from London Bridge. George Warde Norman was a Liberal, a well-read, cultivated man, and a

* See page 27.

friend of Charles Darwin at Down. Director of the Bank of England for fifty years and a member of the Committee of Treasury, he was also closely connected with banking and the City by friendship and family. His wife was the daughter of a banker, three of his sons entered banking, while his grandson Montagu Norman, was Governor of the Bank of England for twenty-four years (1920–44).

Norman had two daughters: the elder, Sibella Charlotte, married Harry Bonham-Carter; the younger, Mary, married Harry's elder brother Alfred. Harry's suit was unpopular at first. Sibella had more eligible admirers, notably John Lubbock (afterwards Lord Avebury) whom, however, she rejected; but her father was adamant on the grounds of Harry's uncertain future. Fortunately other Normans came to the rescue, and by their influence he was offered the post of Sitting or Managing Director of the Guardian Fire and Life Assurance Company in 1861: a duty that he proceeded to discharge with solid success for the next forty years, during which time the premium income of the Company multiplied many times, and the value of the shares increased by over 100 per cent.

Harry and Sibella were married on June 10th, 1862. Harry kept a diary for most of his life, but it was a terse unromantic document—he was not an imaginative man—and the entry for this memorable occasion reads as follows:

> Married this day at Bromley Common Church by Mr. Rawson. All my people there. Except Frances. Rained in the evening.

The honeymoon was spent at his brother Jack's house at Adhurst, and not long afterwards the couple removed to London—first to Seymour Street, then to 91 Gloucester Terrace (now 145), Paddington—where they raised an immense Victorian family, which is the principal reason why there are so many Bonham-Carters alive today.

About the time that Harry was courting Sibella, Florence Nightingale was setting up her headquarters at the Burlington

Hotel in London, whence she conducted her campaign for nursing reform. An important aid was the Nightingale Fund, a large sum of money publicly subscribed as a mark of the nation's gratitude for her work in the Crimea, and which had accumulated by 1859 to over £45,000. As a result of her experiences, Florence decided to use this money to supply a fundamental need not only of the Army but of the nation as a whole—qualified nurses of decent character. She therefore drafted two schemes—both of which were financed from the Fund—for the training of nurses and of midwives. The former was the more important and immediate project, and was worked out in collaboration with St. Thomas' Hospital, for whose resident medical officer, Dr. Whitfield, and matron, Mrs. Wardroper, Florence had the highest regard. As a result of their efforts the Training School was opened in June 1860 with fifteen probationers in residence.

The aims were clear and specific: 'that nurses should have their technical training in hospitals specially organised for the purpose; and that they should live in a home fit to form their moral life and discipline'. The School began in an atmosphere of criticism, for the eyes of all were fastened upon this daring experiment. But Florence was determined it should not fail. Not only had the candidates been thoroughly scrutinised, but their subsequent progress and behaviour were watched with the minutest attention—by Florence herself. The girls wore a uniform, received practical instruction in the wards, attended lectures, took notes and even kept diaries (which Florence looked at), and were subjected to confidential reports of the strictest standard and detail. In contrast to this severity, every attempt was made to make the girls feel 'at home'. They lived in an upper wing of St. Thomas', pleasantly furnished and decorated with flowers, supplied with books and other comforts, and were looked after by a sister in charge. Thirteen out of the original fifteen probationers received graduation certificates at the end of their year's course. They were the pioneers of the modern profession of nursing, not only in Britain. They and their successors 'were sent out singly or in parties to carry and communicate their skill and their high character to other hospitals and other countries; new training centres were founded . . . a very large number became matrons, superintendents and ward sisters, and in later years many trained as district nurses'.* Wherever they were—in Britain, parts of the Empire, the United States, or Germany—Florence kept up an immense correspondence with them all, almost until the end of the century.

But not even she could have sustained this mighty effort without willing and efficient helpers. When the Nightingale Fund was first formed, Florence had appointed as Secretary Aunt Mai's son-in-law Arthur Clough, the poet. Clough was one of Florence's most devoted slaves, but he was a sick man and died soon after taking up the appointment in 1861. His place was then taken by Harry Bonham-Carter who held the post until 1914; to be succeeded by Walter, one of *his* sons, who continued the work until 1947: a grand total of just under eighty-six years between them. The work was voluntary—it carried an honorarium of £50 a year—and for some time it was onerous. Harry's diaries, laconic though they are, are sufficiently revealing. There were innumerable committees, visits to St. Thomas', interviews, correspondence, accounts—all these took up his time after the office several days a week, and other spare time as well. It was his form of public service: part of the common duty which, he thought, everyone should try to perform. Sibella bore his absence with patience but she did not find it easy. However, she admired and liked Florence, who in turn took an affectionate interest in her family.

Harry's good head for business was of inestimable value to all Florence's work. It was he who drafted the original rules for the Training School, which remain basically unaltered to this day, and later became a governor of the Hospital. He also helped found the District Nursing Association in London, and

* Quoted from *A Sketch of the Life of Florence Nightingale*, by Rosalind Nash. (S.P.C.K.)

worked closely with William Rathbone, Florence's friend and colleague, the pioneer of nursing in Liverpool. But Harry was no slave. When a session became protracted, he would say to Florence quite firmly, 'Now I must go home to dinner'—and went. For a long time she refused to see him at all, simply because she was so busy, but kept in touch by letter or messenger. A commissionaire, an old soldier, would bring a note to Gloucester Terrace about breakfast time and wait for an answer. Eventually Harry found this method inadequate as a sole means of contact, and threatened to resign. Florence then consented to see him, receiving him in her bedroom at No. 35 South Street, which had been her home since 1865. On August 8th, 1873, Harry noted in his diary:

> Saw Florence by appointment, for the first time for at least 14 years. Sitting up in bed, face much filled out and fat-looking. Voice much the same and expression very affectionate.

After that there were regular visits, at least once a month. Joan—Harry's only daughter—vividly remembered these occasions:

> We used to walk across the Park to South Street on a Sunday. Walking in London was pleasanter then, the traffic more leisurely, all horse-drawn vehicles of course, but the streets were dirtier and had to be constantly cleaned. The Park itself was much the same as now, but only private carriages were allowed. The paths were not tarmaced and had to be watered to keep down the dust. South Street was a modest quiet street off Park Lane, and we children used to wait in the dining-room while my father went upstairs to see Miss Nightingale. I remember the downstairs room well. It was full of improving books, of no interest to us. I was quite young then.*

Although Florence Nightingale had to contend with a tough and tenacious opposition, her prestige was already immense

* From a broadcast talk given in December 1949.

and her advice sought on all sides. In 1864 she drafted the instructions for the British delegates to the Geneva Convention which provided for the neutrality of wounded in war, and led to the foundation of Red Cross Societies in practically every country in Europe except, strangely enough, England. The idea, however, did not die, and was forcefully revived at the outset of the Franco-Prussian war in July 1870. Thanks mainly to the efforts of Col. Robert Loyd-Lindsay, V.C.,* an organisation sprang into being with the provisional and cumbrous title of the *British National Society for Aid to the Sick and Wounded in War*. Large funds poured in from the public, and at the end of August a representative visited both sides to offer money, supplies, and the services of surgeons. This offer was accepted. The battle of Sedan was fought on September 1st, and ten days later Harry Bonham-Carter accompanied Capt. Douglas Galton, R.E.,† on a mission to the German hospitals. In fact the two men soon separated, each following his own itinerary. Both returned to England about the end of the month.

Harry kept a meticulous journal and wrote a number of informative letters home, all of which have survived. Characteristically, they lacked imaginative and descriptive power—which is sad for the historian—but overflowed with facts and figures, which presumably he was sent out to obtain. He was immensely conscientious and industrious, travelling down the Rhine to Düsseldorf, Cologne, Bonn, Coblenz, and Mainz; and making rail trips to Frankfurt, Darmstadt, Mannheim, Heidelberg, and Karlsruhe. He paid a visit to the Fliedner Institute at Kaiserswerth, where he found a great effort being made to send nurses to the front. And he was generally impressed by the comparative efficiency of the rear hospitals and compounds, where the wounded of both sides were being treated with equal humanity. Occasionally he encountered a rabid nationalist, who reminded him of the treatment of

* Later Lord Wantage.

† Husband of Marianne Nicholson, Harry's first cousin.

Germany by Napoleon I, but in the main the atmosphere was seemly and civilised. The Germans were of course jubilant at their early successes. Although medicines and stores were in fair abundance, the demands of the campaign were such that by the end of his first week in Germany, Harry had made grants of no less than £8000—part of the grand total of £220,000 contributed by the Society to the war.

Harry's excellent command of German made his task in the Rhine area comparatively straightforward. But he talked French less well, and naturally enough found conditions in the occupied part of France less easy to cope with. On September 24th he was at Saarbrücken where he boarded a crowded military train to Remilly.

> Lucky in finding a first-class carriage with three officers, a young Prussian cuirassier going to join his regiment before Paris after recovering from a wound obtained at Gravelotte; and two Landwehr, captain and doctor, bound for the Army before Metz. The train enormously long with provisions and troops went at a snail's pace till we reached the highest level, passing by Styring, a coal and iron mining town close to Forbach, the houses on both sides covered with bullet marks, the roofs of the large workshops and furnace chimneys considerably damaged. Entered France between Saarbrücken and Styring about 3 miles from the former, the boundary marked by a clearance cut through the Forest. My companions somewhat excited at seeing the graves of the fallen on the field which were visible in many places from the Railway.
>
> Every station occupied with a detachment of troops, every house for pointsmen or policemen occupied by two or three soldiers and patrols at other places, especially above the deep cuttings. At several stations herds of sheep and cattle feeding in the adjoining meadows. The trains made up of waggons and carriages bearing the names of every railway in Germany, besides many of the 'Est'—the Paris and Strasburg through-line.
>
> At Remilly got out some hundred yards from the station

and shouldered my traps and basket of provisions till a blue bloused extemporised porter relieved me. No Frenchman, but a German from Magdeburg. I addressed a soldier at the door of the Hotel de France (Café et Restaurant. Ecurie et Remise pour 40 Chevaux) and discovered the object of my search. Passing through a lower room devoid of furniture, beyond a small table and chair and about a dozen mattresses piled in one corner, I followed my soldier up a narrow dark staircase with a shaky handrail, the unceiled roof above, and was shown two doors on the first floor, on which 'Times Correspondent' was written in pencil in large letters. In one of these I found . . . Mr. Woods, the well-known newspaper writer, now sub-editor of *The Times* . . . and other gentlemen. My hosts were satisfied with mattresses on the floor of the sitting-room, and offered me a third, not divesting themselves of much of their clothes. I was however accommodated in the adjoining room with a handsome bedstead, part of the remaining furniture of the house. I however soon discovered the cause of my friends' preference in the very powerful odour which permeated my apartment from a stable beneath, mingled with that of carbolic acid which had been plenteously applied as a remedy. I turned in at a somewhat late hour leaving my companions still engaged, the one in dictating, the other in writing a brilliant account of the sortie from Metz on the previous day at which the whole party had by a lucky chance assisted.

And so on, and so forth. The narrative poises tantalisingly on the edge of some really graphic piece of description, which it never quite achieves. One has the impression that Harry was the perfect phlegmatic Englishman, seemingly unmoved by any horror or inconvenience, and pursuing his dogged course with 'traps and basket of provisions'.

He managed to reach Sedan, by hired carriage, but left no account of it. A letter found among his papers, however, from an unknown correspondent provides this brief but vivid appendix. It is dated September 11th, ten days after the battle.

I heard that a portion of the French army which had surrendered itself was to pass through Sedan this morning, and I heard these men were dying of hunger. Col. Dalton told me that he had seen them shut up on an island with a gun pointing down the bridge which led to the mainland, and they were starving. They had only about one biscuit (and that a small one) to each man every eight days, so some of the Prisoners told me themselves today, and horseflesh, and even that they were now being forbidden to kill. I had bought some loaves of bread coming here yesterday hearing there was very little in the town, and I determined to cut them up and have them ready, but they came before I was ready, thousands of them. I passed down with them giving cigars which I had. Their gratitude knew no bounds—'ah monsieur, we are hungry! They have nearly starved us, many have died. The rain poured down on us, as we lay on the ground—we have only had some boiled horse and no salt. Oh for a bit of bread.'

Harry was home again by October, and found a delighted Sibella awaiting him. She had feared he might catch cholera, and had written some anxious and touching letters. He would never again have to face such an ordeal, for this was at the height of Victorian progress and prosperity, when war was no longer part of the prospect. He could have no idea that forty years later five of his sons would take part in a far greater German war, or that one of them, Charles—my father—would rise to become a senior general in the British Army.

* * *

As recorded, Harry and Sibella were married in June 1862. When their last child was born in October 1880, their family amounted to twelve—eleven sons and one daughter: a classical example of a mid-Victorian middle-class household. Yet, although large families are often the product of comfortable circumstances and a firm faith in the future, Harry Bonham-Carter was not at the outset particularly well off. His salary at the 'Guardian' never exceeded £1500 a year, while his private income at this stage was about £400. No doubt Sibella had some money of her own as well. None the less their combined resources were not so large as to afford a luxurious way of life; nor were they by nature self-indulgent. Later, when Harry became comparatively rich through a fortunate investment in a Welsh coal-mine, he behaved with the utmost generosity towards his children and dependents. Until then, to raise and educate twelve children called for careful living, even in the 1880s with income tax at 7d. in the £. Moreover, the domestic staff was considerable, as befitting the station of the family and the custom of the age.

My father, Charles, the third from youngest, was born in 1876. It was always a puzzle to him to remember how they all fitted in during the holidays, and before his eldest brothers had left home. Fortunately 91 Gloucester Terrace, although a narrow house like its neighbours in that part of Paddington, was tall and rose to five storeys. The top floor was allotted to bedrooms for his only sister Joan, the cook, and three or four maids. The third floor consisted of a day nursery, and of a night nursery in which he slept with his two younger brothers and their nurse. Harry and Sibella slept on the second floor, and had a boy with them. Adjoining were two other rooms, always full of boys. The first floor consisted of front and back drawing-rooms; the ground floor of dining-room, school-room, and a dressing-room; while the basement was the preserve of the footman. As the boys got bigger, some of them had to be boarded out. Such was the crowded ménage until 1886 when the whole family removed to 5 Hyde Park Square, a much more commodious house, convenient for the Park, and a 'better address'. Harry modernised it too. At 91 Gloucester Terrace all hot and cold water had to be carried up endless stairs in cans, and saucer baths taken in the bedrooms. At 5 Hyde Park Square he installed two bathrooms and a hot water and central heating system. On the ground floor there was a proper cloakroom, with a screen of stringed beads in the window, and a flush lavatory with a small placard bearing a discreet message which read, 'Do the deed that must be done'.

Charles was just able to remember his nursery days. There were no lying-down prams then. All children were carried until they could sit upright, side by side, in a mail-cart, iron-tyred, and pushed with resounding clangs over the joints of the stone pavements. He recollected the daily walk to the Albert Memorial, mornings spent under the shade of the trees in the summer, the 11 o'clock drink of milk, and nurse sitting on a camp-stool always sewing. At noon the younger children were brought home and put to rest in a dark room. The nurse was Catherine Outram.

Charles wrote:

> She came to our mother towards the end of 1863 from Bromley Common. She was the daughter of a roadman and very decently educated, though I dont think she had time to read anything but the Bible. To this she was devoted, and to the end of her life she was a member of the Bible Class under the Vicar of St. James' Church, Paddington. She was the salt of the earth and we loved her dearly. She was always equable in temper and practical, and suffered from only one drawback. Being very short-sighted, she saw very little of what we were doing, and to this I attribute my incurable habit of bolting my food. When we were grown up, she became the perfect valet and kept all our clothes in faultless order. The nursemaid was always French or Swiss.
>
> Another firm friend was William Simmons, who came as footman in 1880. He was a little man, and very plain. He was a kind guide and guardian who used to take us rowing on the Serpentine, and to see the Varsity Boat Race from the towpath at the point of the bend above Putney. Later when we used to spend the Easter and summer holidays in the country, he would join us in our games of 'stump' cricket, and was our popular companion. He died in 1928, not long after he was pensioned. I remember William too as the perfect buffoon who gave us many hilarious moments, play-acting and singing. He had a close friend, Fred Roberts, a

postman who rendered patriotic ditties at our annual servants' dance, suiting actions to the words:

Here upon guard am I
Willing to do or die
Fighting for Queen and Country too
Fighting for home so dear
Cannon are there in sight
Bayonets to left and right
Hands, true and steady
Are willing and ready
And hearts that know no fear.*

Our life as children conformed to the pattern followed by most other families of our sort. I remember going to the dining-room for family prayers before breakfast, sitting with the servants on chairs along the wall. Father would read a passage from the Bible, and then say the Lord's Prayer and a few other simple prayers. This was the custom in practically all the houses I visited until I grew up, and for long after that. Grace would be said at dinner parties, if not at other meals. At home we did not see much of our parents again until the evening, when we spent the two hours after tea in the drawing-room. Father often did not return from work till late, having so much to do for Miss Nightingale. His long absences, his retiring character, and the fact that he wore a beard made him seem rather remote; and we stood in awe of him. But he was, we discovered, the gentlest of men; and as we grew up we got to know him far better and respected his fine intelligence and keen sense of duty. On Sundays we all went to church, and in the afternoon walked with our parents to visit friends.

In matters of formal religion, Father was extremely broad-minded. Although he no longer attended chapel, he subscribed all his life to the High Street Unitarian Chapel at Portsmouth, and in certain matters of dogma declared his Nonconformity even in church. For instance, he would never turn to the east nor genuflect, while any reference to the Trinity, in the Creed or elsewhere, would elicit from him an audible 'No, no.' Our mother, on the other hand,

* Words by Harry Adams (Howard & Co.). Music by E. Jongmans.

was a strong churchwoman and brought us all up in the orthodox Anglican faith. If for some reason we were unable to go to church on Sundays, we would go through the service at home. She would often read the Bible to us, and poetry in the evenings, especially Milton which some of us never forgot. She never ceased to educate herself, was a fair artist and took drawing lessons in middle life. She wrote to all her children every week when they were away from home, and at her suggestion we ran a family newspaper, the *BCNews*, which circulated for about five years in the 1890s. Like Father, she did some form of public service—mainly visiting in the Paddington Infirmary—almost all her life. She was almost a saint.

After leaving the nursery, we were allowed much freedom and became self-reliant and independent, travelling about London in pairs or even alone. You cannot imagine how different it was then. Horses everywhere, gangs of men always at work cleaning the streets—the muck used to be sent in railway trucks, I believe, to the market gardens of Essex and Bedford—street criers and hawkers of every kind. I once saw a Jack-in-the-Green coming down Chilworth Street: about the size of a telephone box, with a man inside covered with greenery, with others dancing or rather trotting around. Sometimes we were given money for a theatre, 2s. 6d. for a seat in the Pit, 4d. for bus fares, and 2d. for buns. The first time I went with an elder brother to a performance of *The Mikado* at the Savoy. I must have been eight or nine, he eighteen months older. Although a considerable queue had formed, we quietly inserted ourselves at the head of it, and were received with laughter. Usually we went early to the Pit door, taking with us a miniature chess board and playing till the doors opened. I saw many of the leading stars of the stage: John Hare, J. L. Toole, Beerbohm Tree, William Terriss, Charles Wyndham, Mary Moore, the Kendals, etc. I never saw Henry Irving, nor Ellen Terry till much later. I saw Marion Terry in three or four beautiful performances. As schoolboys we went out frequently, eating first at a restaurant, often Gatti's, where we had a chop or steak, Welsh rarebit and a tankard of beer. Father always kept a horse and pony in the mews behind our house. He rode in the Row in Hyde Park every morning before breakfast, taking a son with him. We were taught to ride in a school off Bishop's Road and learned well enough to come to no harm.

We spent our holidays at Easter and in the summer out of London. Sometimes we stayed with our grandmother (Joanna) at Ravensbourne where a nursery and extra bedrooms had been added for our benefit. The nursery walls were all papered with drawings cut from the *Illustrated London News*, well varnished over so that they were protected from picking fingers: an unending joy to us. The pond below the house was full of sticklebacks which gave us hours of good sport with a worm tied on to a length of thread. At the outflow there was a noisy ram which pumped water to the house and which, until I was well past nursery age, filled me with terror. It was there that I saw Cousin Flo Nightingale for the first time, walking in the garden with a stick, appearing to me very old. She was actually 64, and lived another 27 years. My next meeting with her was as a cadet at Sandhurst, some ten years later, when she showed great interest in me and told me I 'would get to the top'. Though mellowed in her old age, she was still a formidable character and frightened many people out of their wits. But she always had a soft spot for soldiers, and in my case she cheerfully abandoned an important appointment if I would go and see her. I kept some of her letters. The one quoted here shows her deep humanity and humour, for she was a very wonderful humane person.

Jan 28/97
10 South Street
Park Lane W.

Dear 'Charlie'

I should be very sorry not to see you before you go.

Would 5.30 or 5 tomorrow (Saturday) or Sunday suit you?? Or have you twenty-five better engagements?

Your affecte

F. Nightingale

This is you!

Je suis le capitaine de vingt cinq soldats
Et sans moi, Paris serait pris

After 1880 Father leased a small house called 'Woodside' at Keston on the Norman estate nearby. Woodside was on the edge of Hayes Common, and had about three acres of land with two cottages attached. The gardener lived in one, and our servants in the other when we came down from London. Behind lay Padmill Wood, through which a path led to Ravensbourne, only a few hundred yards away. It was a good place for boys for, besides a tennis court and a meadow for cricket, we were free to wander over the neighbouring land. We used to ride down there occasionally by way of Herne Hill and Dulwich. After our grandmother died in 1884, Ravensbourne was let, and we all squeezed into Woodside. Notwithstanding our large numbers, there was room for visitors, we boys crowding together into dormitories much like we used to do at Gloucester Terrace. We were quite comfortable and very happy. Under each bed by day was a hip bath. These were put in a row in the morning, and we filled them with cold water with a hose from the tap in the garden below the window, and after our baths we siphoned the water out.

We were mad on games. There was a boys' cricket club at Hayes, while the Keston village team was largely manned by schoolboys in the holidays, and many of the large houses had cricket grounds of their own. I played at Chilston (Akers Douglas), Iden (Hoare), Ledgers (Buxton) and Chelsfield, where my uncle Ned Norman always played for the village. The Normans also ran the West Kent cricket club at Chislehurst for many years, where we often played. All these and others, such as the Lubbocks, Hambros and Goschens were close friends or relatives, in the main City families of substance much like ourselves. Willie Hoare was a queer fellow, but very kind. He once sent us a remarkable postcard:

'Will you come and shoot partridges on Saturday, so-and-so has chucked. Yrs W.H. P.S. I have just heard that so-and-so can come after all, so dont trouble.'

* * *

When still a small boy, Charles attended a day-school in London owned by a clergyman called Topham, and largely staffed by members of his own family. The youngest children were taught by the three Misses Topham.

They must have been efficient teachers. From them I learned to write clearly and quickly. I have not seen their method adopted elsewhere. A pencil was tied across the palm of my hand with the end protruding beyond the base of my little finger. This had the effect of keeping my hand straight and forced me to use my fingers. Of the other two Rs., I was slow at reading and quick at sums. We also had lessons in geography and natural history.

In April 1886, when I was ten years old, I went to a boarding school at Rottingdean, then a charming unspoiled Sussex village. A long straight street led inland from the seashore to the green, which was flanked on one side by a flint Norman church and on the other by houses occupied by the gentry. Burne Jones lived in one, and Rudyard Kipling for a time in another. When I arrived, the school took up three houses in the centre of the village. The only grounds consisted of a strip, far from level, approximately 60 × 20 yards, used as a playground, with a gymnasium at one end of it and two fives courts. There was also a large private garden. In those days far less was demanded of private schools. The food was ample but roughly served. There were practically no organised games, and to change into flannels was an event. We never had matches against other schools. Instead on half-holidays we played football among ourselves in the next valley and cricket on Beacon Hill, about ¾ mile distant. These grounds were no more than open downland, quite rough and grazed by thousands of sheep. There were no shelters of any sort. Doubtless the absence of luxury did us no harm, and we certainly had no idea that we suffered from any hardship. The sanitary arrangements were old-fashioned. Once a week we had baths filled with hot water by Solomon, the general handyman, who presided over the ceremony. When his turn came, each boy left class for the necessary time and returned duly scrubbed and polished.

In 1887 the school was taken over by Thomas and George

Mason who made great changes. They gave up the old houses and erected new buildings at the end of the village, furnishing them properly. So far as possible they introduced modern ideas, not only in material things. Games were organised, food improved, and so did the teaching which was provided by four assistant masters for the 50-60 pupils. Above all they established friendly relations with their boys. Both the Masons were excellent teachers. Thomas was a sound headmaster and a firm disciplinarian, though not so good a judge of character as his brother George. Once he discovered some boys guilty of immoral tricks. He got rid of them quite rightly, but then proceeded to cross-examine the whole school, asking questions on matters of which they were completely ignorant and innocent, thereby merely arousing but not satisfying their curiosity.

In September 1889 Charles went to Clifton, following an elder brother and a cousin. Clifton College was then a comparatively new Public School. It had been founded in 1862 on the initiative of some leading Bristol families who frankly wanted a school for the 'sons of gentry', in preference to the ancient grammar school. This unashamed piece of snobbery led to the grotesque position whereby if one brother at the college met another at the grammar school in the street, they were forbidden to speak to each other! With the granting of a charter in 1877, however, the scope and aims were enlarged, and Clifton became a broad-based liberal type of school in contrast to the older and more orthodox foundations which leaned heavily on classics and custom. Science had been included in the curriculum almost from the start, and proper regard was given to History, English, and Modern Languages. At the same time, following Arnold, much emphasis was laid on character and leadership, the value of team games, and the exercise of authority by members of the Sixth Form. A startling innovation was the separate house for Jews, maintained to this day.

Charles' school career was happy but not distinguished. For several years his reports made indifferent reading, but

Harry never played the heavy Victorian parent, only admonishing him in a gentle way.

I started in the bottom form but one and moved slowly up the school to the Upper Fifth, where I stuck—the only one in our family not to spend a year at least in the top form of his Public School—and so never became a prefect. I was a big fellow and growing fast, slow in the uptake and at times frankly lazy. Fortunately it all went with an easy temper, for I was continually ragged by my brothers and did not resent it in the least. I was known as 'Hunk'.

One episode I remember well. It was in the holidays and we were playing a game which required each of us to write a poem. I said I was no good at that sort of thing. 'Yes, you can,' said one of the others, 'its easy, like this:

There is a man
Who can
Blow his nose
With his toes'

So I gave in. After five minutes all had finished but me. I asked for more time—more than once. At last after much impatience and cries of 'Charlie have'nt you finished *yet*?' I read out my effort. It was

There is a man
Who can
Blow his nose
With his toes

My mind simply refused to work!

There were several remarkable masters at Clifton in those days. My first headmaster, who was also my housemaster, was James Maurice Wilson. He was a tall spare man, with a dome of a head, great width between the eyes, and a beard then turning grey down to his waist. Of outstanding intellect he was a distinguished scientist, a senior Wrangler, and it was said only failed to take a First in Classics through illness. He was one of the first Anglican churchmen to bridge the gap between science and the Christian religion. He was in sympathy with both masters and boys, full of wisdom and human kindness and understanding; likewise, his wife, formerly a Miss Talbot, who was a remarkable person, able, cultivated and with a great sense of humour. Our only criticism of the Wilsons was that their thoughts were so devoted to things of the mind that they never noticed what they ate or drank. So the food in School House was indifferent, and after the midday meal any boys who had money hurried to the grub shop to assuage their hunger. Expenditure on food ceased to be necessary with the arrival of Wilson's successor Michael George Glazebrook, a great scholar, and an athlete who was said to have been the first Englishman to jump 6 feet. He tightened up the discipline of the school, which was probably necessary, but was not otherwise a success at Clifton. His weakness was a lack of understanding of both men and boys. I had an interview with him once when he questioned me for half-an-hour about the characters of other boys in the house; needless to say none of them was guilty of anything worse than bad language. On another occasion he was seen by a couple of boys to embrace his wife in the garden. They cheered; whereupon he rushed in and made all sorts of trouble. Wilson was called 'Jimmy', Glazebrook the 'Bogey Man'.

There are some good stories told about Jimmy Wilson at the end of his life: of his other-worldliness and wonderfully active brain. His wife died before him, and during her last illness, when he was sitting by her bedside, she asked him, 'What is troubling you?' He replied, 'We have been here such a short time that I dont know a reliable undertaker!' He then asked her how she wished to go to the place where she was to be buried. 'By motor car.' 'What,' he asked, 'all the way?' 'Yes, all the way.' 'In that case,' he replied, 'I shall come too.' When he died at the age of 95, three letters were found in his desk. One gave the solution to a mathematical problem sent him by a schoolmaster who wrote that neither he nor his pupils could solve it. The second was the translation of part of a Latin missal sent him by the Librarian of Worcester Cathedral. The third was the reply to a crammer who wanted a jingle to help his pupils remember something by rote.

The tutor of School House was W. W. Asquith, brother of the Liberal Prime Minister. He was almost a dwarf, but he balanced his diminutive size by a devastating quickness of repartee, and maintained discipline by mordant criticism. We were fond of him but feared him. The man to whom I owed most was H. S. Hall, the mathematician. He was a teacher of superlative skill, able to reduce every problem to its simplest terms, and make clear the logical sequence of mathematical processes. Thanks to him I not only became proficient in mathematics, reaching scholarship standard soon after leaving Clifton, but learned for the first time the satisfaction of analysing and completely understanding a problem, and presenting it clearly to others.

I was above average at games, though not a star, except perhaps at boxing. I was given my cricket colours in 1893 by W. G. Grace junior, son of the great Dr. The old fellow used sometimes to stand behind the nets and give us tips. He taught me to play forward to a yorker and make it a full pitch, and I cannot remember being bowled by one in consequence. I played racquets for the school in my last year, and also won the Public School heavy weight boxing competition at Aldershot in 1893, when I was 17. I boxed a bye with an instructor who knocked me about a good deal, but in the final I was too quick and powerful for my Harrovian opponent. My weight was then over 13 stone in singlet and flannel trousers!

As I was destined for the Army, I was a keen member of the Cadet Corps, an active organisation at Clifton, then attached to the Bristol Engineer Corps. I became a 2nd Lieut. in 1893 and senior cadet in the following year. The Corps was in the charge of Col. E. C. Plant, who was also our art master. He died some time after I left, and the manner of his death was unfortunate. His wife was a confirmed invalid, and for his comfort he set up a second, weekend, establishment somewhere in Somerset. In Bristol he was Col. E. C. Plant CB, our much respected citizen; at weekends he was Mr Hall, commercial traveller and enthusiastic bee-keeper. His wife died some time before him and he continued to live in Bristol during the week as the saddened widower he undoubtedly was. Unfortunately he himself died at the weekend, and his country wife came in great distress to his friends and explained the circumstances. They did their best to conceal the fact of his double life, but he was a very prominent volunteer officer, and his funeral was a local event. His coffin left his weekend home with a brass plate bearing the name of Hall engraved upon it, but arrived in Bristol with that of Plant. This was noticed by a reporter and published both in the local papers and in a pamphlet; and so poor Col. Plant's reputation was dragged through the mud. I may add that Plant's invalid wife knew all about the double arrangement, and is said to have employed her time making things for the Hall family.

Charles left Clifton at the end of the summer term 1894, and went to the Royal Military College, Sandhurst, on the following September 1st. He was the second of Harry's sons to enter the regular Army.

* * *

These extracts from Charles' personal memoir, describing his Victorian boyhood, are significant for several reasons. Not only are they an authentic unaffected record of an age and aspect of society, but they indicate some of the immense changes that had overtaken the middle class as a whole, and the Bonham-Carters in particular, since the name was first adopted in 1827.

In the 1820s the family was still 'Portsmouth commercial', firmly Unitarian, politically in opposition, and reformist in outlook. Indeed it was zealously opposed to the Establishment in many of its forms: all those relics of 18th-century Toryism embedded in Parliament, the Court, the Church, the Public Schools, and other privileged institutions of English life. It was into this world that Harry had been born, and in which he had grown up with personal experience of some of its handicaps. After all he had only attended a small obscure boarding school, pursued his studies as best he could abroad, before going up to Cambridge where he was prevented from taking his degree on a matter of religious principle. But the Reform Act had been the turning-point, and it exerted an influence until the end of the century, by which time all the major aspects of public life had been transformed. By 1900 every man had the vote; the squirearchy had been broken by the agricultural depression and the massive growth of industry; thanks to the Evangelicals and the Tractarians the Church had been rejuvenated and reformed; a system of public education was in force, while the example of Arnold had opened up new prospects for the independent schools and more than doubled their numbers. In short the urban middle class had come to power. In so doing it had not abolished the Establishment, but taken possession of it and reinvigorated it; and had lost some of its own edges in the process.

Harry's was a case in point. Although he never quite lost the habits and beliefs of his provincial background, his children belonged entirely to the new metropolitan orthodoxy. They were born and bred in London, and were brought up as Anglicans, not Unitarians. They all attended Public Schools: either new ones such as Clifton, or old ones such as Rugby and Winchester, now broadened and remodelled. Several of the younger sons went to Oxford, for by then Harry could afford to send them there. The majority entered the Services and professions, and took their place as leaders and administrators of an Empire approaching the zenith of its influence and power. A list of Harry's eleven sons, with an indication of their education and careers, underlines this point:

Herman: born 1863. Winchester, RMA Woolwich, Army (R.E.) and Indian Railways.
Gerard: born 1865. Rugby, brewer, farmer, Red Cross Commissioner.
Walter: born 1866. Winchester, family solicitor.
Norman: born 1867. Rugby, Oxford, Indian Civil Service.
Edgar: born 1870. Clifton, Oxford, barrister, Legal Secretary to the Sudan Government.
Reginald: born 1872. Winchester, mining engineer in Spain.

Octavius: born 1873. H.M.S. *Britannia*, Dartmouth, Royal Navy.

Philip: born 1874. Died as a boy at Winchester.

Charles: born 1876. Clifton, RMC Sandhurst, Army.

Frederick: born 1877. Winchester, Oxford, accountancy and banking.

Maurice: born 1880. Winchester, Oxford, barrister, secretary to H. H. Asquith, the City.

The only daughter, Joan, born 1864, lived with her parents at home, was active in public welfare work, and became in her time the figurehead of the family. She was much loved and respected, and was an authority on Bonham-Carter relationships and records.

As for politics, Harry was of course by heritage and humour a Liberal, although always an unassuming one. However, after Mr. Gladstone's attempt to enact Home Rule for Ireland in 1886, he became a Liberal Unionist, and so took the first step towards a form of Conservatism, adopted by all his children except one. The exception was the youngest, Maurice, who acted as principal private secretary to H. H. Asquith, Liberal Prime Minister 1908–16, and who married Asquith's daughter, Violet. There is little doubt that the man who converted Harry on the subject of Irish Home Rule was his brother-in-law, Albert Venn Dicey, husband of his youngest sister, Elinor. Dicey was a mild affectionate and witty man, with a brilliant and forceful mind. He was a distinguished barrister, a Fellow of All Souls, and Vinerian Professor of English Law at Oxford for twenty-seven years. He wrote a series of works on constitutional law: classics in their day and still highly regarded as sources of authority, notably *The Law of the Constitution* and *Law and Opinion in England*. Dicey was a powerful controversialist and exerted a measurable influence on political thinking, both through his books and his contributions to *The Times*, most of them polemics on current issues. He undoubtedly hastened the near-extinction of Liberalism in the Bonham-Carter family, and caused Harry and Sibella to 'disapprove' of cousin Johnny's activities as a Gladstonian Liberal at Petersfield.

* * *

Although the family's political loyalties shifted, its essential liberalism or liberal-mindedness did not. By that I mean a fundamental attitude of mind—an attitude towards liberty—which revealed itself in a fearless individualism tempered by a keen sense of social responsibility and practical humanity, and in a genuine belief in democracy as a reasonable and workable system of government, both in Parliament and outside.

This theme has already been amply and variously illustrated in all that has been related so far, from the early John Carters down to Harry himself. From now on, however, the narrative takes a new form. Instead of drawing on the lives of different people in different generations, I propose to develop the theme in terms of the life of one man—my father, Charles. This is not just filial devotion. The plain reason is that he was the epitome of liberal character, in the sense defined, and expressed its personal meaning better than almost any other member of his generation.

Moreover, he rose to the heights of a profession which, when he entered it, was perhaps the least liberal of all, and was still the preserve of privilege and hidebound amateurs. Inside forty years he and some of his colleagues transformed not only the technical proficiency of the Army, but also the social and mental atmosphere of the whole organisation—his own achievements in training and education being outstanding. Here was the liberal leaven at work, for this was not merely a matter of efficiency, but of wisdom and vision and humanity. Furthermore, as a member of a great public service which he helped to fashion, and as Governor of Malta just before the last war, Charles influenced some of the critical events which have determined the course of this country, and its place in world history.

The narrative proceeds therefore as an account of Charles' career and largely in his own words. It is both an historical record and a continuing illustration of the theme of the book, which is implicit in his actions and ideas.

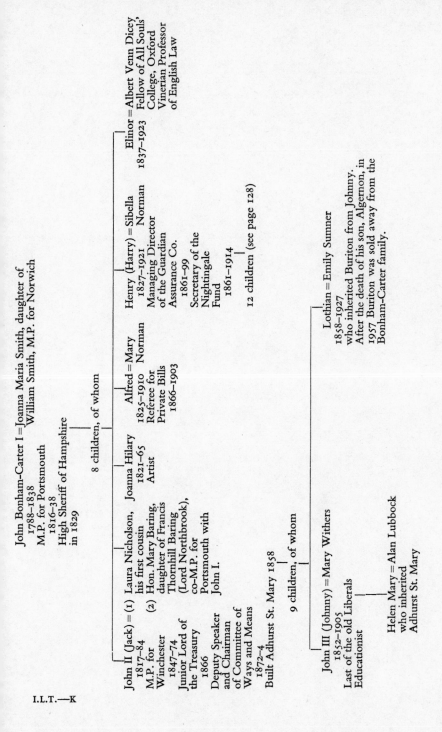

John Bonham-Carter I = Joanna Maria Smith, daughter of William Smith, M.P. for Norwich
1788–1838
M.P. for Portsmouth
1816–38
High Sheriff of Hampshire
in 1829

8 children, of whom

John II (Jack) = (1) Laura Nicholson, his first cousin
(2) Hon. Mary Baring, daughter of Francis Thornhill Baring (Lord Northbrook), co-M.P. for Portsmouth with John I.
1817–84
M.P. for Winchester
1847–74
Junior Lord of the Treasury
1866
Deputy Speaker and Chairman of Committee of Ways and Means
1872–4
Built Adhurst St. Mary 1858

Joanna Hilary
1821–65
Artist

Alfred = Mary Norman
1825–1910
Referee for Private Bills
1866–1903

Henry (Harry) = Sibella Norman
1827–1921
Managing Director of the Guardian Assurance Co.
1861–99
Secretary of the Nightingale Fund
1861–1914

12 children (see page 128)

Elinor = Albert Venn Dicey
1837–1923
Fellow of All Souls' College, Oxford
Vinerian Professor of English Law

9 children, of whom (children of John II)

John III (Johnny) = Mary Withers
1852–1905
Last of the old Liberals
Educationist

Helen Mary = Alan Lubbock
who inherited
Adhurst St. Mary

Lothian = Emily Sumner
1858–1927
who inherited Buriton from Johnny.
After the death of his son, Algernon, in 1957 Buriton was sold away from the Bonham-Carter family.

PART TWO

CHARLES

General Sir Charles Bonham-Carter, GCB, CMG, DSO

CHAPTER I

OFFICER

I HAVE already stated that, at the end of the last century, the British Army was morally and materially a highly conservative organisation. No major war had been fought since the Crimea, 1854–6, and the Indian Mutiny, 1857–8. Since then the long years of peace had been punctuated only by a number of minor campaigns in the Middle and Far East, and in South Africa, where a small British force had been humiliatingly defeated by an irregular but more skilful band of Boers at Majuba Hill in 1881. It was a familiar story. The economies and apathy of peace had destroyed incentive and undermined efficiency, particularly in tactical training and equipment. On the other hand, an important reorganisation had taken place under Edward Cardwell, Liberal Secretary of State for War. Purchase of commissions and corporal punishment had been abolished, short service engagement introduced, a reserve created, regiments localised in the counties where the regular battalions were linked together, and associated with the militia (home service units) and the volunteers. However, no general staff was yet in being. The direction of the Army was divided between the Commander-in-Chief sitting in the Horse Guards (then the Duke of Cambridge who only retired in 1895 after forty years in the post) and the War Office, where the Quartermaster-General and the Adjutant-General were regarded as the chief planners. Few general officers, other than Roberts, Kitchener and Wolseley, had commanded so much as a division in the field, and there was no proper organisation for war. Moreover, as Charles describes, although the quality of regimental officers was beginning to improve, the majority still regarded soldiering as a social convenience and an opportunity for sport. As for Tommy Atkins, while a hero in wartime, he was regarded almost with contempt in peace. In Kipling's words:

Oh, it's Tommy this, an' Tommy that, an' 'Tommy, go away';
But it's 'Thank you, Mister Atkins', when the band begins
to play.

This was the general state of affairs reflected in Charles' recollections of Sandhurst and of the early years of his service.

The Sandhurst course lasted for three terms, roughly a year and a half. The cadets were organised into six companies, each under the command of a major, chosen from among the instructors, but responsible only for discipline and administration.

The instruction (I avoid the word education) was the responsibility of three colonels, given the very unsuitable title of 'Professors'. Each was responsible for a collection of subjects—fortification, topography, and an oddly assorted group of tactics, administration, and law. These subjects were taught in water-tight compartments, and it was some time before I began to grasp the intimate connexion between them all. I cannot remember any lectures on military history, though there may have been some. Privately I read a good deal from the very beginning of my career. I spent many hours drawing plans of fortifications, and learning about scarps and counterscarps, traverses, parados, parapets, trenches, ditches and glacis; curiously enough some of this proved useful to me, but not much.

I cannot recall learning anything about the siting of fortifications, nor of how fortifications are the servants of strategy and tactics. We did some useful practical work on the ground, digging, directing labour, bridging with trestle and pontoon, and demolitions. Our instruction in topography included map reading, and the making of sketch maps. This certainly made us observant of ground, but again it was some time before I realised that the study of topography was intended to show how ground affected the application of tactical principles. The fact that tactics, administration and law were lumped together, rather than grouping tactics with topography, is an indication of the muddled thinking behind the whole system for training officers.

The Riding School loomed large. In our last term we must have spent four or five hours a week under the Riding Master. At the end of my time I was not a skilled horseman, but had a tight seat and hands sufficiently good not to harm a horse. We did a good deal of drill, weapon training (rifle and bayonet only), and physical training. The latter was designed more to develop muscle than an active and well balanced body. It was some years before the Swedish system was introduced.

The post of Commandant was regarded as a suitable niche where a distinguished old soldier might end his service. His assistant however was really efficient, and on the whole the instructors were well chosen. They knew their limited work and were enthusiastic. There were some fine men among them. One of our first tasks on joining was to obtain our uniform. This was made by local tradesmen and was of excellent quality. It consisted of:

Scarlet tunic, trousers, helmet and cap.
Scarlet Mess jacket, blue waistcoat and overalls.
Service Dress of two blue serge jackets and two pairs of trousers.
One pair of riding overalls.
An overcoat.
A flannel blazer in RMC colours.
Two pairs of service boots, one pair of Mess wellingtons, one pair of ankle gaiters, and one pair of gym shoes.

My father kept the bills sent to him at the end of each term, and I discovered that the tailor's bill amounted to £26–12s.–4d., and the bootmaker's to £4–17s.–od. Altogether my three terms at Sandhurst cost £40–12s.–10d. Of course he gave me an allowance as well, but I forget how much that was.

As cadets, we were paid 3s. per day, and this was credited in our termly bills. At the end of each month we paid our mess bill, and were paraded after dinner for the purpose.

The messing was adequate but monotonous. I don't suppose the Mess Secretary knew much about catering or the purchase of food for large numbers.

I was very happy at Sandhurst and had a successful time there. I passed out only 46th on the list, after being much higher at the end of my first and second terms. I was promoted Corporal at the beginning of my second term and Under Officer my last term. As a result a good deal of administrative work was thrown on me, and I like to think that my comparatively low passing-out place was due to that, and not to lack of industry! My parents came down to watch the passing-out parade, a simpler ceremony than nowadays, and to see me given the Sword of Honour by Lord Wolseley.

What I got from Sandhurst was a sound acquaintance of the elements of soldiering, upon which it was possible to built later. But of real education there was very little.

Charles was gazetted 2nd Lieutenant on February 29th, 1896, and was posted to the 2nd Battalion Queen's Own Royal West Kent Regiment, then stationed in Dublin. Previously he had spent his leave in London, taking singing lessons with Luigi Parisotti, one of the best teachers of the day and a great friend of the family. Parisotti was impressed by Charles' fine bass-baritone voice, and tried seriously to persuade him to exchange the Army for a professional career as a singer—to no avail, although Charles continued to sing as an amateur, and enjoyed music all his life. In London also he had a good time doing the social round.

There were many dances in private houses, and young men were welcomed by hostesses. The custom was, on hearing that a dance was to be given and that an invitation would be forthcoming, to pay a formal call at once and leave cards. After the dance one called again. By day the normal dress for a young man was a frock coat and top hat. In the evening at home it was a dinner jacket with a stiff-fronted shirt, but a guest always wore a tail coat. Soft-fronted shirts did not exist, so one wore on the following day the shirt put on clean the previous evening. The cost of laundry was low. When paying formal calls, top hat and frock coat were obligatory. One took one's hat and gloves into the drawing-room, and placed them at the side of or under the chair.

Life in Dublin as an infantry subaltern was almost as pleasant as in London, and a young man found no difficulty at all in passing the time away. In the winter there was a 'season' led from the Castle by the Lord-Lieutenant, the Earl of Cadogan and his family, and there were four or five dances every week. In the summer Charles played cricket for the battalion and garrison, and in the autumn obtained leave to go and shoot game with his relations. He was less keen on riding.

The minds of a large proportion of Irish men and women were dominated by the horse; perhaps they are still. I was never keen on racing, but we all went to the Punchestown meeting in the spring, where the battalion had a tent, to make some return for the generous hospitality we had received during the year. These races were exceptionally interesting because they were steeplechases and we knew most of the riders. They also provided a glorious picnic for every Irishman within reach, and for the garrisons of Dublin and the Curragh. There was a great deal of horse talk in the mess, and a battalion polo club—a rich man's pastime—organised by the two senior subalterns for whom we had few kindly feelings. They brought pressure on some of us to play, but without result; and when the battalion left Ireland, the club came to an end—much to our relief. In these days when the horse has almost disappeared from the roads and farms, and survives almost solely to give pleasant recreation, it is difficult to realise its former importance in the Army and the value placed upon riding. It was of course the chief means of transport until long after the first World War, longer perhaps than was necessary, but there were social implications attached to riding which queered the issue.

Although Charles took full advantage of the good life around him, he was not lazy, and took his regimental duties as seriously as he was allowed.

I had not been taught at Sandhurst, and I certainly did not understand, the organisation of the Army. The garrison in Dublin consisted of a cavalry regiment and five battalions of infantry, commanded by Major-General Viscount Frankfort de Montmorency. The Commander-in-Chief in Ireland was Lord Roberts. For manoeuvres in 1896 and 1897 infantry brigades were formed, but the brigade commanders were appointed only for the exercises; there was no divisional organisation. The reason for this omission was presumably that the Army had not been called upon to undertake a campaign for many years.

My acting battalion commander was a splendid officer, not exceptional as a tactician, but in every other way efficient, firm in character and quiet in manner. Under him I gained a thorough knowledge of the pay, clothing, feeding and general care of the men. In other administrative matters and in drill we were well trained by the adjutant. On the whole all twelve subalterns knew their work thoroughly, but with a few exceptions the captains and majors were inadequate, some of them frequently the worse for drink by the time they went to bed. In truth before the Boer War many regimental officers were little better than ignorant amateurs, and would have received short shrift by later standards. For them the Army was an excuse for sport and a pleasant social life. They learned no more of their profession than was sufficient to keep them out of trouble. None the less they were often good leaders. One, but not the only, explanation of this attitude was the low pay, and it remained so until after the first World War. My pay as a 2nd Lieutenant was 5s 3d a day, as a Lieutenant 6s 9d. In 1914, when I was a senior captain of eighteen years' service I received £212 a year. Of necessity every infantry officer had some private means. My father made me an allowance of £150. I think the smallest any of my brother subalterns had was £50. Any subaltern without private means transferred to the Army Service Corps or the Pay Corps, or found employment in the colonies.

I cannot pretend that the work was arduous. We paraded under the adjutant at 7.0 am and trained till 3 pm. We were then free till the evening when we usually had an hour's work before dinner. I remember teaching the only two illiterates in my company to read and write during that hour. There were of course periods when a good day's work was demanded, such as battalion and weapon training, then called musketry. For officers the latter consisted of firing a course with a revolver, and learning a ridiculous sword exercise. This was performed by all the officers together as one of the set pieces at the General's Inspection. It was always very nearly too much for my powers of self-control, for being a junior in the rear rank the figures of the seniors were exposed to my view in all their grotesqueness. Of course subalterns fired the rifle course with their companies. It consisted merely of normal target practice at various ranges, fire being frequently applied by volleys on a word of command. Tactical training was carried out in Phoenix Park in close order.* Wider extensions and the scientific use of ground were not adopted until heavy casualties in the early part of the Boer War made them necessary. I may add that our uniform for work in the field was a red serge jacket and blue trousers tucked into ankle gaiters.

In the mid-summer of 1898 the battalion moved into camp at Aldershot, and took part in the manoeuvres held in September on Salisbury Plain. I had the good fortune to be in temporary command of a company, the only other officer being a particular friend of mine. Since we were to march long distances, we were determined that our unit should do as well as any, and that there should be no sickness or falling-out. We provided ourselves with a supply of plaster, lint, and boracic powder, and every evening we examined the men's feet with the utmost care and carefully patched up lame dogs. No one went sick, and we received a good chit. At the end of the manoeuvres there was a grand parade at which the old Duke of Cambridge took the salute. He was mounted on a great heavy horse, and his orderly carried his umbrella! He was the last Royal Commander-in-Chief, and had held the post from 1856 to 1895. When the Government demanded his resignation and refused to

* Lord Wolseley called it 'barrack square ballets'!

appoint the Duke of Connaught in his place, it was said that Queen Victoria was deeply disappointed. The old Duke had been born in 1819, so when I saw him he was 79. He was a fine old fellow, but needless to say a wonderful old Tory!

1899 was the last year in which I took my soldiering pretty light-heartedly. In August to stimulate recruiting the battalion went for a ten days' march in west Kent. We did not gather many recruits, but good results appeared later. The normal routine was to strike camp early and march to our next halt, arriving before noon. The rest of the day was occupied with a cricket match or an entertainment of some sort given by the battalion or for the men. In the evenings there was usually a torchlight tattoo. I ran the cricket. We did well at Tonbridge and Tunbridge Wells, but by the time we got to Westerham we were getting tired, and finished by being beaten by St. Mary Cray. By that time our bowlers could scarcely raise a run. We had quite a triumph at Tunbridge Wells. It was a hot day and we were entertained by the Mayor with much wine. Our opponents put us in under the urge of hospitality, and I opened with a brother officer, who refused to take the first ball, being unfit he said owing to his libations at lunch. They had merely made me courageous! I hit the first ball over the bowler's head, escaped being caught, and we then made 140 runs in 45 minutes. At that point we succumbed exhausted. The match was drawn!

Charles was in Egypt when the Boer War broke out in October 1899, but returned home at once to help mobilise a mounted infantry unit, arriving in South Africa on April 6th, 1900. By that time the first disastrous phase of the campaign was over. To the general amazement Britain, the most powerful country in the world, had been soundly beaten in a number of battles by two tiny states of veld farmers. The British generals had been slow and incompetent, the men no match for their opponents in ground-craft and marksmanship, even the military equipment was inferior. All this was the outcome of the defects noticed by Charles, even in his first few years' service, and of many other failings inherent not only in the military system but in the whole attitude of the nation towards its army. Fortunately the Boers, on their side made grave mistakes too, for they had strong initial advantages. They were more numerous in the field, better prepared and knew the country, but lacked a proper strategic plan. Instead of following up their early successes and exploiting their temporary superiority, they allowed themselves to be immobilised in fruitless sieges—a form of warfare for which they were least suited—and so gave the British time to reorganise and recover.

In December 1899 command in South Africa was taken over by Lord Roberts, with Kitchener as his Chief of Staff; and together they planned and executed a campaign which soon transformed the whole course of the war. An army corps was assembled, transport and artillery reformed, a deception scheme put into operation, preparatory to launching the main force across the Modder river into the western part of the Orange Free State. The plan succeeded admirably. Kimberley, where Rhodes had been bickering with the garrison commander in a most unseemly manner, was relieved on February 15th. A large force of Boers under Cronje surrendered at Paardeberg on February 27th, and Bloemfontein was entered on March 3rd. At the same time Buller, who had suffered some of the worst defeats in the early part of the war, finally raised the siege of Ladysmith in Natal. During the next three months the campaign was prosecuted with equal vigour and success in the Transvaal. Mafeking, so long and brilliantly defended by Baden Powell, was relieved on May 17th; and with the capture of Johannesburg and Pretoria a few weeks later, the war seemed almost over, nine months after it had started. Almost, but not quite. As is well known, the Boers then resorted to guerilla tactics, a form of warfare in which they excelled. Small bands or commandos ranged over the whole vast territory, some penetrating deep into Cape Colony itself, raiding, ambushing, and seriously disrupting the British lines of communication. It was not thought that these tactics would win the war, but the Boers were hopeful that the uncertainty and stalemate so caused would postpone the final decision, and possibly bring about a change of policy in Britain.

On their side the British adopted a campaign of attrition. Kitchener, who had succeeded Roberts, began the construction of 4000 miles of blockhouses, fencing off the Boer territory into corrals, with a view to rounding up the commandos by a series of 'drives'. At the same time he established refugee camps for Boer families (with their livestock) who wished to contract out of the war. Later all families were brought in from large areas in order to deny their use to the enemy, and the farms burned. Strategically it is hard to see how Kitchener could have acted otherwise, and as Botha himself admitted the blockhouse and camp system was in fact mainly responsible for the final defeat of the Boers in May 1902. But the camps caused a great outcry, for they were at first overcrowded and badly administered. This and the fact that most of the Boer families were ignorant in matters of hygiene caused much suffering, and a high death-rate from enteric fever and other epidemics. In other respects the war was honourably and humanely conducted by both sides; and once the camps had been improved—largely at the instance of Miss Emily Hobhouse who came out from England in the early part of 1901—it was possible to reach a settlement without undue bitterness. And this in turn was the prelude to that far greater act of mutual trust and magnanimity, the formation of the Union in 1910, with Botha as first Prime Minister.

Charles served nineteen months in South Africa as a regimental officer with mounted infantry. He gained invaluable experience as a fighting soldier, often on detachment with his own command. In the latter part of his time it was a war of small actions, in which all depended upon initiative, skill, and the power of quick decision to meet a tactical emergency. He excelled in this, as well as in the management of men and the administration of the unit. Mounted infantry, as the name implies, meant 'foot soldiers on horses'. It was not a term synonymous with cavalry—indeed the difference between the two arms was most marked. Although the cavalry played a useful part in the war, especially under General French, they were still the traditional shock troops, depending upon the charge and their ability to use lances and sabres to cut down the enemy at close quarters: in fact the historical rôle dating from the earliest days of warfare and already out-dated. A mounted infantryman used his horse as a means of transport, to travel quickly from one point to another, ready to dismount, use ground, and attack by fire and movement in the ordinary way. But in the earliest days of the campaign there was not only tactical mishandling and unreadiness to make troops mobile in this way, but a lack of horses and of troops able to ride. After Buller's defeat at Colenso in December 1899, this was gradually made good, but serious shortages continued well into 1900, as Charles related, when his unit joined the 17th Infantry Brigade at Reddersburg in the Orange Free State.

Though my company was equipped as mounted infantry, no horses were ready for us, so we marched with the rest of the battalion with our equipment tied on with string. This added considerably to the strain of long marches. My company commander was an able man, but with a distaste for unpleasant duties and completely allergic to marching. It was not long before he disappeared to try to collect our equipment as a mounted unit and some horses. As the senior subaltern also went sick, I soon found myself in command of the company again.

We did some hard marching in April and May, and were in action two or three times. On April 28th we took part in an attack on Thabanchu mountain. Starting from our camp at the bottom, we spent a very cold night half way up the hill. On the following morning I was sent with my section to protect the left flank of the attack. We went down into the valley again, and after going forward about three-quarters of a mile came under heavy rifle fire, and were held up all day in a dry watercourse, quite isolated. However we certainly gave the protection asked for, and had only one man wounded. We got away after dark. On May 29th my battalion took part in an attack by the brigade on a Boer position at Biddulphs Berg, four miles east of Senekal. The attack was carried out by the Grenadier and Scots Guards, but was not successful. Casualties were fairly heavy and we covered the withdrawal. The veld was quite dry, after a rainless winter, and the grass was set alight by shell fire, causing many of the wounded to be burnt. We left behind doctors and orderlies to look after them, both ours and the enemy. The war was conducted in a comparatively gentlemanly way.

A further but successful action took place at the end of July near the Caledon river on the borders of Basutoland, involving heavy marching and resulting in the surrender of 4000 Boers. Soon afterwards the unit came into its full complement of horses and equipment, and spent the autumn on escort duties and patrols before going into garrison at Frankfort from November till February. This was the hottest season of the year, when thunderstorms occurred of extraordinary severity. 'I actually saw a mule killed by lightning a few yards from the tent in which I was sheltering. The flame appeared to have travelled from his withers down his forelegs and to have killed him instantly.' Early in 1901 a mobile column was formed which moved about the Orange Free State, clearing the country of cattle, sheep, and foodstuffs, and bringing the farm families into the camps. Another more congenial operation was the holding of a defensive line, against which other columns drove the enemy.

We never had much success, but I enjoyed my time as a mounted infantry company commander enormously. We had few casualties, but there was great fascination in the high veld country of wide grassy valleys and low hills, to which there seemed no limit. I was proud of my command. Certainly too I gained enormously in knowledge and in the ability to act rapidly and correctly. When acting as the advanced guard to the column, I always had to decide quickly how to deal with opposition—by encirclement, flanking, or simply rushing it at a gallop, avoiding if possible any delay to the main body. I got quite skilled at the game and never made any very serious mistake. I also learned how thoroughly to look after my men in the field.

After a short spell as adjutant, Charles had a bad attack of enteric fever, and was invalided home in November 1901. He was met by his father at Waterloo with an ambulance, 'which was of course quite unnecessary'. Just over a year later he entered the Staff College, Camberley, gaining 585 marks out of 600 in the higher mathematics papers, and otherwise giving promise of remarkable abilities. By then he was nearly 27 years old and a married man. He was in truth at the real beginning of his career, in which he emerged not only as a fine staff officer and commander, but as a thinker, teacher, and man of vision, who inspired his colleagues and subordinates in a service which is benefiting today from some of his actions and ideas.

* * *

The course at the Staff College lasted two years, 1902–4.

The first year was devoted to the duties of a staff officer of formations up to a division and the tactics concerned. In the second year we studied the staff duties of higher formations, imperial strategy and in some degree the higher direction of war. Naturally we read a lot of military history and wrote essays on every conceivable subject. We also took part in a number of exercises on the ground without troops, and during one vacation in each year we were attached to a unit of an arm to which we did not ourselves belong. In my case—a field battery at Easter 1903, and a cavalry regiment in 1904.

Most of our work was performed in syndicates, both indoors and out, each man being given experience as a commander and in every position on the staff. Later I had considerable acquaintance of directing work carried out by syndicates, and found with interest how quickly one was able to spot the work for which each member was responsible. We were put through a severe test during the last few months of the course, being given more work than was possible to get through in the time allotted. It was a test of our judgment in choosing essentials and leaving out non-essentials, and of our power to stand up to long hours of work with stamina and spirit. A staff officer who allows a difficult task to depress him is useless.

Among the students were experts on most subjects—men who had been on one side or the other in the Russo-Japanese war, and those who had special knowledge of parts of the empire. Lecturers from outside sometimes had to face difficult questioners. We also made a close study of the armies of Germany and France, for even then there were signs of serious rivalry and tension between them.

Our batch of students numbered thirty-two, but for the second year we were joined by half-a-dozen men who had served on the staff in South Africa. They were older than the rest of us, who ranged between 25 and 35 in age. But age or seniority made no difference. We were all treated exactly alike. The standard of ability was high, and we learned as much from each other as from our teachers—which was right. One of the most important assets we acquired was the power to work together, and the knowledge we gained of the way any Staff College graduate was likely to act in any circumstance. We left Camberley, not fully educated in the sense of a man who has got full value from his time at the university, but with enormously increased power of using our wits logically and with knowledge. We were not narrow-minded soldiers.

Shortly after leaving the Staff College, Charles was posted as an instructor to the Royal Military College, Sandhurst, for two years. Considerable changes had taken place since his own days as a cadet there ten years previously.

The training at Sandhurst had improved enormously, but it was still limited to making a young officer technically proficient. Educationally, all depended upon the company he was attached to. Far the best instructor was Major Charles

Ross, brother of Ronald Ross, the great medical pioneer who discovered the cause of malaria. Charles Ross was a remarkable man, a true educationalist, trying always to stimulate and train the minds of his pupils and excite enthusiasm for their chosen profession, and leaving as much as possible to their own efforts. He certainly stirred in me a deep interest in education that never left me. I was sent to him to teach military law and administration, not the best use to make of a man straight from the Staff College. Evidently Ross thought so too, for he handed over to me military history, saying that he did not mind how the boys passed so long as they did pass, for he intended to talk to them on 'war'. He also gave me the job of preparing outdoor tactical schemes, and when they were carried out he and I argued over the possible solutions in front of the cadets. For a time, too, I taught topography and tactics. The former had been taught without much imagination—it can be a very dull subject indeed—and I tried to bring it to life. However my first lesson was a complete failure because I attempted too much—combining the study of physical features with tactics and the influence of ground upon operations. I then recalled a conversation I'd once had with old uncle Albert Dicey, who told me he was quite content if he could drive home one or at most two ideas to his listeners. Only a very intelligent audience could grasp and retain as many as three or four. So I made a fresh start and carved three lessons out of my original one. As to tactics—the only innovation I introduced was to make a cadet explain to the rest of the class the reasons for his solution to a problem. The object was, of course, to make him articulate and marshal his ideas in an orderly way.

* * *

In January 1906, exactly twelve months after Charles had gone back to Sandhurst as an instructor, a Liberal Government was returned to power with an overwhelming majority in the House of Commons. Since this is not primarily a political history book, there is no need to discuss in detail the parliamentary loyalties and policies which distinguished the parties and their component elements. Suffice it to say that the two main parties were in themselves divided. The Conservatives, now permanently allied to the Liberal Unionists, were torn between traditional free trade and protection, as advocated by Joseph Chamberlain; in the main they stood for a strong empire and the *status quo* at home. The Liberals, backed uncertainly * by Labour and the Irish Nationalists, were committed to Irish Home Rule and various social reforms (some of which they succeeded in enacting); but they were divided between an enlightened imperialism (as instanced by the creation of the Union of South Africa) and a radical pacifism which detested the whole idea of empire. So far as the Army was concerned, the outlook in 1906 must have seemed dark, for all those who had served in South Africa keenly resented 'the civil abuse showered upon our generalship and the anathemas launched against the chivalry which our soldiers had shown to the enemy'.† Such hostility was associated predominantly with the section of Liberal opinion led by Lloyd George, and it did much to strengthen the reactionary and discourage the progressive elements of the Army itself.

As it turned out, however, the Liberal administration, with Haldane as Secretary of State for War, was responsible for the most important series of military reforms since those introduced by Cardwell, another Liberal, in 1871–2. It is true that, immediately after the Boer War, various commissions had been set up to enquire into the state of the Army, and had found an urgent need for reform: notably, the reorganisation of the War Office, the training of a general staff for the study of strategy and the preparation of war plans, and the replacement of the Commander-in-Chief by an Army Council with the Chief of the General Staff as first military member. But it was not until 1907 that the main reforms were agreed, whereby the Army as a whole was remodelled, though within the

* In 1906 the Liberals had a clear working majority, but from 1910 onwards they depended upon their allies to stay in power.

† *The Army in My Time*, by J. F. C. Fuller. (Rich & Cowan.)

Cardwell system. This provided for a first line army of regular units, with its own reserve (incorporating the old militia), composed of six infantry divisions, four cavalry brigades, and supporting arms and services—the total strength to be raised to over 160,000 men on mobilisation. It also provided for a second line or Territorial army of part-time soldiers, replacing the old yeomanry and volunteers, amounting to fourteen divisions. In addition there was to be preliminary training of officers at the universities and public schools.

Although this reorganisation did not, in the opinion of some, go far enough, yet it was undoubtedly a major step forward of enormous consequence. Had it not happened, the small but highly efficient expeditionary force would never have been sent to France in August 1914, and it is possible that the German advance upon Paris would not have been halted on the Marne. Moreover, reform was not confined to the framework of the Army. The new dispensation encouraged the technical development of arms and equipment and the general improvement in training, staff work, and command, which had been born out of hard but salutary experience in South Africa. Intelligent and devoted men were finding their way into key positions. As noted by Charles, the quality of instruction at the Staff College and other training schools perceptibly improved, and officers were encouraged to study other armies and other methods. It was no longer always considered 'bad form' to talk 'shop' in the mess, or to take the profession of arms seriously. The Territorials set a *general* standard of efficiency never achieved by the militia and the volunteers, and in other ways did much to break down the barriers between army and civil life. Although much remained to criticise, by 1914 the British Army was not on balance inferior in quality either to the French or to the German armies which, despite their size, contained many weaknesses soon to be revealed on the field of battle. As time went on, few responsible officers doubted that a clash with Germany would come, although not all—like Lord Roberts—preached the need for universal service.

Such was the mood and movement of events in the decade before 1914, when Charles was approaching the prime of his career. However, despite the improved organisation of the Army and his own undoubted qualities, advancement was painfully slow. When war broke out, he was still only a senior captain after eighteen years' service. There were several reasons for this. One, simply, was the slow tempo of peace-time soldiering, common to all armies. Another was the reduction, under the Haldane scheme, of the number of battalions in certain line regiments. This resulted in a large surplus of officers who had to be found employment, and reduced the rate of promotion even further. Charles, however, did not return to regimental duty for eight years, during which time he was holding staff appointments: first as brigade major at Gibraltar, and then as DAA/QMG to the Coast Defences of Southern Command, based on Portsmouth. At Gibraltar there were only two battalions of infantry and few opportunities for training, but Charles used his ingenuity to conduct two simple tactical exercises in Spain, 'doing them very quietly so as to avoid the attention of the Spanish authorities'. At Portsmouth, he had to master and make known the new regulations for the administration of the army in the field, and at times take charge of training as well, acting as chief staff officer to his commander. All this was routine duty, but invaluable experience. A curious incident occurred in September 1910.

> I was called up directly I arrived at my office by H. de C. Martelli, then a captain serving in one of the forts on Portsdown, who told me that during a morning ride he had come across a young man making a sketch of the fort and its approaches. The young man said his name was Helm, and that he was an officer in a Prussian Pioneer Regiment who had come to this country to learn English. Martelli asked what he should do with the youth, who was then in the Depot mess. I told him to bring me any papers his guest had, and to continue to entertain him. The law about espionage

at the time was that, before a man could be arrested and prosecuted for spying, permission had first to be obtained from the Attorney General. I therefore took Helm's papers straight up to the War Office and handed them over to Lord Edward Gleichen, head of the German section of the Intelligence Directorate. In the meantime Helm stayed at the Depot mess as an involuntary guest. A few days later permission to prosecute him was received, but action had to be taken by the police. Martelli therefore explained to Helm that, owing to a curiosity of the law, he would now be arrested at the gates of the fort by the civil power and brought before the magistrate. This duly took place and Helm was remanded for trial at the Assizes at Winchester some weeks later. The lad had not done any serious harm, so the Judge told him that as he had been kept in custody for some time already he would be released forthwith—but that he was not to repeat his silly behaviour. The sequel to this case was the passing of the Official Secrets Act, which is now the law of the land dealing with such matters.

Charles returned to regimental duty in November 1910, and was soon after posted to India where he spent two years as a company commander in the 2nd battalion of the Royal West Kent regiment, then stationed on the North-West Frontier. It was straight regimental soldiering, edged with the reality of active service against the tribesmen—a mobile column was always on call—and of hard training in wild territory. Early in 1913 he received a private warning from a friend in the War Office, to the effect that the Germans were now expected to make war at an earlier date than anticipated, and advised him to come home. Not long afterwards an opportunity occurred, and he secured a posting to the regimental depot at Maidstone. He was still there on July 27th, 1914, when a telegram arrived ordering him to report to London at once and be ready to travel by night mail in plain clothes. He hoped that his destination might be France; in fact it turned out to be in exactly the opposite direction—Scotland. He had been appointed as GSO2 to help organise the Cromarty Firth as a Defended

Port, and it was there he heard the declaration of war on August 4th.

* * *

The posting to Cromarty probably saved Charles' life. The 1st battalion of the Royal West Kent regiment was engaged in heavy fighting in France from the outset, and at Neuve Chapelle on October 28th lost practically all its officers. It was brought out of action by two subalterns, both of whom became casualties soon afterwards. On hearing this news, Charles immediately applied to be sent to France, and a successor being found he arrived at Le Havre on November 14th. A week later he took a draft up to the front, and assumed command of a company, the battalion moving into trenches at Wulverghem opposite Messines Ridge. Before leaving camp they were inspected by the Commander-in-Chief, Sir John French. 'He gave us a "pep" talk and I remember feeling that he was doing more harm than good, for he talked high-falutin' nonsense which failed completely to impress the men in my company.'

Taking over the front line was an eerie business. There was bright moonlight and so no difficulty in finding the way. We moved in file across very muddy fields, parallel to and about fifty yards from the main road to Messines. From time to time a shell would burst over or in some ruined buildings on the road. We halted near some farm buildings and awaited the arrival of an officer and guides from the Royal Scots whom we were relieving. The buildings consisted of a small house and two barns. The roofs had practically disappeared and the rafters stood out like gaunt skeletons against the sky—an impressive picture of desolation. After a short time the guides appeared, and as soon as the platoons had moved off I joined the Royal Scots officer under cover, where he explained his dispositions by means of a sketch plan which he handed to me.

The trenches which we took over had been dug by troops in the positions they happened to occupy, when they halted the last German attacks in the battle of Ypres. No chosen defensive position had been prepared, for the character of the operations had made that impossible. In many parts of the long line the Germans had partially seized some high ground to our disadvantage, and my own company's trenches were overlooked from Messines Ridge which gave perfect observation to the enemy. It would have been far better to have adjusted our line, withdrawing where necessary to ground suitable for defence. I know application was made by some commanders to do this, but were met by a peremptory order from the Commander-in-Chief that not a yard was to be given up. I have often wondered how many lives this cost us quite unnecessarily.

Directly my platoons were in position, two in front and two in support, I visited them. The trenches were frightfully wet, and in places parties of men were separated from their neighbours by deep impassable mud. I found too there was a gap where no trench had been dug, and no covered way up to our position. Owing to the prevalence of 'trench feet', a painful and crippling swelling of the feet and ankles due to standing in water, companies remained forward for 24 hours only, and then moved to a support position about 600 yards back on fairly dry ground out of sight of the enemy. All men who could be spared were employed at night improving the defences which were vastly better after the first 48 hours, though still poor. However the enemy was as exhausted as we were, and there was no real danger of attack, only intermittent shelling and sniping. Apart from supervising the defences, posting sentries and maintaining contact with troops on our flanks, my most important job—I found—was to keep the men in good health and fettle, by encouraging them to keep warm by physical work, guarding against numb feet, getting up the rations, and making reasonable though primitive sanitary arrangements. When the unit was relieved, we went back to Neuve Eglise where there were still a number of undamaged houses. My subaltern and I put up at the house of a Madame Houssein who had refused to leave her home, and who was most kind to us. I then went to Bn. HQ. to give the CO a chance to get some rest. A short spell to sleep and get clean put us all on our feet again, ready for the next tour of duty in front.

It rained almost continuously during the first half of December, and the trenches quickly deteriorated. It was quite normal to stand in mud over the ankles, and in places men got bogged down and had to be helped out. We tried many experiments: deep drains and sump holes which soon became flooded, and faggots and boards which though better sometimes disappeared completely. We always returned from the front soaked to the skin, and some of the men became exhausted. There was a good deal of sickness, mostly from 'trench feet', though we managed to have a lighter sick list than any other company through observing a strict routine. Not only did I have a keen and efficient subaltern and an admirable sergeant-major to help me in this, but the battalion quartermaster was superb—the perfect example of a regular NCO who had got his commission. As a result we were soundly equipped and properly fed and supplied, whatever the circumstances.

On January 1st, 1915, Charles was transferred to HQ. First Army for duty as a liaison officer to the commander, Sir Douglas Haig. The short time he had spent as a company commander in the front line had, however, been long enough to learn conditions well, and to know what made life bearable in the trenches and what did not. Moreover, although he did not serve as a regimental officer again until 1919, it did not mean that his life was henceforward always safe and comfortable. The main reason for his posting was the severe shortage of trained staff officers—no less than 25 per cent became casualties—and an order had to be issued that no graduate of the Staff College was to continue serving with a regiment unless he already had a command. The Army as a whole was to suffer from this scarcity—particularly of first-grade appointments—for at least eighteen months. Meanwhile, until new men could be trained, the few experienced officers bore a tremendous responsibility. Nor was this always confined to their normal duties as planners and administrators, for in several cases they had to watch over inadequate commanders. On taking over an appointment later in the war, Charles came upon the following message from his predecessor: 'Never let X out of your sight. If you do, he will either give an order you cannot carry out, or give a promise you cannot fulfil.'

In January 1915 liaison at any but the highest level was a novelty. Briefly a liaison officer was a dual-purpose being. He had both to communicate the orders of the commander to subordinate formations, and keep the commander informed of the needs of these formations and of the operational situation at any point. In the latter case efficient liaison was invaluable, since reports from units in actual contact with the enemy often altered—after passing through two or three headquarters—in emphasis if not in statement of fact; moreover their passage to the senior commander took time.

> It took a little time, however, before we liaison officers were welcomed and treated with confidence. It was feared we might be the commander's private snoopers. So it was necessary to exercise tact and make sure that one's contact knew the gist of the report it was proposed to take back. Fortunately my task was made easy in that I knew most of the men I had to deal with already; but in any event all went smoothly quite soon, and in due course we were welcomed as sympathetic listeners to troubles and anxieties, and as bearers of news. At first I used to see Haig every evening, when he asked me questions on every conceivable subject—the defences, the state of the units, their morale, their physical condition, equipment, clothing, and so forth. All this made my work intensely interesting and worthwhile, but later when he knew his Army well I became little more than a messenger. However, when operations blew up in March, all the interest returned.

On March 10th, 1915, the First Army launched an attack at Neuve Chapelle, with the object of occupying Aubers Ridge. After an initial break-in, the attack petered out with considerable casualties.

> It was the first occasion when liaison officers were used in battle, but the best use was not made of them, as they were

not sent far enough forward. Certainly I never went further than Brigade HQ. It was after this battle that Sir John French told the *Times* correspondent that if he had sufficient ammunition, he could blast his way through any defences, or words to that effect.* This led to an attack on the Government. French was talking nonsense. Heavy and sustained preparation by artillery for an attack by infantry, if skilfully planned, could always enable an initial advance to be made. But for various reasons the depth of the advance was limited in every case, until the last phase of the war when the enemy began to break. It was, however, true that there was a grave shortage of ammunition which was not overcome for many months. The cause of this was that shells were expended in a quantity which before the war had been considered quite impossible. During the first winter, for the ordinary support of the infantry, guns were limited to as little as two or three rounds a day.

Charles had a good deal to do with Haig, both then and later. He respected him for his probity, selflessness, and steadfastness, and for the deep care and thought which he devoted to his work. But he realised at once that Haig did himself less than justice by his inability to express himself in speech (though not on paper), and that this gave an impression of aloofness and woodenness, much disliked by the politicians. As a commander in the field he instilled immense loyalty, but through conservatism was limited as a strategist. For instance, Haig retained an instinctive belief in cavalry (he was a cavalryman himself) despite its known vulnerability to machine-gun fire and barbed wire; and he was generally distrustful of new ideas until they had more than proved their value. Moreover, some of his chief staff officers stayed with him too long, were over-optimistic, and at times allowed themselves—and him—to get out of touch with developments.

However, Haig was not concerned with holding on to

* In his book *1914* (Constable) French reported his words as: 'The protraction of the war depends entirely upon the supply of men and munitions'. This gives a different impression.

ground for its own sake, by contrast with the Commander-in-Chief, Sir John French (another cavalryman), who had small conception of modern warfare. An example of this took place in April 1915 at the second battle of Ypres, when the Germans made a successful surprise attack with poison gas. They were finally held by the Second Army under Smith-Dorrien, 'an exceptionally gifted commander'; but when the latter wished to withdraw from the salient which was 'nothing but a shell-trap', he was relieved of his command. Later, after large losses, a small withdrawal was sanctioned, but the position continued to favour the enemy at a high cost of British lives.

Charles took part in this battle as GSO2 to the 50th Division, which had only recently arrived from England and, being thrown in untried, suffered heavily. It duly recovered, thanks to the innate toughness of the men and strong leadership. Charles remarked then, as he did again and again, that the character of a commander could make or break a formation. A good man made himself felt all the way down, and could offset serious weaknesses or the most adverse situation —and vice versa. Of Lord Cavan, who commanded the 50th Division for a time, he wrote:

> When he first arrived, I was shocked at his ignorance of the functions of other arms than infantry, and of the organisation of higher formations. However he told us frankly that we must not demand of him difficult decisions until he had learned his task thoroughly, and he soon became an efficient commander. I realised that, during stationary warfare at any rate, the most necessary qualities in a general are a gift for command, unerring judgment, a personality that impresses his subordinates, a quick brain and a retentive memory. Charm of manner is a great asset and a perfect sense of justice essential. Such a commander must, however, learn to trust his staff, who must be skilled and educated, and be allowed to do their work free of interference.

The 50th Division was not involved in either of the British offensives of the spring and autumn of 1915, but continued to hold the Ypres salient. It was in an exposed and vulnerable position with two brigades forward, and Charles was detailed to work out a co-ordinated scheme of defence, making full use of the machine-guns then becoming available in larger numbers.

The system I introduced was to establish a zone of fire from machine-guns, sited sufficiently far from the front line to have a chance of escaping hostile artillery in case of attack. These guns were arranged to cover the ground in front of them with flanking and cross-fire—very few firing directly to their front—while receiving protection from hostile frontal fire. Many other divisions took up the idea, I feel sure, quite independently, for it was only commonsense to provide a support line behind the forward defences, and this was no more than an application of the principle of defence in depth. However, I must confess I was pleased when staff officers were sent from other HQs to find out what we were doing.

January 1st 1916 was a red letter day for me. On that day I was promoted Brevet Lieut-Colonel, appointed GSO1 to the 7th Division, and I got out of the Ypres salient at last!

The 7th Division had already earned a wonderful reputation. Originally commanded by Thompson Capper, one of my teachers at the Staff College, it had held its ground in the face of fearful odds at the first battle of Ypres in October and November 1914, and had again performed great deeds at Loos in September 1915 when the divisional commander was killed. Capper's place was taken by Herbert Watts, a born leader of infinite courage who had done well with a brigade, but he was not an efficient divisional commander. I doubt if he ever grasped fully what his artillery could do, or what he might expect of his engineers or signals; nor did he properly understand the system of supply. On the other hand he was a charming chief to work for and he trusted his staff.

Here then was a classical example of that combination which, although by no means ideal, was quite practicable in the conditions of trench warfare—namely, a brave and respected but otherwise inadequate commander, supported by an efficient staff.

My colleagues included Lt-Col. the Hon. Maurice Wingfield, the AA/QMG, who was one of the ablest staff officers I ever met. He and I always shared the same billet to ensure that we each had complete knowledge of the work of the other, and could agree on our advice to the general. We both had excellent assistants, one of whom, Riddell-Webster, became Quartermaster-General in the second world war. The CRE, CRA and the other specialists all knew their work, likewise the three brigade commanders. Of these Cyril Deverell was in a class by himself. When I first met him early in 1915 he was a junior major, but by September 1916 he was commanding a division. He deserved his extraordinarily rapid promotion. His plans were always drawn with the utmost care, and his men well trained. He also saw to it that they had the best conditions possible in which to carry out their tasks. His physical appearance was striking. With rather humped shoulders, a long sallow face and a large nose, he was no beauty and his expression in repose was grim, but often lighted up with a charming smile. He finished his career as a field-marshal and CIGS, but was unfortunate in falling foul of Hore-Belisha, when the latter was Secretary of State for War. I must mention one other officer, C. C. Foss, one of the brigade majors. I think he was as brave a man as any I have known. He earned a V.C. at the battle of Neuve Chapelle in 1915. The story was told me by General Watts. At that time Foss was adjutant to a battalion of the Bedfordshire regiment which had just been pushed back by a German counter-attack and lost some newly won positions. When Foss reported this, Watts (his brigade commander) replied in an airy sort of way: 'Oh, lost them have you, young fellow? Well, you had better get them back again.' Foss saluted and said, 'Yes, sir.' He went off, collected a dozen men or less, and heroically retook the lost ground. He was a highly strung nervous man. I saw him once receive an order from Deverell to reconnoitre a particularly unpleasant place, and as he listened he began to shake. He then went straight off and did the job perfectly.

Early in 1916 the 7th Division, then part of the Fourth Army commanded by General Sir Henry Rawlinson, was told that it would share in a big attack to be launched in the summer. This was to be the battle of the Somme, the first full-scale British offensive in France, and marked the point at which the main burden of the war in the west was taken over by the British from the French. Before then the French had been engaged in a series of unsuccessful and highly costly offensives, and in a long defensive campaign of attrition at Verdun, which ultimately went their way. As a result they had sustained immense losses in men and materials, and apart from a massive attempt at the Chemin des Dames in May 1917 which failed, they played a comparatively small part in subsequent offensives on the western front. The British on the other hand, although they lost over half a million men between August 1914 and July 1916, were mainly engaged in preparations: assembling and training some forty new divisions and increasing their frontage in a critical part of the line.

The battle of the Somme was thus a turning-point in more senses than one. However, this is not the place to discuss its larger significance, nor to include Charles' specialised account as part of the general narrative. This account will be found in Appendix B at the end of the book. It is the first-hand record of a man intimately concerned with the planning of one section of the battle, and—despite the disappointment of the result—it indicates the care with which preparations were made, the size of the effort expended, and some of the lessons learned.

* * *

On October 7th, 1916, Charles received the news of the death of his mother, Sibella, at Buriton. She was in her 80th year. It was in a sense a climacteric in the history of the family. Although all the sons had long dispersed from home (five of them were now in the Army), and that sublimely happy era of Victorian youth was long long past, yet the survival of their parents—'the old people'—had kept the memory and reality of it steadfastly and serenely alive. Sibella above all had kept it so. Seated at her writing-table in the library, in her long black dress reaching to the ground with a jabot of lace and a cameo brooch at the throat, she had written to them all without fail every week, wherever they were in the world. They adored her, and remembered her now for her love, her simplicity, her saintliness, and her few little foibles. Though 'proper' in the plainest sense, she was never shocked nor surprised at anything, she never talked down to young people, she never did a mean thing. Dying, she gave this advice to a young grandson who just remembers her: 'Never steal a pin'. Though ten years her senior, Harry survived another five years to the great age of 94. The day she died he wrote in his diary: 'My dear wife died, in her bed in this house, her hand in mine, but not conscious. 52 years of married life—how short!'

It was a climacteric too for Charles. Hardly had he returned from England and seen his own wife and three young sons, when he found an order to report to GHQ. There he was instructed to take charge of the senior of two staff schools at Hesdin, with the task of training GSO2s to fit themselves for first grade appointments. This posting was the direct outcome of his own work as GSO1 to the 7th Division during the battle of the Somme. It was the recognition of his outstanding qualities, both as a skilled and visionary planner who saw far beyond the immediate technicalities of the situation, and who commanded the affection and respect of superiors and subordinates alike. These qualities were later to be given full expression in the highest posts in the Army. Now and for most of the rest of the war, they were to be devoted to training and, as will be described, to education in the widest sense.

It was planned that I should give three courses during the coming winter at Hesdin, each lasting six to seven weeks. I said I could'nt do much in so short a time, and so had best concentrate on one sort of operation. Since I had been told we were to go on attacking in 1917, it was agreed I should teach the staff duties of the division in attack, from the preliminary preparations to the final break-through of the enemy's defences and the early operations of open warfare.

At Hesdin I found the necessary accommodation had been prepared and a young adjutant who ran our affairs admirably, so I was little troubled with administrative arrangements. The students were to assemble in a very few days, so I worked long hours in preparing lectures and schemes. One of the lectures, I remember, was finished at 3.30 am and delivered at 9.0 am the same morning. It was like that all through the first course, and only by going full out was I able to keep ahead of the work. I had two assistants, both good men. One of them, Robert Haining, taught gunnery—which he insisted should not be an abstruse science when practised in the field, but only so to those engaged in research. It was easy to grasp the potentialities of the various guns, and thus the best means of employing them. This approach was characteristic of most of our work—analytical, getting rid of unnecessary complexities, and concentrating upon the essentials. Certainly the courses went well, and our pupils told us honestly that they had learned a great deal.

At the end of each course I sent in a confidential report on each officer. I only reported completely adversely on one man, and surprisingly enough he was the first 'graduate' to be given a first grade appointment afterwards! When I complained about this, I was told it was all for the best as he was to be on the personal staff of one of the higher commanders, who knew him well, and would give him a minimum of responsibility! But most of the students were efficient officers, with considerable experience already. Some of them made big reputations later, mostly in the second world war: notably 'Jumbo' Wilson (Field-Marshal, Supreme Commander in the Middle East), and Bernard Montgomery (Field-Marshal, Viscount Montgomery of Alamein). Montgomery had been a pupil of mine at Sandhurst, and I had also met him regimentally. As I knew him, he was a very studious hard-working officer, devoted to his profession—and modest. One officer who made an impression on me was J. H. Peck, an Australian, and completely self-made. He told me he got his education from the hoardings! He was one of the best of fellows and very able. To his surprise he found himself most popular. At dinner at the end of one course, he insisted on speaking. He then told us that when he first arrived, he was like a nervous foal, bucking and blowing through its nostrils, for fear he should be treated with discourtesy by a lot of stiff regular officers. Instead he found himself among the friendliest and most generous-minded lot of men he had ever met. Henceforward no Australian would be allowed to run down the 'Imperial' army in his presence.

It was during the third course that the 4th Division, in which my elder brother Norman was serving as a regimental officer, passed fairly close to Hesdin on its way to the battle of Arras. Norman got in touch with me. He was in camp some sixteen miles away. I sent a car for him, but it missed him. I then sent my groom with a spare horse, but he missed him too. Eventually Norman walked the whole distance. He stayed the night and we spent a very happy evening together. He was 49, the most magnificent physical specimen, and appeared much younger. Moreover he had given up a high position in the Indian Civil Service to volunteer for the army. I had tried to get him transferred to the Provost Marshal's department, but he said he wished to take his platoon into action twice before leaving the battalion. He was killed leading his men for the second time in an attack at Arras soon afterwards—in March 1917.

Between April and October 1917 Charles acted as chief of staff (BGS) to General Pulteney, commander of III Corps.

Putty was a dear old man (not so old), but the most completely ignorant general I served during the war, and that is saying a lot. An attractive trait was his love of birds. There was a swallow's nest in his hut, and he used to explain to us the careful sanitary arrangements of the parent birds. . . . During my six months with the corps we were never asked to undertake any active operations, but I was detailed to draw up an offensive plan for the capture of Cambrai. I made a very careful reconnaissance, and reported there would be no difficulty in occupying a position on the left flank where counter-attacks could be held, but for the same reason it was essential the right flank should reach and rest on the Canal de l'Escaut, an obstacle of great strength. When the battle took place at the end of November, about five weeks after I had left, the right flank unfortunately was not able to gain the canal, though much progress was made by the tanks, the first time they were used *in force*. Later the Germans counter-attacked at this point, and we lost a large part of what had been won by the offensive.

Service with III Corps was, however, at a tangent to the main direction in which Charles was to be employed. In October 1917 he was posted to GHQ to take charge of the training of the whole of the British Army in France. His chief assistant for a time was Lt.-Col. John Dill who was to become CIGS 1940–1.

When I arrived I was horrified by the lack of knowledge at GHQ of the conditions under which fighting in the Ypres salient (the Passchendaele campaign, July–November) was being carried out. During the last month they were very bad indeed, and I do not believe for a moment they were realised. The main reason for the battle being prolonged, after the weather had broken and turned the ground into a quagmire, was Haig's conviction that we must keep up the pressure on the Germans in order to give the French time to recover from the mutiny, following the failure of their attack in May. But Haig was being ill served by his staff. Kiggell, the Chief-of-Staff, was stale and worn out. Davidson at Operations was likewise overdriven. Charteris at Intelligence was much too optimistic. In all there was a dreadful lack of reality and first-hand contact. When Jack Dill left me for Operations, he did much to put this right. He told me later that at first he was kept completely in the dark about future plans. He then tackled Davidson and told him that if he was treated with confidence, he could do useful work. If not, then he demanded to return to some formation in front. He also told Davidson that it was useless to have at GHQ keen young liaison officers, unless he made use of them and really listened to what had been told them by people at the front—much of which could not possibly appear in a written report.

For some time I had myself been aware of this gap between GHQ and forward formations and units, and the general depression of morale following the casualties and failures in Flanders. Besides this, drafts from home were but partially trained, and there was need to learn new techniques and to restore confidence in training methods and the use of arms. Once therefore the fighting died down, we could begin serious work.

First of all, I handed over to Dill the job of training infantry to work with tanks. As his subsequent career proved, Jack Dill was a splendid staff officer, so I had no qualms in that direction, and that left me free to visit subordinate commanders and staffs to find out what they knew and what they wanted.

A sound training organisation already existed, with schools of instruction at various levels of command, and courses of all kinds. My job was to be certain that instructors knew the latest ideas, agree the principles and ensure uniformity of instruction once agreement had been reached. One way of doing this was to issue pamphlets based on the most recent battle experience. Another was to have stationed at each Army a small unit to give practical demonstrations under various conditions.

Two tasks I considered to be of extreme importance. One was to improve the use of the rifle. Standards had sadly fallen away since August 1914 when a trained man could fire fifteen aimed rounds per minute, and when the Germans mistook our rifle fire for machine guns. The rifle remained the infantryman's *personal* weapon, proficiency in which was the basis of his confidence in his own all-round efficiency. The second task was to make better use of the machine-gun, especially the heavy Vickers now available in quantity. At that time each infantry brigade had one machine-gun company, the handling of which was supposed to be dealt with by the divisional staff. I felt strongly that the only way to ensure this was done properly, was to form the three companies into a divisional machine-gun battalion; and I pressed continually for this reorganisation. The decision, however, was delayed for week after week. At last I managed to get it through by pointing out that special courses would have to be run for the officers appointed to command, and that unless something was done at once we would not be ready for the German onslaught which we knew was bound to come early in 1918. I then enlisted the help of R. H. Leyland, Maurice Wingfield's brother-in-law, and a captain on the Adjutant-General's staff, whose job it was to deal with M.G.Corps postings and promotions. He was a fine character. He had the complete confidence of the officers in the Corps; indeed they accepted his rulings without a backward thought, although he was often their junior in rank. A year later he was killed when commanding a battalion himself. Leyland and I sat in my office all through one afternoon and selected most of the men to take over the new units. We completed the business quickly with free use of telegram and telephone, confirming only by letter. In a matter of days we had courses running in England and France. Of course many of these officers needed no training, but all benefited by discussions. So much time had been wasted that some of the battalions were formed only a few days before the German attack of March 21st 1918, but all were in position by then and gave invaluable service.

At this time also I had my first contacts with the American army, which I soon got to know well. By January 1918 only a few trained formations had arrived, but there was a GHQ under Pershing and a training staff. The head of the American Mission was Col. Robert Bacon, formerly ambassador to France, and a partner of Pierpont Morgan. He was a charming cultivated man with wide interests, and we became very friendly. He arranged for me to visit their HQ, so that they might learn something about our practical experiences. Accordingly on January 30th I went down to Chaumont and had a long sitting with the head of the training branch Col. Malone. The organisation he had drawn up was very complete, though rather academic and inelastic, but capable of improvement with experience. I then visited a number of schools, where some of the instructors were British. Their criticism was that not enough discussion or freedom of opinion were allowed, and I do not think this characteristic has altered with the years. In April, after the German advance, several more American divisions * were brought over in a hurry to complete their training in northern France, in the rear of the British Second Army, with the help of British instructors. This move gave us a great deal of intensive work. The Americans were then as now great hustlers, and they were impatient to finish their training. The troops learned fast, especially the junior officers who were excellent, but the NCOs were less good. Their discipline was curious. The punishments were fierce, and the private soldier did not seem to give his officer the automatic respect due to a man holding a commission, nor even trust to a leader who had really proved his worth. They always seemed to me to be keeping their end up. The staff too were indifferent, and I had the general impression that the higher ranks were not willing to give full value to our experience. This meant that in the end they had to learn the hard way, by taking a lot of punishment from the enemy. None the less there were really very few cases of resentment towards us. I do remember one rather difficult interview between one of our young divisional commanders and his opposite number, an older but far less experienced officer. Another case was a brigade commander, a Southerner I think, who clearly disliked 'the goddam British'. This man was a prodigy in his powers of expectoration, an unerring shot through a half-open door. I told his superior, very mildly,

* Haig made the following entry in his diary for May 7th, 1918. 'General Bonham-Carter (Dir. of Training) reported on the arrangements made to receive and train the Americans. We are using the cadres of our 39th, 66th, 30th and 34th Divisions to help in the training of the Infantry of four American Divisions. I impressed on Bonham-Carter that our Officers are not to command, and order the Americans about, but must only *help* American Officers by their advice and experience to become both *leaders* in the field, as well as *instructors*. For the moment, *training as leaders* should take first place.' Quoted from *The Private Papers of Douglas Haig, 1914–1919*. Edited by Robert Blake. (Eyre and Spottiswoode, 1952.)

that I did not think he was making the best use of the help we were trying to give him, and the poor man was out on his ear in 48 hours.

Training in the strict military sense was not Charles' only preoccupation in the position he held at GHQ in 1917–18. The loss of morale in the Army, evident after Passchendaele and widely reported by the censor, could not be met merely by courses and by weapon training. The troops were anxious about their families and conditions at home. The U-boat campaign was at its height and food was short. The reports of air-raids (though as nothing compared to the second World War) were disturbing. The men themselves were war weary. They were depressed by the sheer mental monotony of life in France, the seeming endlessness of the fighting, and the exhaustion of the autumn battles. Of course the great majority of them were civilians in uniform, 'possessed of minds, interests and prospects which neither the preparation for war nor war itself could wholly divert or destroy'.* Moreover, many had forgotten what the war was about—if they ever really knew—but they all wanted to know what was to become of them when it was all over.

'It is to the lasting credit of Brigadier-General C. Bonham-Carter, then in charge of the Training Branch of the General Staff of GHQ, that he first foresaw the nature of this demand, and afterwards was indefatigable in his endeavours to satisfy it.' * So wrote Lord Gorell, who was serving under Charles in 1917, and later had much to do with the general reorganisation of army education and the formation of the Army Educational Corps in 1920. It is not widely known that the army has had a long history of educational enterprise, dating from as far back as the 18th century when schooling was first provided for young soldiers and the children of soldiers. In 1860 certificates for educational proficiency were introduced, and integrated a few years later with the whole system of promotion. Adult education proper, however, was not seriously

* *Education and the Army*, by Lord Gorell. (O.U.P., 1921.)

fostered until the early 1900s, notably when Haldane was at the War Office; but most activity was suspended in 1914. None the less sporadic efforts at lectures and evening classes continued, mainly at training camps in England, for example at the White City in London, and at Brocton Camp, Cannock Chase. In France very little was done, other than a few lectures organised by the Y.M.C.A., practically the only body that catered for the soldier in his off moments. Certainly nothing was formally initiated or approved by the army itself, which was totally engaged in the problems of fighting. This was Charles' great contribution, for it was he who launched the whole enterprise, not as a small pilot experiment, but as a full-scale official scheme for the whole Army in France. But he had his difficulties.

My ideas were not received with favour by the Adjutant-General, in fact he was frightened of them and thought that the discipline of the army would be imperilled. After making various objections, he looked at me and said: 'I can see that Bonham-Carter thinks I'm a B. . F. .' I could only reply: 'Not quite that, sir, but mistaken.' Of course he did not realise he was dealing with ordinary citizens who had put on uniform for a time, and was completely lacking in vision on this point. Thanks to the help of Butler, Deputy CGS and Burnett-Stuart, Deputy A-G, we got approval on January 1st 1918. I then went over to London to recruit lecturers. My brother Maurice, then working in the Ministry of Reconstruction, helped prepare the way, and I had a busy but profitable time. My diary for January 9th reads as follows:

11.0 am. Ministry of Reconstruction—saw Maurice, Vaughan Nash, and the Minister, Dr Addison.
12 noon. Ministry of Labour—saw Sir D. Shackleton.
12.30 pm. Ministry of Reconstruction, for conference with Arthur Greenwood (afterwards a Minister) and Dr Basil Yeaxlee.
1.15 pm. Lunch at my club with John Buchan.
2.30 pm. Ministry of Pensions—saw the Minister, Mr Hodge.

3. pm. Board of Education—saw the President, H. A. L. Fisher, Selby Bigge, and Gilbert Murray.
4. pm. Board of Agriculture—saw Sir Daniel Hall.
4.30 pm. War Office—saw Lynden-Bell, Director of Staff Duties.

I had a similar round on January 10th and returned to France on the 11th. All my contacts were most helpful, and before long a stream of specialists began to arrive, giving lectures to units all over the area occupied by our army. I attended some of them, and felt sure that a great deal of good was being done. Of course not all the lecturers were equally successful in answering the many very searching questions put to them.

Fortunately I found exactly the right officer to administer the scheme in Douglas Borden Turner, a most energetic and gifted man, whose chief interests in life lay in education and social service. Before coming to my staff he was serving as a remount officer in Gough's Army, but how he got on there I cannot think. He knew very little about a horse, but did admirable work for me.

Another scheme I put forward was only adopted after some delay by direct intervention of the Commander-in-Chief himself. This offered general education and vocational training to anyone in the army fitted and willing to receive it. At first I considered the scheme need not come into operation until the war was over—the purpose being to keep men contented while waiting for demobilisation and train them for civil life. On second thoughts I decided to go ahead at once, but allow for expansion when the fighting ceased. Douglas Borden Turner worked out the details, and based it on a similar scheme operated by the Canadians. However this time the A-G defeated us, and the scheme was shelved.

Fortunately Haig himself came to hear of the Canadian scheme shortly afterwards.

At an historic dinner one night at Lord Haig's chateau his personal enthusiasm was aroused, and he gave orders for the preparation of a scheme for general education throughout the army in France with the object (1) of making men better citizens of the Empire, by widening their outlook and knowledge, (2) of helping them by preparing them for their return to civil life.*

Charles noted:

I found on my desk one evening a note signed 'D.H.' instructing me to draw up a scheme for educating the army similar to that of the Canadian Corps. Since this had already been done, he had it the very next morning, and approved of it at once. So, in spite of great difficulties, education began. It entailed an extra staff officer at every Army and Corps HQ to organise the work, obtain men willing to teach, find accommodation, and so forth. We were desperately short of such mundane things as paper, pencils and books. Moreover the scheme was formally promulgated barely a week before the great German attack on the Fifth Army. But we kept going, and when the emergency died down, we made great strides. At the end of the war the number of students rose to fully three quarters of a million. Not only did the scheme help maintain morale before and after the Armistice, the latter a very difficult time when excellent demobilisation plans were upset by political pressure, but it also stimulated the general desire for education, which was such a feature between the wars.

On March 21st the German attack began. When the situation became serious, practically all training ceased, and I was sent to Third Army HQ at Beauquesne (commander, Sir Julian Byng; chief staff officer, Louis Vaughan) whose staff were very hard pressed. I was able to relieve Vaughan to some extent. The whole of the Fifth Army was retreating pretty rapidly, while the right of the Third Army was also retiring, partly under pressure, in order to keep contact. Despite this the morale of the troops remained high. A colleague told me of one case of panic. He was passing a brigade headquarters, when the senior officers were away, and saw a young staff captain rushing in and out of his office

* *GHQ*, by 'GSO', page 200.

throwing papers into his car, evidently badly frightened. He took the lad and shook him, saying: 'Think, think, dont get excited', and the boy got hold of himself again, deeply ashamed.

On March 26th, we had some excitement. Byng and Vaughan had gone to their billet to get some food, and I was holding the fort. They were away for an hour and a half, I suppose, and during their absence reports came in from Corps. It became apparent that there was a gap of a couple of miles at least at Serre, and that there were no troops available to fill it till the arrival of the New Zealand division, which could not possibly reach the front till the following morning. When the Army commander returned I explained the situation, and suggested that the Germans were probably just as exhausted as our troops, and that nothing would happen for some hours. He took the news quite calmly of course, though naturally anxious, and all he said was: 'I agree we can do nothing but wait, and direct the New Zealanders to the right place. Anyhow you've given me a first-class thrill.' I noticed however that he found waiting a trial, so I gave him a copy of Marcus Aurelius which I always carried in my pocket. He began to read it, and seemed to find relief. After his death in 1935 Lady Byng returned the book to me. I have always found the meditations of this soldier-philosopher soothing in times of anxiety.

The defeat of the Fifth Army naturally led to some anxiety at home and to questions in the House of Commons. In defending himself and the Government, Lloyd George made certain statements, strictly accurate in themselves, but intended to deceive. One was that the ration strength of the army was greater at the beginning of 1918 than it had been a year earlier. This was indeed true, but included a large number of Womens' Army Auxiliary Corps and of German prisoners. The fighting strength was much lower. It is a matter of history that after the speech a letter appeared in the *Morning Post* under the signature of F. B. Maurice, in which he wrote that the Prime Minister's statement did not reveal the truth. Maurice had been Director of Operations at the War Office, and was awaiting appointment to command a division. He undoubtedly had the promise of a brilliant career, but there could only be one result for such insubordination—compulsory retirement. He wrote the letter, I know, fearing that the P.M. intended to replace Haig, a step which we were all convinced would have had a disastrous effect on the morale of the army. A number of officers of my seniority at GHQ were equally anxious that the truth should be known. So I was deputed to take to London a statement showing the exact statistics. I may say that neither Haig nor his CGS had any knowledge of our action. I gave the figures to Mr Asquith, who did not use them however, for although there was a division in the House, no enquiry of any sort took place.

Some time in the early summer of 1918 Charles began to feel that adequate progress was not being made towards uniformity of training methods, and that he was not senior enough to obtain it. On his recommendation an Inspector-General of Training was appointed,* the training branch of GHQ reduced and given the task of implementing the policy of this officer. Charles himself was anxious to secure a command, for he had been continuously on the staff since early 1915. He was promised a brigade, with a view to quick promotion to a division; but it was not to be. Owing to the decline in man-power available for the Army, it was decided to cut down the number of formations and reduce their strength, thus diminishing the opportunities for command. His hopes were therefore disappointed. In August he returned to duty as chief staff officer with a corps, and he served in this capacity until the end of the war and the subsequent entry into Germany with the Army of Occupation.

* Lieut.-Gen. Sir Ivor F. Maxse.

CHAPTER 2

SENIOR GENERAL

It is a curious fact that when a war has been successfully concluded—as many have been in the course of British history—we are prone to cast away our arms and advantages beyond all prudence and common sense; so that when the next emergency arises we find ourselves as unprepared as ever we were. We comfort ourselves with the cliché that we are an unmilitary nation, as indeed we are. When peace comes, many people are so heartily sick of bloodshed or bored by routine or otherwise frustrated that they become exaggeratedly pacific and, more foolish still, cannot believe that every other nation will fail to follow suit. At such times the professional soldier suffers an eclipse. He reverts to his substantive rank and loses pay. Promotion is retarded, and work blunted by the absence of action. Often he becomes unpopular, as Kipling so pithily recorded. Army Estimates are cut to an extent which stifle initiative and render the profession precarious to a middle-aged officer. One false step or a long illness or merely enforced superannuation may bring his career to a premature end, and he finds himself in an overcrowded world on an inadequate pension.

This was particularly true of the 1920s, when Charles was fortunate to survive a period of uncertainty. In his case it culminated in a serious sickness, the aftermath of enteric fever contracted during the Boer War, and a condition exacerbated by the long strain of service in France. Meanwhile he at last obtained command of troops, the 2nd battalion Royal Dublin Fusiliers; and in December 1919 he sailed with this unit for Constantinople, taking my mother with him. They were met at the quay by the Commander-in-Chief, the Army of the Black Sea, General Sir George Milne, and the battalion marched to quarters at the Military Medical School, Haidar Pasha, adjoining Florence Nightingale's former Barrack Hospital.

Living conditions were primitive, the winter was exceptionally cold, and it needed resilience and resource to resist depression. My parents rented a comfortless house at Feneraki, formerly the *summer* home of a French merchant, with all the disadvantages implicit in that description.

On the day we took possession there were eighteen inches of snow on the ground. The only means of getting warm was to crouch over an oil stove in great-coats. We also had another larger stove for heating water and for cooking. We used to toss for who should have a bath before going to bed, the loser having the bath. Madge [my mother] had managed to get as cook an old Russian woman whose husband had made a living in Salonika by buying clothing from British soldiers and selling it to great advantage. My soldier servant rushed in one day and announced in great excitement: 'Her vest's army, too.' Certainly her skirt and jacket were! Soon Madge replaced her with a Greek man, who cooked quite well but was a little weak in the head, and Kyrieki, a pretty Greek girl who acted as maid. Kyrieki had the habit of doing her work in her 'undies', with her hair down, and bare feet. She was highly amused when Madge insisted that when answering the front door she wear a dress and have her hair up. When she contracted malaria, she was attended by our regimental doctor, a Scot, who heard his patient's symptoms via the Albanian gardener who spoke Greek and a little French, re-translated into English by Madge.

The Dublin Fusiliers were a mixture of the best type of volunteers, some with war experience, (compulsory service never applied to Ireland), and raw recruits, including the lowest type of corner boys from Dublin. This made for difficulties at the outset, and they were far from improved by conditions in Turkey. The barrack rooms were cold and badly lit, and it was impossible at first to provide regimental institutions. So it was not surprising that the men were attracted in the evenings to saloons where there was light, warmth, music and 'kind ladies'. These places sold a form of spirits, *mastik*, which had no immediate effect but brought on delayed drunkenness. After drinking, my Irishmen either passed out or went berserk. We also had many cases of venereal disease and some serious crime, including manslaughter and murder. In addition morale was weakened by the nature of our work. On arrival we were ordered to provide a host of men for detached employment—storemen, batmen, orderlies, etc.—all jobs normally done by soldiers in a garrison town, and many others besides. Naturally we sent away only the trustworthy men, and this allowed more rope for the bad characters left behind. We had more crime, civil and military, than I had ever experienced, and the punishments I had to give, both in number and severity, filled me with dismay. Eventually I had a notice posted in every barrack room stating the penalties attached to each type of crime, and this had some effect. For example: Private Murphy was brought before me for drunkenness.

'Murphy, were you drunk?'

'Well, sir, it was this way . . .'

'I did not ask you how or why, but only if you were drunk.'

'Maybe, sir, I had some drink taken.'

'That wont do, Murphy, you know quite well what it is to be drunk. Were you drunk?'

'Yes, sir, I was.'

'Very well then, I need not hear any witnesses. Do you know what is your punishment?'

'Yes, sir, fourteen days.'

'Quite right.'

Murphy was marched out of the room. Outside he said to the escort:

'Well, anyway, that's justice.' All in the thickest brogue.

One of the difficulties in dealing with delinquents in the orderly room was the horror they had of speaking the truth. One lad of about 20 told me a real fairy tale. I put down my pen, looked at him and said:

'You cant really expect me to believe that, can you? Come, tell the truth and shame the Devil.'

With a broad grin he did so, and I let him off on that occasion 'pour encourager les autres'.

The most serious results of drunkenness, as I have said, were that it led to a high incidence of V.D. and to extreme violence. So in addition to the cases with which I was able to deal myself, there were many courts-martial. In one instance two men stole some live ammunition, visited a neighbouring village, and took pot shots at the inhabitants, killing one. The trial resulted in a death sentence which had to be confirmed by the Commander-in-Chief. Before confirming the sentence, Sir George Milne sent for me. He was shortly to leave the command, and was most unwilling to give his consent, as this would be one of his last acts. I had to convince him otherwise, first because murder had been done without any valid extenuating circumstances; secondly an example had to be made to prevent it happening again.

When I took the battalion to India at the end of 1920, I was able to get rid of two hundred really bad characters,* and after that all our troubles ceased. However by then things had already much improved, for various reasons. One was that we were able to do some training and also saw a little active service against the Turkish nationalists. Another was the help given me by our chaplain Father Barry Doyle, an Irishman himself, and devoted to his work and to the men. He used to keep me posted of their state of mind, and warned me at times if mischief was brewing. I was able to do him a service. I interviewed the Papal Legate, and asked him to recommend Barry Doyle's appointment as a Domestic Prelate to the Pope. I told Doyle of what I had done, and he said he would certainly get the honour, as they would hope I should join the fold. It turned out just as he said, and he became Monsignor Barry Doyle just after we

* Charles used to tell the story of the typically Irish incident at the disbandment parade of the regiment several years later. When the ceremony was over, he was walking off the parade ground when several rough-looking characters made a rush at him. He awaited the worst, but found they were all men he had sacked from Turkey, who were delightedly wanting to shake hands with him!

left for India! A third reason was the improvement in regimental institutions. In particular I started a National Savings Group, in the hope of diverting some of the men's money away from drink. This had a resounding success, and within twelve months over £10,000 was saved.

In this last instance there was a remarkable parallel with the work of Charles' illustrious cousin, Florence Nightingale, at Scutari. In the absence of any official scheme, Miss Nightingale acted as private banker to anyone who wanted to send their money home, £71,000 was sent in six months. All money, she said, saved from the drink shops.

A few weeks before Charles left Turkey, I was brought out to Constantinople by train by my mother, who had returned to England the previous summer. It was a most adventuresome journey and took us nearly a week. I was not quite six years old, but sufficiently grown up to retain some vivid though disjointed memories of my short sojourn. By then my parents had taken a house at Moda, within a mile of Feneraki and likewise on the Anatolian side of the Bosphorous. It was a medium-sized villa in a respectable suburb, but there were things about it which resembled no villa in England. At night my bed had to be pulled out from the wall, which oozed bugs, fat black blobs that bit to distraction if given the chance. I remember well the fears of the night: above all the eerie cry of the watchman as he banged his staff on the pavement and called out the hours. I remember too the villainous-looking boatmen at the quays of the Golden Horn; the polite merchants in the bazaar who invited us into their little low shops to sit on a carpet and drink black coffee—one of them gave me a fez; the British military policemen directing the traffic; St. Sofia; butter at 18s. a pound, and bananas 6s. each. I remember going for a walk, protected by a soldier. He bought me sweetmeats from a travelling trolley, quite forbidden, but so was the cigarette he gave me. I remember the terrible ships from Sebastopol and Odessa, crammed with White Russian refugees of Wrangel's retreating army. They were so over-crowded and ill loaded that they steamed up the Bosphorous listing so heavily that it looked as if they were bound to turn turtle. At night ghastly murmurs and yells emanated from these hulks, and in day-time Moda was besieged by haggard Russian officers and their families seeking shelter.

Despite the physical discomforts, life in Constantinople at this time was intensely interesting to anyone with a sense of history and who looked beyond the immediate horizon of Service duty. The political position was precarious. Thanks to a humiliating peace treaty * and to the ambitions of the Greeks under Venizelos, who hoped to carve out a new empire in Asia Minor, a strong nationalist movement had sprung up under Mustapha Kemal in central Anatolia. This movement was in opposition to the 'legal' government of the Sultan in Constantinople, who was supported by the Allies and who naturally had to defer to them. But the Allies were already in disagreement among themselves, and were tired of the occupation. Some of them even had a secret understanding with the nationalists, who daily gained ground and penetrated ever nearer to the shores of the Bosphorous. In this area most of the military responsibilities rested with the British. Thus it was that Charles was involved in several minor actions, both with his battalion and as the commander for a short time of a mixed brigade of Allied units, with headquarters at Beykos. Although these encounters were of small tactical importance, they presaged the growing strength of Kemal, his utter rout of the Greeks, and the ultimate evacuation of all foreign troops from Turkey in 1922–3. Meanwhile my parents enjoyed to the full that extraordinary and exhilarating company of men and women, who composed Constantinople society during the last days of the Sultanate: diplomats and officers of the Allied missions; journalists—among them Philip Graves of *The Times* who became a firm friend; savants; churchmen, Orthodox and Unorthodox; refugees from Poland and Russia; the powerful community of Levantine merchants led by the

* The Treaty of Sévres, signed by the Sultan in August 1920.

Charnauds and the Whittalls; and prominent members of the régime. Among these was Abdul Mejid, cousin of the reigning Sultan, whom he succeeded in the anomalous position of Khalif in 1922. Abdul Mejid was a charming and cultivated man, of liberal character, and a true patriot who was finally driven into exile when the Khalifate was abolished from Turkey in 1924. He had many interests, among them the breeding of magnificent Arab horses which he paraded before Charles. He was also a keen rider to hounds; and regularly went out with a small company, which included my mother, to hunt jackal on the slopes of Kaish Dagh with a pack of foxhounds specially imported from England. That alone was a comment of a kind!

* * *

Charles' service in Turkey under General Sir George Milne was to bear fruit later, as I shall describe. Meanwhile he had to face one of those dispiriting periods, familiar to successful men, when his career all but petered out. That he survived was due to his own resilience in body as well as in mind, and to the benevolence of friends.

In November 1920 he was posted with his battalion to India, where he was to remain only a few months before returning to England to take command of the 129th South Wessex Infantry Brigade, Territorial Army. This was only a part-time post, with appropriately reduced pay, and professionally a backwater. Most of his time was taken up visiting detachments in Dorset, Wiltshire, and Somerset, and in directing training schemes. The staff work was performed by a brigade major. This left Charles free to adopt an unorthodox but characteristic view of his other duties. As the commander of citizen soldiers, he felt it was his business to meet people in as many different walks of life as possible. He bought a house near Bath, joined the local rotary and literary clubs, and together with my mother gave up much time to Citizen House. This was a social settlement for young people which became an important dramatic centre and school under its gifted director, Consuelo de Reyes. Charles commented: 'The old gossips of Bath were shocked by Citizen House, or pretended to be. We could never understand why; perhaps the girls, most of whom came from very poor homes, danced in pretty dresses!' As a small boy, I retain two sharp memories of this time. One was taking part as a black page in *The Ballad of Bath Ghosts*, a pageant recalling the glories of 18th-century Bath, and produced by Citizen House at the Pump Room. The other was sitting immediately behind G. K. Chesterton at a Citizen House play. He was so large that he occupied two seats to himself, and entirely prevented my seeing the stage. But he so oscillated and gibbered with laughter that he gave me a performance all to myself. Charles also made contact with the Royal School (for the Daughters of Officers of the Army), of which he was later to become a governor. In these and other ways he maintained his profound interest in the humanities and in education, which was shortly to be given full scope in the Army itself. Nothing, however, could have been further from his mind when he was suddenly struck down by serious illness, necessitating four major operations in two and a half years. He should have died. Not only did he make a miraculous recovery, thanks to a tough constitution and will, to the skill of the surgeons and the devotion of my mother, but once recovered he enjoyed good health almost for the remainder of his life. Meanwhile his job was preserved through the good offices of Sir Louis Bols, his divisional commander, and of Sir George Milne, without whose intervention he would undoubtedly have had to leave the Army.

* * *

1924 was an *annus mirabilis* for Charles. By April he had fully recovered in health and prospects, and was actively installed as chief staff officer to Sir George Milne, GOC Eastern Command, at the Horse Guards in London. This was the first of two spells of service under 'that truly remarkable man, Uncle George'. The second spell, the account of which brings this chapter to an end, lasted 1927–31, and occurred at the War Office when Milne was CIGS, and Charles Director of Staff Duties. Although not his last military appointment, it was in several senses the apex and fulfilment of Charles' career in the Army. As often happens in life, it came his way by accident. After leaving the Horse Guards, he was offered the post of commandant of the Royal Military College, Sandhurst, which he had long desired. 'I wrote to Uncle George thanking him for the appointment. In reply he sent me a postcard saying, "Are you taking Sandhurst or DSD?" I went up to London at once to find out what he meant. I discovered that an unexpected vacancy had occurred and that I was free to make my choice. Naturally I chose the more important position of DSD, saying—not entirely in jest—that I would have been the first commandant of the RMC to have made a serious study of education. To which Uncle George replied that as DSD I should be able to make any changes at Sandhurst that I liked.'

Thus it was that Charles found himself finally so placed as to influence the basic organisation and education of the Army: subjects with which he had long been intimately concerned, and about which he had thought deeply for most of his professional life. More important still, he had the good fortune to serve under Milne at a critical time when the British Army was qualitatively and technically in advance of other European armies, and when it was still being directed to that end. For this, Milne—a man of vision and a strong character—was largely responsible. This is an important matter of record, still not widely recognised, and which was the subject of misrepresentation during the second World War. But here first is Charles' assessment of his chief.

Milne's judgement was exceptionally sound; it was based on deep knowledge and a gift of imagination and foresight—qualities essential to a successful military commander. Once during a discussion, when I was reporting to him on the development of tanks, he outlined with remarkable accuracy the tactics of the second world war. He demanded a high standard of work from his subordinates and always obtained it, for his staff was carefully selected, and to those whom he trusted he delegated authority to a remarkable degree. He also had the power of getting men to work in harmony, not only his own staff but colleagues too. While he was CIGS, the military and civil sides of the War Office learned to work together, and gave up that suppressed hostility which had so often been the case in the past. He never hesitated to accept responsibility for the decisions or actions of his staff, and he invariably backed us. At the same time he threw an enormous responsibility on his senior officers. His treatment of me will serve as an example.

When I first arrived at the War Office, and for four or five weeks afterwards, I was called in to see him two or three times a week. He then explained to me his policy on every subject and problem with which I had to deal. Once satisfied that I had absorbed his views, it was quite difficult to see him as often as I wished. I remember particularly one occasion when I asked for an interview. He enquired through his military secretary what it was that I wanted to talk about. I said that as I had not seen him for some time, I felt he ought to know what I was doing. He merely replied that he was confident that I was doing right, that he was quite satisfied, but that he could not see me. Such trust not only brought him devoted service, but also allowed him to concentrate on his work for the Committee of Imperial Defence and for the Cabinet, and through frequent inspections to keep in close touch with the army itself.

Of course he had his weaknesses. He would sometimes give way to pressure of old friends or comrades; and he could occasionally be vindictive. He was a shy man and at first sight appeared reserved and forbidding, particularly to those who showed fear of him. He also had a strong streak of caution in his make-up, perhaps because he was a Scot! But it was not so strong as to affect his broad and visionary view of what the army was and what it should become. He was absolutely single-minded in his devotion to this cause, and it is significant that his term as CIGS was twice extended, lasting from 1926 to 1933. Although his position on the Army Council was not officially higher than the other military members, he soon became 'primus inter pares'; as a result every CIGS is now recognised as the true head of the army.

These are weighty words in any context. Here they should be closely related to Charles' own work as DSD, which was always materially affected by the decisions of the CIGS, and to the whole question of military preparedness before 1939. At least they should puncture those critics, who generalise fatuously about the 'military mind', and condemn out of hand the whole direction of the Army between the wars.

Broadly and briefly the Staff Duties directorate was concerned with two main groups of subjects: one—technical; the other—personal.

The organisation of the Army for war: chiefly the war establishments of units and formations; the development policy of weapons (not artillery), tanks, vehicles, and equipment; the preparation and issue of training regulations; and the formation of new services.

The supply of officers: their recruitment, education (not training), and selection for staff appointments.

The mass of detail which make up these headings cannot of course be discussed here. Instead I propose only to comment on one or two subjects of historical importance. First, the technical aspect.

In 1939 the Army found itself grossly under-manned, under-trained, and under-equipped by comparison with the Germans. This condition was tragically emphasised by the campaigns of 1940, when above all the enemy demonstrated his immense superiority in the handling of armoured forces. Despite strenuous efforts, this discrepancy had not been made good two years later, when Rommel captured Tobruk and swept the Eighth Army back to El Alamein. These disasters provoked an anxious and acrimonious enquiry in the Press and in Parliament, which sought *inter alia* to trace the origin of British inferiority in tank development; especially since the tank had been a British invention and an important factor in the final victory in France in 1918. In a heated exchange between Churchill and Hore-Belisha during the debate on a Vote of Censure on July 1st–2nd, 1942, two mis-statements of fact were made. One by Churchill, when he attributed the successful use of armour to ideas first expressed by General de Gaulle,* and thereafter exploited by the Germans. The other by Hore-Belisha, in defending himself against the accusation that, when Secretary of State for War, he had failed to produce an efficient tank, able to stand up to gunfire. Hore-Belisha stated that he had inherited an official policy which was only 'concerned with advocating a tank capable of resisting armour-piercing bullets, not artillery fire'; and that this had been laid down by the staff pamphlet of 1929, known colloquially as the *Purple Primer*.

Both these statements were incorrect and highly misleading. The latter was immediately disproved in two letters written in August 1942 by Charles to Hore-Belisha, who duly admitted he had been misinformed. The true story can be outlined as follows.

Despite the formation of the Royal Tank Corps in 1923, and the efforts of a few enthusiasts,† the lessons and potentialities of tank warfare were not seriously considered by the General Staff until 1926. In that year Milne was appointed CIGS, and soon afterwards 'expressed his intention to carry out the mechanisation of the army, with the tank in the principal role'.† An experimental force was formed of tanks and other armoured fighting vehicles, and tried out in manoeuvres at Tidworth in 1927. The success of this trial gave practical proof of the new policy and encouraged further steps. In 1929 a start was made in mechanising infantry and cavalry, and close study was given to the co-operation of tanks with other arms. By this time Charles had taken over as DSD and

* Notably in his book *Vers l'armée de métier*, published in 1934.

† The full story from the tank point of view is related in *The Tanks*, by Liddell Hart (Cassell), from which these quotations are taken.

was fully involved. In January 1929 he delivered a directive which envisaged three main functions of armour:

A light armoured brigade of armoured cars and light tanks, with close support, for strategical reconnaissance.

A medium armoured brigade of medium and light tanks and supporting troops, for manoeuvre in a set battle.

A similar group, strengthened as to infantry, artillery and engineers, for long range penetration.

These proposals were incorporated and expanded in *Mechanised and Armoured Formations*, the so-called *Purple Primer*, from the colour of its cover, (revised and republished in 1931 as *Modern Formations*), a staff pamphlet, barely 40 pages long, first produced in March 1929. This was an historic document. It was drafted by Col. C. N. F. Broad, head of SD2, 'and embodied the main ideas that had been formulated in theory during the decade since the war, checked by the experience of the last two years' practice. It was issued not only to the Army but to the Press, as a means of educating public opinion —on which military progress depended for its backing. Its purpose was described as being "to stimulate thought in the army . . . on the whole subject of what war in the future is going to be like".' *

This was the pamphlet misquoted by Hore-Belisha, for it never advocated any hard and fast policy for tanks, neither as to construction nor as to use. *It merely stated the position reached in 1931*, when many problems awaited solution. Two types of tank had by then been evolved—the light and the medium. The latter weighed 16 tons, was clad in armour thick enough to stop small arms but not gunfire, and carried a gun capable of destroying similar machines. Since no field bridge then existed, capable of supporting a heavier tonnage, and since processes of hardening steel were insufficiently developed, it was plainly impossible to make progress by thickening the armour. But the future was left open. And eight years were to

* The full story from the tank point of view is related in *The Tanks*, by Liddell Hart (Cassell), from which these quotations are taken.

elapse before war actually broke out, during which time it was anticipated that these problems would be largely overcome. Likewise many far-seeing speculations were advanced as to the handling of armoured formations—their mobility, rapidity of manoeuvre, penetrating power, material and moral effect, etc.—all of which anticipated de Gaulle, and were turned to good account by the Germans who had made a careful study of the pamphlet and developed its ideas in practice.

Why then were British tanks inferior in the early part of the war? There were two main causes, both dating from soon after this time.

First, financial economy. This was a matter of Government policy, which was influenced partly by the economic depression, and partly by the pacific opinions of the majority of the electorate. Before 1935 less than £400,000 a year was spent on tanks and tracked vehicles, while the total cost of the regular and territorial armies was only a little over £30 millions. Twenty years later the figure exceeded £500 milllions. Charles was closely connected with finance, for it was his duty to advise where economies could be made with least harm to the efficiency of the Army. It drove him almost to desperation, especially when after the estimates had been agreed the Treasury would frequently demand a fresh cut. 'I remember one particular occasion when I was suddenly asked to make a further reduction of a quarter of a million. I was at my wits' end, when the Quartermaster-General came into my office to tell me that the cost of the soldier's ration had dropped by 1d, making a saving of £150,000. I dont remember how we found the balance, nor even whether it was necessary to do so.' Alas, no such miracle occurred in the case of tanks, and at one point three armament firms were compelled to disperse their skilled workmen and scrap their machine tools for lack of orders. This had a delayed effect, for when rearmament began it was some time before the men and the tools could be reassembled.

Secondly, opposition. Milne fought a continuous battle

against conservative elements in the Army, especially the cavalry, and he was worn down at times. Undoubtedly he showed caution, too much for the tank enthusiasts, but he never gave in; and so long as he was in office, some progress was made. Unfortunately Sir Archibald Montgomery-Massingberd, his successor in 1933 (the year that Hitler came to power) thought—in Charles' words—'of the future only in the terms of the past. He failed to press forward research in the development of weapons, and failed completely to visualise in what manner tactics were likely to evolve. Nor did he realise the rapidly increasing power of the aeroplane. Milne on the other hand was determined that, even though the Government refused to provide the weapons he asked for, officers should have some knowledge of how they should be used when they did become available.'

Two other references illustrate the technical difficulties of those days, and how Charles worked to overcome them, sometimes successfully, sometimes not.

> Another subject which we were anxious to settle was the light machine-gun, what gun should be adopted, on what scale issued, and so on. We found it hard to persuade the small arms experts to get a move on. So to force their hands we brought over a Danish 'Madsen' and demonstrated it. At the trial it came in for aggressive criticism from the research men, which was exactly what we had hoped, for in a comparatively short time they produced an adaptation of the Czech 'Bren', an admirable weapon.

Conservative opinion and vested interests, however, combined to defeat a progressive move in another direction.

> The more complicated weapons developed after 1918 and the arrival of mechanisation required a high standard of maintenance and repair, and a unified system of control. The situation was unsatisfactory because responsibility had become divided—between the Royal Army Service Corps which supplied the general transport of the army, and the Royal Army Ordnance Corps which looked after the

weapons and all the vehicles which served those weapons. This duplication was not only costly, unnecessary and inefficient, but highly dangerous in wartime leading to confusion, delay and loss of life. The solution lay either in forming a new corps of mechanical engineers or in allotting all the duties to an existing corps. At first I advocated that the job should be given to the Royal Engineers, whose younger officers were highly trained, all having taken an honours degree in Mechanical Sciences at Cambridge. But the senior RE officers showed little understanding or appreciation of the problem, and so put themselves out of court. The matter was then thrashed out again, and Milne asked Shinwell, then Financial Secretary, to preside over a committee to decide the issue. Various officers were nominated to state the case for the RASC and the RAOC, who wished to keep the *status quo*, while I and one or two colleagues spoke for the General Staff.

I accompanied Shinwell during his visits to workshops, and ensured that the officers whom he questioned told him the whole truth. I became confident that he realised what was at stake. Reduced to the simplest terms it meant that a lorry carrying supplies would have to go for repairs to one type of workshop (RASC), while a similar lorry carrying or dragging a gun would have to go to another (RAOC). I urged him to recommend the only workable solution—a new corps to have sole responsibility, staffed by the best trained mechanics. But it was to no avail, and he reported in favour of leaving things as they were. The result was that during the second world war the Royal Electrical and Mechanical Engineers (REME) had to be formed in a hurry, but by then much time and valuable material had been lost, and no doubt many lives sacrificed as well.

Finally, the educational aspect. Here Charles was able to do the most important work of his military career, for he broadened the whole conception of education within the Army, gave new form, purpose, and quality to the preparation of young officers, and generally exerted so vital an influence that some of his plans only matured after the end of the second World War, nearly twenty years after he had left office.

When I went to the War Office in October 1927, there was a serious shortage of candidates for Sandhurst, less so for Woolwich. My predecessor had decided to lower the standard of entry, with the result that instructors were complaining they had to spend far too much time teaching cadets subjects they should have known already. I insisted that a proper standard should be re-established, and to obtain quality rather than quantity. I made up for the shortage by attracting more candidates from the universities, and incidentally remedied a long-standing injustice, by allowing everyone holding a degree to have eighteen months seniority. This action duly bore fruit, and the number of candidates gradually rose. It was also noticeable that the university men were on average better educated and more efficient than the others. In addition, I fully supported the scheme whereby young RE officers were sent to Cambridge, where they took the Mechanical Sciences Tripos in two years and qualified as civil engineers.* A high proportion gained first-class honours, and I never heard of a failure.

These university commissions were looked after most competently by a captain on my staff. I shall call him Smith. He left the War Office shortly before I did in 1931, and it was then that I came to hear of his 'unfortunate experience'. One Friday afternoon, just as he was off to catch a train for the weekend, a letter came in from a friend, Mrs A. saying, 'My son Ted, who has just taken his degree, wants to go into the army. What must he do to get a commission?' Smith, in a terrific hurry, called in a shorthand-typist and dictated, 'Dear Mrs A. I am so glad Ted wants to go into the army. There is no difficulty about it. All we shall want with his application is a certificate of character from his Varsity.' He then told the girl to type the letter as quickly as possible for his signature, and to leave a copy on his table. She returned quickly enough, he signed the letter without reading

* This scheme had come into force in 1924.

it, and rushed off. On Monday morning he read through the copy at leisure, and to his horror it ran as follows: 'All that we shall want is a certificate of character for the Bastard'.

In regard to the curriculum at Sandhurst and Woolwich, it was my firm aim to make it less instructional and more truly educational. At Sandhurst far too much time was spent on drill and weapon training, at Woolwich on examinations. I did not have much success with the commandant at Woolwich, although I did persuade him to reduce examination time from nine to three weeks in a course of only 47 working weeks, and to give far more weight to the reports of his teaching staff in deciding the final order of the cadets at passing-out. At Sandhurst, however, I had a real ally in the assistant-commandant, Col. E. D. H. Tollemache, who warmly supported my ideas and put them into practice. My first point was that, whereas fitness and smartness are essential, they should not become obtrusive. Tollemache got over this by working the newly-joined cadets really hard on the square for the first six weeks, but after that he cut down parades to an hour a week. Weapon training was treated in a similar way. Cadets learned to handle their weapons with safety, but no more was demanded. By this means he was able to free the course from practical subjects, better taught *after* a cadet had joined his unit. Secondly I wanted to be sure that enough attention was paid to those subjects, of which every soldier should have a basic understanding, e.g. the principles of tactics, army organisation, administration and law, military history and geography. The object was to produce a young officer equipped with this knowledge, and able to take an alert and intelligent interest in other subjects, not necessarily strictly military. I suggested that there should be a wide choice, and that their application or influence in war should be carefully explained. I was not so much interested in the acquisition of facts as to teach a man to think quickly and logically, especially under pressure, and to express his opinions clearly both in speech and in writing. For all this Tollemache became an enthusiast. He consulted many leading authorities on education, and drew up an admirable syllabus, which had a measurable effect.

Of course there is nothing new in this system. It is only applying to the profession of soldiering principles adopted by other professions—the Law, Medicine, Engineering—whereby theory is studied first, and then tested in practice. I tried hard to get approval for the amalgamation of Woolwich and Sandhurst, and was not far from persuading Uncle George to agree. However when it became known what was afoot, the attack from diehard old gunners became so fierce that he was unable to force it through. The amalgamation had to wait until well after my time; but now there is one principal cadet college, the Royal Military College, Sandhurst.

One of the most fruitful aspects of our work was the contact I and my staff had with headmasters. Uncle George held at least two conferences, when we discussed the entry to Woolwich and Sandhurst, the courses there, and the work of the Officers Training Corps. In addition to discussions, we had some first-rate lectures from such notabilities as Sir Maurice Hankey, secretary to the Committee of Imperial Defence, Sir Warren Fisher, head of the Civil Service, and others. I remember two incidents, both with pleasure. One was the statement by G. C. Turner, headmaster of Marlborough, who said that if he had a son he would send him to Sandhurst rather than to Woolwich for his military education. The other was the resentment of the other headmasters of the conduct of Alington, headmaster of Eton, who clearly thought we were all beneath him. He refused to stay at the Staff College, where we were meeting, and he arrived late for every session. Last of all I remember with delight the final speech given by W. W. Vaughan, headmaster of Rugby, who used to teach me at Clifton—it was a gem in every sense. When he left, I and Sidney Clive* carried his bags to the car. He said he felt very proud to be waited on by *two* major-generals!

* * *

Charles completed his tour of duty as DSD in 1931. Although he had five more years ahead of him, as commander

* Major-General Sir Sidney Clive.

Charles Bonham-Carter as a cadet at Sandhurst, 1894

As a student at the Staff College, 1903

Charles Bonham-Carter, France 1916

of the 4th Division and then as Director-General of the Territorial Army, I do not propose to relate this part of his career, for it would add but little to the tenor of the story. The essence of his work for the Army as a teacher and thinker was largely complete.

The personal impact that he made was of a strong character who never tried to dominate because he never had to; a deeply human man, with whom you would never dream of taking liberties; and above all a man of vision. He had great physical presence, which made his foibles and acute sense of humour all the more disarming. His handsome, rather stern, face was punctuated by an eye-glass—an unnaturally blimpish badge for such an enlightened man—but he wore it simply to equalise his sight. His friends never ceased to wonder at its immovability, and knew that when he fixed you with a penetrating stare—which intimidated some people—he was not looking at you at all, but was in some distant world of his own. The eye-glass was his gimmick, his sorcery.

That stern look was really kindness itself. Young officers soon realised that he was entirely on their side, for he believed in the young and was not discouraged when they failed him now and again. He delighted in forgetting about rank. Once, just before a ceremonial parade, he electrified a foreign mission by obeying his batman's urgent demand that he put on a smarter pair of boots! His habit, too, of writing himself postcards—and of stamping and posting them—as an *aide-memoire* entranced his staff.

The incident of the boots was often quoted against him by his French friends. He loved France and had many contacts, professional and private. In the first World War he got to know a number of French officers, and learned to admire their ability in planning and staff work in the field; and he followed this up afterwards by attending the course for senior allied officers, held at Versailles in 1925, where he met Gouraud, Franchet d'Esperey, and Weygand. But the most permanent contact was his friendship with André Haviland, when the latter was acting as Liaison Officer to the 50th Division in 1916. The two men became firmly attached, and their families have maintained the attachment ever since.

Finally—a word about his visionary quality. He foresaw difficulties and developments, and faced them squarely; and did his uttermost and beyond to achieve what he thought was right. But if he failed, he never showed disappointment, nor allowed it to affect his outlook or his humour. That was real humility.

Such was Charles when in February 1936, at the age of 60, he was appointed Governor and Commander-in-Chief of Malta.

CHAPTER 3

STATESMAN

WHEN my father and mother arrived at Valetta on April 5th, 1936, they were received with all the pomp and honour customarily accorded to a new Governor. Their liner, the P. & O. *Strathmore*, was dressed, and escorted for the last stage of the journey into the Grand Harbour by two destroyers under the command of Commander Lord Louis Mountbatten, and by three squadrons of aircraft. On board they received the Lieutenant-Governor, Sir Harry Luke, who presented other notables on their arrival at the Customs House Quay, where a magnificent guard of honour was drawn up by the Royal Malta Artillery. The following day was devoted to the full panoply of the swearing-in at the Governor's Palace, Valetta. Here, after a formal entry by crowded streets lined with troops, my parents took their places on canopied thrones in the glittering Hall of St. Michael and St. George. Awaiting them was an audience of all the leading people of Malta—the Lieutenant-Governor and his staff, the Archbishop, the Bishop of Gozo, the Chief Justice, the commanders of the three Services, and very many others—all attending in an official capacity but also keen to take a good look at the new Governor and his wife. After the commission of office had been read out, and the swearing-in completed, Charles made his first speech; and then with Madge received the entire company in person in the drawing-room adjoining. It was a splendid performance, splendidly done, and nothing marred the dignity or the harmony of the occasion.

Yet all was not well with Malta. The constitution had been in suspense for three years, and the political situation was confused. Superficially at least, there was some resemblance to events twenty-two years later, when the Governor, Major-General Sir Robert Laycock, was compelled to take over the administration of the island, after the resignation of the Prime Minister, Mr. Dominic Mintoff. On both occasions, relations between the British and Maltese, though not dramatic, were unsatisfactory. There was great need not only for goodwill but for clear unemotional understanding, free of all prejudice, of the facts and feelings of both sides. For this, the first approach must always rest upon a proper knowledge of Malta—its history, its geography, and its ethnic peculiarities.

* * *

The Maltese archipelago consists of three inhabited islands—Malta itself, seventeen miles long by nine wide, where lives the bulk of the population; Gozo nine miles by five; and Comino about a square mile in extent. These islands lie in the centre of the Mediterranean, halfway between Gibraltar and Port Said, in the narrow seas between Sicily and North Africa. The former is less than sixty miles away, the latter about three times that distance. Malta is all that is left of the land bridge that once connected the two continents of Europe and Africa, at a time when the Mediterranean was a series of fresh-water lakes. For that reason Malta contains some of the most valuable and interesting relics of prehistory—the bones of large beasts (such as elephants and hippopotami) trapped by climatic change and geological upheaval, artifacts and souvenirs of Neanderthal man, grandiose and elaborate Stone Age sanctuaries including the famous Hypogeum at Pawla, ancient cart-tracks and other evidence of traffic and human activity in the second and third millennia before Christ.

There is no doubt, too, that it was the geographical position of Malta, and its magnificent natural harbours and bays, that attracted the early settlers of modern times. These were the Phoenicians, traders and sailors of Tyre and Sidon, a white race, speaking a Semitic language, who spread westwards into the Atlantic, and who founded the meteoric empire of Carthage. *It is from Phoenician stock that the present-day Maltese are descended both in race and language*. This is a cardinal and indisputable point of history, for all subsequent rulers of Malta occupied the islands for strategic and administrative reasons only, not for colonisation: the Romans to whom Hamilcar surrendered in 218 B.C.; the Byzantines to whom Malta was apportioned at the division of the Roman Empire towards the end of the fourth century A.D.; the Saracens who conquered it in 870; and Roger the Norman, Count of Sicily, who became suzerain in 1090. After him the Kingdom of Sicily passed to successive royal houses—Anjou, Aragon, Castile—and finally to Charles V, Holy Roman Emperor. He it was who devised Malta in 1530 to the Knights of the Order of the Hospital of St. John of Jerusalem, to hold the island for Christendom and to police the Mediterranean against Moslem marauders.

The Knights of St. John (or Hospitallers) belonged to one of the two * great Crusading Orders who campaigned for the possession of the Holy Places. On their final expulsion from Palestine in 1291, they retired first to Cyprus, then to Rhodes, where for 200 years they continued their offensive against Islam. However, when the Turks became the dominant race among the Moslems in the Middle East, the battle against the Knights was renewed, and in 1522–3 Suleiman the Magnificent turned them out of Rhodes. Seven years later the Knights came to Malta, which remained their home and their fortress until 1798.

The Knights were not welcomed at first by the Maltese, who at that time amounted to about 12,000 peasants and fishermen, ruled by a handful of Siculo-Aragonese families, whose names are perpetuated by descendants today. The sturdy islanders seemed to the Knights a rude unresponsive folk, 'speaking a sort of Moorish', and scratching a scanty living from the thin and stony soil. Apart from Mdina, the ancient capital in the centre of the island, there was no populous settlement, no port

* The other being the Knights of the Temple (or Templars).

proper, and no seaward defences. The Knights therefore, at the height of their warrior and puritanical career, set themselves at once to make a new beginning. They were an extraordinary body, composed of stern men dedicated to celibacy and war, and organised on a basis of nationality into eight distinct Langues, each later with its own Auberge—three for France, two for Spain, and one each for Italy, Germany, and England. Under the vigorous direction of the first Grand Master, L'Isle Adam, they settled on the east side of the present Grand Harbour and proceeded to hew immense fortifications out of the solid limestone rock. Their energy was well rewarded, for the main works were completed in the nick of time. In 1565 Suleiman the Magnificent, now an old man, returned to the assault with an army of 31,000 men borne by a fleet of 181 sail, and laid siege to Malta for four months. It was the last major effort of the Moslems to dominate the Mediterranean, and all Christendom gave prayers for the outcome. Eventually, after immense exertions and losses on both sides, Suleiman withdrew. Malta and the Mediterranean were saved, and the Knights reigned undisturbed for more than 200 years.

Those two centuries of peace were an era of material and civilised prosperity, burgeoning into the late Renaissance and Baroque glories that we see today. Enriched by gifts from grateful sovereigns, the Knights became supreme builders. To them we owe a wonderful galaxy of palaces, auberges, churches, monuments, gardens, and public works, and in the main the five settlements surrounding the Grand Harbour which compose the capital and chief concentration of the island: Valetta and Floriana on one side; Cospicua, Senglea, and Vittoriosa (known as the Three Cities) on the other: the whole enclosed by forts and bastions which rise massive and lustre-white from the deep blue of the Mediterranean. Inevitably, the Knights themselves shed something of their early robust fortitude and self-denial. They lived a collegiate rather than a monastic life, celibacy became a matter of form not fact, and they delighted more and more in elaborate finery and ceremonial. Perhaps their greatest asset was their internationality and the comparative harmony in which they all lived together. Frenchmen might war with Spaniards in Europe, and Spaniards with Englishmen, but not in Malta; and this trait persisted almost to the end. A stricter, more dangerous tension developed at times between the Grand Masters and the representatives of the Church, but without causing any overt breach. There seemed no valid reason why this fortunate and enlightened state of affairs should not continue indefinitely.

But it was not to be. The outbreak of the French Revolution, and the contagion of French militarism and grandeur, rather than any social ideas about liberty and equality, found a response in Malta. There the young Knights of the French Auberges, always in the majority, formed themselves into a Fifth Column. By their agency, the defences were deceived and the island surrendered to Bonaparte on his way to Egypt in June 1798. Thus ended the reign of the Knights. However, the French were not their successors for long. Soon the Maltese rose in rebellion, drove the soldiers of the garrison into Valetta and imprisoned them there until September 1800, when they were finally ejected with the help of the British. In their turn, the British were at first reluctant occupiers; and by the Treaty of Amiens in 1802 it was agreed to restore Malta to the Knights. But the renewal of hostilities made this impracticable, while the Maltese themselves were unwilling to return to the old order of government. At their express wish, Malta was placed under the permanent protection of Britain, and in 1814 became part of the Empire. This arrangement was confirmed by the Congress of Vienna a year later.

That, in the briefest of terms, was how Malta came into the British orbit: a characteristic process, for the motives of both sides were mixed. The desire of the Maltese for protection and other assistance was balanced by the importance of the island to Britain as a naval base, and later as an essential link in the route to the East. It was this strategic aspect that shaped the British attitude to Malta more than any other, and in a manner strongly similar to that adopted by previous powers. Occupation, not colonisation, was the aim; and apart from the initial reorganisation of the legal and administrative system—a measure long overdue, and in any event necessary to conform with British practice—there was very little interference with indigenous life and institutions.

In terms of government, Malta became a Crown Colony and remained so until 1921. Before then all legislative and executive powers were vested in the Governor and Commander-in-Chief—with one exception, the post was always a military appointment—but were tempered after 1849 by a Council of Government composed both of nominated or official members and of elected members. Later a small executive body was also set up. Although the proportion of elected to official members was altered from time to time, and certain other variations made, this was the limit of decentralisation during the first century of British rule. Power remained securely in the hands of the British Government acting through the Secretary of State for the Colonies and the Governor for the time being.

There is no doubt that the great majority of the Maltese people were quite content with these arrangements, at any rate until the end of the first World War. The peasants, dockyard workmen, and small traders—the bulk of the population—were not interested in politics. They were and are thrifty, hard-working, law-abiding people, and far less volatile than their Mediterranean neighbours. Many of them were illiterate, but generally they made no complaint so long as the British connexion guaranteed their personal freedon and a reasonably stable economy: in other words, a market for their goods and an outlet for their labour. In the main this was satisfactorily provided by the Navy, and by Servicemen and officials, together with their families, stationed on the island. Likewise the few aristocratic families, with one notable exception, held aloof from public affairs. It was the small professional class who, as might be expected, took an active interest in politics and stood for election to the Council of Government, It was they who by 1900 were making claims for wider Maltese representation, and were even claiming self-government.

None the less the public administration, though autocratic, was honest and enlightened, in the context of 19th-century imperialism and *laisser-faire*. Public works, education, health defence, and other measures were all introduced, taxation was low, and amicable relations were established with the Roman Catholic Church, the most powerful institution in Malta outside the British Government itself. But here lay the cause of future dissensions. Culturally, as well as spiritually, the influence of the Church was very strong. Since 1831 the dioceses of Malta and Gozo had been placed directly under the Vatican, and a number of the priests trained in and guided by Italy. Italian was the formal speech of the Church, as also of the Law, and had been since the Middle Ages. Moreover, since Italy was the nearest European country and frequently visited by the educated Maltese, the Italian language was often polite parlance in educated circles. English, on the other hand, was a comparatively recent introduction, though predominant in commerce and government affairs. With all this, Maltese itself was the language (often the only one) spoken by the great majority of the population. As explained, this was no Italian patois, but an ancient Semitic speech which had attracted certain foreign accretions during the centuries. Some Maltese, it is true, affected to despise it as the parlance of the pantry; but there were also certain scholars who had begun to purify and enlarge the vocabulary, and generally adapt the language to modern needs by drawing upon its own and allied sources. As an illustration of its Semitic character and of its profound dissimilarity to Italian, here is a rendering in Maltese of the Lord's Prayer:

Missierna li inti fis-smewwiet,
Jitqaddes ismek,
Tigi saltnatek,
Ikun li trid Int, kif fis-sema hekda fl-art.

Hobzna ta' kull jum aghtina l-lum,
Ahfrilna dnubietna, bhalma nahfru lil min hu hati ghalina.
U la ddahhalniex fit-tigrib,
Izda ehlisna mid-deni. Hekk ikun.

The fall of prices at the end of the first World War, and the sudden reduction of employment by the Services, the chief employers in an over-populated island, were the cause of great economic distress, one of the few occasions when violence occurred in Malta. The riots of 1919 also brought to a head the general desire of the Maltese to manage their own affairs, and this led in turn to the granting of self-government in 1921. In fact the new constitution was a dyarchy, and demonstrated very clearly the different interests of the British Government and the Maltese people. Since Malta was a strategic base, certain powers were 'reserved' to the Governor (aided by a nominated council), and these included defence, foreign relations, immigration, coinage, and the like. All other matters relating to the internal welfare of the island were made the province of a Maltese Parliament. This consisted of a Senate of seventeen members, an elected Legislative Assembly of thirty-two with a life of three years, and a Ministry of not more than seven ministers. The elections were contested by two main parties—the Nationalists and the Constitutionalists. The former gained the majority and were in power for the first six years, during which time economic conditions generally improved and relations remained reasonably stable, although politics at all times in a tiny Mediterranean country such as Malta are bedevilled by personal passions and vendettas. The Nationalists furthermore were orientated towards an extension of Maltese independence, both socially and politically, and included a small number of adherents of extreme views who looked to Italy for salvation. The first serious signal of these intentions was the Pari Passu Act, passed in 1923, which made the Italian language compulsory alongside English in the higher classes of the elementary schools.

In 1927 the Nationalists were ousted by the Constitutional Party under Sir Gerald (later Lord) Strickland, who had been Chief Secretary of Malta, next a Colonial and subsequently an Australian State Governor. He was a man of wealth and large possessions both in Britain and in Malta, of great intelligence and personal force, by birth an aristocrat of mixed British and Maltese descent, and fanatically attached to the British connexion. On all counts he was a formidable opponent. Although a Roman Catholic himself, he quite soon became involved in a serious dispute with the Church in Malta, which grew to such dimensions that it involved both the British Government and the Holy See. It culminated, shortly before the General Elections of 1930, in a Pastoral Letter issued by the Archbishop which strictly forbade members of the Church to vote for Strickland or his candidates, and indeed ordered them to support his opponents. The penalty for disobedience was complete excommunication—the withholding of baptism, marriage, and burial rights, as well as communion. Since the Maltese are almost without exception devout Roman Catholics the implications of this Letter were authoritative and absolute. Moreover it constituted direct interference by the Church with affairs of State, and led inevitably to the suspension of the constitution.

In the interim a Royal Commission was sent out from England to make a report, of which the eventual outcome was the restoration of the constitution and the holding of new Elections in 1932. This time the Nationalists came back into power. However, the political atmosphere, already prejudiced, now further deteriorated under the actions of the new Ministry, which deliberately substituted Italian for British interests, particularly in the matter of language, and even removed Maltese as a subject of examination for certain posts in the Government service. Since these actions were openly supported and to some extent financed by Mussolini and Fascist propaganda, deeper and more dangerous issues were at stake. Further temporising was out of the question, and the constitution was once more suspended in November 1933. It was not restored until 1947.

* * *

To all intents and purposes this was still the situation when my parents arrived in Malta in April 1936. Charles' predecessor, General Sir David Campbell, had been ruling the island single-handed, advised only by officials, for over two years. Towards the end of 1935, however, he had contracted a fatal illness, was invalided home, but was able to see Charles only once before he died. This single interview and a briefing at the Colonial Office as to recent events was the only preliminary information Charles received. He could discover no up-to-date and authoritative book, and he admitted openly that when he arrived at Valetta he had only the most sketchy impressions of the history of Malta and its people. But he learned fast, and not only through books.

Fortunately he had the support of a strong Service entourage and of a loyal and efficient team of civil servants, all but three of them Maltese, led by Sir Harry Luke, a man of wide and sympathetic interests, whose encyclopaedic knowledge of Mediterranean affairs was probably unique. Luke furthermore had had to bear the chief burden during Campbell's illness and the tensest moments of the Abyssinian crisis, when it seemed quite likely that Italy would make a sudden attack upon Malta. This latter threat had temporarily subsided, and although the island's defences were still dangerously weak (especially in anti-aircraft artillery and in fighters), purely military measures were no longer the most urgent concern. Opinion in Malta had been severely shaken by recent events: in general by the appeasement policy of the British Government towards the dictators and by the apparent weakness of the Empire, whose approaching dissolution was the constant theme of Fascist propaganda; and in particular by the constitutional débâcle and all its ramifications. Permeating all this was the virus of social relations. Many British people living in Malta—most of them

Servicemen and their families, stationed there for only a short time and continually being replaced—were extraordinarily ignorant of the island, its history, and its inhabitants. Their clubs, their tennis and bridge parties, and the usual social round which occurs in any part of the world where British people are gathered together, imprisoned them within their own self-sufficiency. They lived an insulated isolated existence, quite detached from the Maltese towards whom they frequently behaved in an indefensibly offhand and arrogant manner—that silent arrogance peculiar to Britons, which is even more effective than Prussian bullying and brutality in the hostility it arouses. Perhaps the most blatant example of this attitude was the practice of referring to the Maltese as 'Malts', a term of contempt bearing the same overtones as 'Wog' or 'Dago', and meaning in effect an inferior probably coloured race, whose place was to serve the British, not to meet or treat with them on equal terms.

In the final reckoning the British have very little to reproach themselves for in Malta, in the matter of democratic government and institutions; indeed they have much to be proud of. Of this many of the Maltese are still insufficiently aware, for they are blinded by that kind of parochialism which seems endemic in any situation where one people is behoven to another, however benevolent the intention. Far more damaging—and criminal because entirely unjustified—are the haughty airs of the officer or petty officer and his wife, reared in the blinkered environment of Aldershot or Portsmouth. They spend six months or six years in an ancient and beautiful city, among friendly people, poor materially but rich (even the poor people) in traditional culture and good taste, and carry on in a manner they would never contemplate, not even in the worst slums, at home. And they express pained surprise when one day the 'Malts' or the 'Wogs' tell them in no uncertain terms to go. How ungrateful! And yet these people wonder why the Empire declines.

Such was the atmosphere in Malta in 1936, and the reasons

that gave rise to it. Charles was thus soon aware of the considerable body of anti-British feeling, and of the distinct but much smaller section of opinion that was secretly or vociferously pro-Italian. He felt that he and Madge had to take action at once and meet the social disgruntlement head-on.

About three weeks after our arrival I asked Briffa de Piro, one of my closest Maltese assistants, who it was who exercised the greatest influence among the people. The Noble Families? The Lawyers? The Landowners? He thought for a time and said: 'Undoubtedly the Parish Priests.' I then told him that Madge and I would visit every parish in Malta and Gozo, and make the acquaintance of every parish priest, and all the prominent residents everywhere as well. I instructed him to arrange for the first visit as soon as possible.

At the time I did not realise the importance of this decision. I learned only much later that no Governor had systematically visited the parishes and villages since Sir Alexander Ball, the first British Governor of Malta, over 120 years earlier. This was a remarkable fact. It was certainly no stroke of genius on my part, because I was only doing what is always the first duty of a commander or staff officer in the army—to gain as quickly as possible a thorough knowledge of the formation and the men he is called upon to command and to serve.

By means of these visits Madge and I learned quickly how people of all classes lived, what were their problems, their hopes and their fears. By the time we had completed our tour—over 60 individual visits—we had a deeper knowledge of Malta and the Maltese than any English person, and than all but a comparatively few Maltese.

One of the most important institutions, we found, was the village club. Most of them had been started as band clubs. By the purchase of a few instruments, a small band would be got together and a room hired for practice. These simple beginnings would then grow into social and in many cases into political gatherings. In the larger places we often found two clubs, each run by the principal political party.

To enable us to meet a complete cross-section of society, Briffa de Piro and Edgar Salomone, my excellent Maltese ADC, arranged that we should be entertained by every club in a position to receive us.

Most village visits were planned on similar lines. On arrival everyone would be out in the streets, dressed in their best, especially the children. We would first call on the priest who would then conduct us to the church, where sometimes a few prayers would be said, followed by a display of the treasures, some of them very fine and of great antiquity—altar cloths, silver plate, jewelled vessels, some beautiful lace worked in Malta, a whole wall hung with magnificent red brocade, vestments of great complication and splendour, and statuettes and pictures. Not all of these were good of course, and once Madge made the mistake of admiring a rather tawdry oleograph hanging in the church vestry; whereupon it was torn off the wall and presented to her! But everything was in the grand tradition, both new and old, and highly decorated, and it made a joyful impression. Certainly the village church in Malta remains, as it used to be in England, the centre of artistic as well as religious life, and the people are genuinely attached to it. The only thing that really worried us were the relics, and the familiar way in which they were shown to us. The priest would cheerfully handle a finger bone or an elbow of a saint, with an apparent and utter absence of veneration.

When we came out of the church, we walked down the street, often amid a deafening roar of petards and fireworks, and visited the clubs for music and refreshments, and after that perhaps a poor man's house or two. Finally, back to the priest's, where we would receive petitions and an address, to which I always replied. Madge would be presented with some lovely bouquets of flowers or a painted wax candle or a piece of embroidery, and be paid some well-intentioned compliments, though the English would sometimes founder on the way. Generally she was referred to as my 'amiable consort': a sentiment with which I heartily agreed. Her part was just as important as mine, and she could often break the ice where it might not seem fitting for the Governor to do so. On one occasion she told the priest she did not think much of his patron saint Julian, who had made a bad start in life by murdering his father and mother. The priest was delighted, but said with a smiling face that the saint had properly repented and then made up for it by starting a lepers' home!

The great thing was to show friendship, and to let them feel that we really wanted to help them if we could. I can only say that the response was terrific. At many places people surged round us, clapping and shaking our hands and just wanting to touch us, and we often had real difficulty in getting back into the car. Those were the occasions when I longed for our enemies to see us—enemies abroad such as Mussolini and his gang, and those enemies at home always ready to make out that the British Empire was merely a polite form of tyranny, and a decaying one at that.

These regular contacts with the plain folk of Malta continued until the outbreak of war, and were balanced by a formidable programme of official receptions at one or other of the Governor's three palaces. Of these the Palace of the Grand Masters in Valetta was the largest and most magnificent. Its simple rectangular exterior was deceptive, for it housed apartments of great splendour—the Hall of St. Michael and St. George with its brocaded walls, frescoes of the Great Siege, and the remarkable musicians' gallery taken from the Knights' Great Carrack of Rhodes; also the vast Armoury and the Council Chamber hung with Gobelins tapestries. This building was generally used for administration, for ceremonial occasions, and for the State balls. The Governor's permanent home was the Palace of St. Anton just outside Valetta, a rambling 17th-century house of great charm, built by the pleasure-loving Grand Master Antoine de Paule, and set in beautiful gardens. In the summer he would retreat to the castle of Verdala in the south of the island: a towering four-square Renaissance fortress, now civilised and rendered altogether delightful by its seclusion among terraced gardens and scented woods.

Verdala and St. Anton were the scene of most of the larger

Charles Bonham-Carter at a village festa in Malta

Charles Bonham-Carter with Anthony Eden in Malta, February 1940

entertainments—about three official dinner-parties a month attended by twenty or thirty guests, and garden parties in the summer.

To these came educated people of all callings, and we were able to meet and talk to anyone we wished, British and Maltese alike, men and women—Service people, officials, professional and business men, churchmen, diplomats, and some of the many visitors to the island. We regarded it as a unique opportunity to bring the British and the Maltese together, and to persuade the Maltese themselves to forget their political differences for a while in a friendly atmosphere—in fact not to allow politics to affect social relationships at all. The visitors were of all kinds, both private people and official delegations, including naval squadrons from most of the Mediterranean powers. Historically the most interesting was the visit of the Turkish Fleet, the first time a Turkish force had landed in Malta since the Great Siege of 1565. Harry Luke prepared a special exhibition of the relics of the Siege commanders which seemed to please our guests a great deal.

The first garden party, held on May 27th, 1936, was a significant one for several reasons: chiefly because Charles was involved in an incident with the Italian Consul General, Ferranti, or at least avoided being so involved. Ferranti was about to be expelled for organising spying and dissension—he had long been a great nuisance—but with typical effrontery turned up at St. Anton, knowing full well that the British authorities had been apprised of all his activities. When he and his American wife came forward to be presented, Charles refused to greet him and pointedly put his hands behind his back. Three days later, Ferranti's nefarious doings were published in the Press. The whole story was noted by Charles in his journal.

The actions of the Italian Consul General, Ferranti di Ruffano, and the enthusiasm he displayed as propagandist for Fascist Italy caused us much trouble during the spring and summer. However he was well watched by the Defence Security Officer, Col. Ede, whose vigilance and industry were unsurpassed. Within a week of my arrival I was given a full brief as to the whole Italian situation in Malta. Briefly there were three ways in which the Italians were trying to exert influence:

(1) They were subsidising three newspapers, *Midday Views*, *Malta*, and *Lehen-es-Sewa*. The first named was unimportant, and although the circulation of *Malta* was quite small (less than 400), it was ably edited by Dr. Enrico Mizzi, the most extreme member of the Nationalist party, a determined man who never tried to conceal his pro-Italian feelings. *Malta*'s articles were quoted verbatim in the Italian press, and the reports gave a purposely misleading impression of events and opinions on the island. It was enabled to pay its way by advertisements from Italy. The third paper, *Lehen-es-Sewa*, was a more formidable and elusive proposition, being the organ of Catholic Action with a wide circulation among priests and laymen. Since it was in some measure the responsibility of the Church, and therefore part of the whole tricky question of ecclesiastical relations, it was difficult to deal with. And although I demanded of the Archbishop from time to time that he should control the exuberance of the editor, who was clever enough to avoid over-stepping the law, I seldom got any satisfactory result. In general the paper was hostile to Britain, tendentious in tone, and continually sniping at the Government.

It was not until Italy declared war in 1940 that the question of subversive publications was cleared up. By that time the atmosphere in Malta had fundamentally changed, and the matter largely solved itself.

(2) They had established the Istituto di Cultura Italiana, a club and social centre, run solely for propaganda purposes, where members of the Italian colony and Maltese sympathisers congregated together, and tried of course to influence others.

(3) The Umberto Primo School had also been founded, by permission of the Government, for the children of Italians, and rightly so for there were not nearly enough

schools in Malta. Some Maltese children were taken in and given free education, and had not the teaching been strongly propagandist instead of educational, we should not have objected. Certain other educational institutions were also receiving financial support in return for teaching Italian ideas. Maltese school children were also sent on free holidays to Italy.

On the other hand the Opera House, which had an Italian company and repertoire, was subsidised by the *British* Government; but this was a *bona fide* cultural subvention, and paid by us.

Besides this, Ferranti was engaged, we knew, in direct spying. It was this that gave us the opportunity to put a stop to practically all Italian activity.

Ferranti took every opportunity of making trouble—with the police, the press, and the authorities generally—often over quite small incidents; which proved that he was behaving in a completely improper manner for a man in his official position. The accumulation of these incidents, gave us the excuse to ask for the removal both of Ferranti and of his confidential secretary; and this was duly agreed, although Ferranti was at first allowed to stay on until the end of the summer.

But there had been other developments. On May 14th two Maltese were arrested for trying to obtain plans from a Dockyard draughtsman: Dr. Delia, a lawyer, and one Flores, who owned a tobacconist's shop. Flores stated definitely that the purchase money for the plans was to be provided by the Italian Consul General. Delia also confessed. The case came before the magistrates on May 24th and was concluded on the 30th, when a full report was published in the press, including the prisoners' confessions. During all this time Ferranti put on a bold front. A couple of days before the case was begun, he complained to the Lieutenant-Governor that the police had behaved improperly when he was embarking on a ship for Italy some little time before. Judging by the police report, he had merely made a commotion in order to draw attention to himself. On the 27th, he came to the garden party. On the afternoon of the

30th, when the papers came out about the spy case, he left his office and walked ostentatiously up and down the Strada Reale, the main street of Valetta.

His final act was likewise in character. He was due to leave on July 3rd, and I warned the Commissioner of Police to ensure that whatever Ferranti did or said was to be treated with scrupulous politeness. The Commissioner then told me that Ferranti had written to him, expressing the hope that his departure would be quiet. Besides this I was asked by the Colonial Office not to make any announcement of his departure. I had no intention of doing so, since it was quite unnecessary in a small island where news spreads like a forest fire. In the event no one paid the slightest attention, and the whole episode fizzled out.

I heard later that Ferranti had declared on his honour as a gentleman that he had never had any dealings with Delia, and that Ciano had assured our ambassador in Rome to this effect. This statement was accepted for what it was worth! At any rate on July 4th, the day after Ferranti left, the licence of the Istituto di Cultura Italiana was withdrawn, and that of the Umberto Primo School varied to forbid the acceptance as pupils of any children of British subjects. The latter step I took with some regret as we were so short of schools. There was one amusing postscript. On June 2nd Mizzi published a violent attack on Delia in his paper *Malta*—part of a plan, we gathered, emanating from Ferranti for his own defence. On the following day Delia's wife went up to Mizzi in a restaurant and belaboured him in the face with her shoe, indicating *inter alia* that she did not consider him fit to be touched by her hand!

So ended the attempt at Italian penetration. Ferranti was succeeded by Casertano, a nice little man, who behaved with the utmost correctness. His wife, Donna Beatrice, was a descendant of Don Carlos of Bourbon, the former Spanish Pretender, and a delightful lady.

The final settlement of the more complicated question of the status of the Italian language in Malta was also not long delayed. Already in 1934 it had been replaced by English and

Maltese as the official medium of the Courts and of any part of the Administration. This had been done despite strong opposition from the lawyers, who deprecated their native language on the grounds that it was only a colloquial form of speech, and who generally feared that the change would restrict their employment. But the Pari Passu Act of 1923 was still on the Statute Book. This, it will be remembered, had forcibly introduced Italian into the curriculum of the elementary schools: a bad measure, if only for the reason that it imposed too great a strain upon the capacities of the children, who thus learned very little of either Italian or English in their early years at school. Formerly, when the parents had a choice, 97 per cent chose English. Charles was determined to repeal this Act, and eventually did so, but his action became closely involved with the larger business of restoring representative government—a pressing and delicate manoeuvre which followed on the heels of the Ferranti episode. Altogether the summer of 1936 was a testing start for the new Governor!

Before we left England, I was told that one of my important tasks would be to bring about conditions favourable for the return of self-government, and that it was the intention of the British Government to take the first step in that direction very soon.

On the very first day after my arrival, I received a telegram from the Colonial Office, asking if I would like the Bill empowering the Crown to vary the constitution to be introduced into the House of Lords a few days hence, or alternatively at a later date. I was of course entirely guided by the leading officials when I replied that there was no objection to its early introduction. At the Second Reading of the Bill it was stated that Malta would be governed by the Governor, assisted by an Executive Council composed of official and unofficial members, the latter to be nominated by me. When the Bill was finally enacted on July 1st, the Secretary of State for the Colonies, The Rt. Hon. W. Ormsby Gore,* (who had succeeded Jimmy Thomas), said

* Later Lord Harlech.

he hoped it would be possible before long to take a further step towards a more representative constitution.

These pronouncements led to active agitation in Malta, as we had expected. It took the form of proposals for the boycotting of the new constitution, and of warnings against anyone agreeing to serve on the Executive Council, and much else in a similar vein. Instead insistent demands were made for the immediate return of full self-government. As I say, none of this came as a surprise, but there was no going back. Letters Patent bringing the new constitution into being were approved on August 20th, and I fixed September 2nd for the Proclamation Ceremony.

Meanwhile I was faced with the knotty problem of finding at least three suitable men, who would accept my invitation to serve along with the five official members on the Executive Council. In view of the agitation I was assured I would have great difficulty in finding anyone at all. Anyone who *did* accept would become the target of violent abuse, and would have a very unpleasant time. However, I was not unduly depressed for I felt sure that an appeal to put country before private interests would succeed with good men. I wished also the unofficial members to represent as many opinions and interests as possible. I therefore decided to try to enlist a prominent member of each of the three political parties—Constitutionalist, Nationalist, and Labour—and two members of the professional and business classes. Five altogether—two more than the legal minimum. To my great delight all my invitations were accepted.

At the outset I considered it unwise to approach the leaders of the two main parties, Lord Strickland and Sir Ugo Mifsud, owing to party passions in the past, but secured two sound lieutenants in their place—Baron De Piro D'Amico, a former President of the Senate, and C. Mifsud-Bonnici, a prominent lawyer and a minister in the previous Nationalist Government; both gave me wise and valuable service. Likewise Dr Paul Boffa, leader of the Labour party; Professor P. P. Debono, a distinguished surgeon; and Edgar Arrigo, President of the Chamber of

Commerce. After consulting their friends, all these men put aside personal scruples and the prospect of public hostility, and came in. Malta owes them much. I also nominated Vice-Admiral Sir Wilfred French to represent the most important employer of labour in the island—the Royal Navy.

As Proclamation Day approached, so public criticism grew in intensity; but this was among the least of Charles' anxieties. Before everything else, he wanted to make sure that the new arrangements would be given a fair trial, and that the Executive Council would not be faced at the outset with having to enact contentious legislation. He therefore strove to complete certain measures before September 2nd, and which would be regarded as his responsibility alone. Most important was the repeal of the Pari Passu Act, already described, for this would terminate the language question, and close an obvious opening for renewed Italian agitation. It was a near-run thing, for the telegram from the Colonial Office approving and legalising his action did not arrive until the afternoon of Proclamation Day itself. However, it had the effect hoped for. The language question was not raised again, and in the revised constitution of 1939 the subject was statutorily debarred from further consideration.

Some time before September 2nd Charles became aware that a boycott of the Proclamation Ceremony was being organised, and that resolutions were being put forward at the meetings of certain professional bodies to forbid the attendance of their representatives. But Charles found a strong ally in an unexpected quarter.

Michael Gonzi, Bishop of Gozo, had given me a promise that he would be present, so I asked him to come and see me. He was on a holiday in Tunis, but returned at once, arriving only a few days before the Ceremony took place. I asked him to do his best to counter the opposition. He ensured that the Church would be well represented, and interviewed the Chairmen of the Chambers of Advocates and others, but with only partial success. However, when the day came, the Hall of St. Michael and St. George was well filled with officials and Service officers, as well as many Maltese notabilities, and the Ceremony passed off smoothly.

It was, however, nearly wrecked by a series of ludicrous incidents.

In the morning I drove down as usual at 6.30 am, from Verdala to St. Anton to bathe in the swimming-pool. On my way back the car ran out of petrol. I was alone and dressed in a shirt and pair of beach trousers of bright hue. I stopped a lorry and managed to persuade the driver to take me back to St. Anton where I picked up another car and returned at full speed to Verdala. By then it was getting late and I barely had time to have breakfast and change into full dress. But this was not all. I found Geoffrey Elliott, my British ADC, in his room green and miserable with an attack of 'Malta tummy', and wearing a pair of trousers twice too big for him. He had sent his to the laundry who had sent him back a pair of mine! He managed to survive the Ceremony, though he nearly fainted and had to leave the Hall. Madge also was not well, but got through all right.

In his speech Charles explained the new constitution and appealed for fair criticism.

I wished to make the people of Malta realise that we were taking the first step on the road back to a form of democratic government. Although the majority of people were happy under the existing system, the educated classes were not and felt they had been unfairly treated. This had led to a fairly widespread anti-British attitude, and to ill-feeling among the Maltese themselves, as between the strong supporters of the British connexion and their opponents, who were accused (often unfairly) of being pro-Italian. I hoped that this comparatively small change would help bring together men of goodwill, even though they held different political opinions, and enable them to co-operate for the good of the community. I also felt that internal strife would be a grave weakness in time of war; in fact I doubted whether Malta could be held as a fortress at all in such circumstances.

The action of Bishop Gonzi was of great significance. Originally Charles had been warned against him, probably because together with the Archbishop he had signed the Pastoral Letter of May 1st, 1930, forbidding votes for Lord Strickland—the step that led directly to the suspension of the constitution. He was therefore reputedly anti-British, and it was a reputation that died hard. Charles, on various grounds, came early and independently to quite a different conclusion, and this was of the utmost relevance for two reasons. First, the reigning Archbishop of Malta, Maurus Caruana, was an elderly man in ill-health, and the question of his succession was already a burning issue. Before the end of 1936, Charles was convinced that Gonzi was the right and obvious choice, although he was never able—during his time as Governor—to overcome the opposition to Gonzi's candidature. Secondly the relationship between Church and State was still equivocal. Mentally it was natural that some Maltese priests should have a bias towards Italy. Some of them had been trained there, most of them spoke Italian (since it was the language of the Church), while the dioceses of Malta and Gozo (then separate) were under the direct jurisdiction of the Holy See. Politically, the quarrel with the Constitutionalist party had driven them into the arms of the Nationalists, and although this did not necessarily make them pro-Italian, it did render them lukewarm towards the British. The number of Italianisers among the priests was actually quite small, but they had a powerful mouthpiece in *Lehen-es-Sewa*, the Catholic Action newspaper, and were thought to constitute a group within the circle of the Archbishop.

Charles did all he could to remedy this dangerous and unnecessary situation. By his visits to the villages, he made the personal acquaintance of the parish priests. He likewise made strenuous efforts to get on good terms with the Archbishop himself, though without much success. Not only was Caruana ailing, but he was a weak man who allowed himself to be governed by his *curia*, or secretariat, of highly conservative churchmen. Gonzi, however, displayed quite different qualities. Not only was he demonstratively loyal and willing to support the Governor, but a man of strong character, capable of dealing with the anomalies of the Church in Malta, and of overhauling its administration. Socially, too, he was progressive. It was not until 1943 that he finally succeeded to the Archbishopric, since which date he has continued to display all the qualities of wisdom and strength that Charles recognised in him.

* * *

For three years Malta was ruled by the Governor and the new Executive Council of ten (five official and five nominated members). Technically the Governor still had absolute powers; in fact he deferred to the Council in practically every instance, other than in 'reserved' subjects, such as defence, which were in any event excluded. The actual administration devolved as always upon the permanent officials. The Executive Council was in fact mainly concerned with local government, and with extraneous interests such as trade development and certain welfare matters.

In agriculture—the main industry of the island—steps were taken to improve pig and poultry breeding, pasteurise milk, immunise the ubiquitous goats against *brucella abortus* (the source of undulent fever), and conserve crops. In public works, there were major operations such as the clearance of an overcrowded quarter in Valetta known as the Manderaggio (this was held up by the war), the expansion of water supplies, the renewal of the electricity power plant, also the collection of refuse and destruction of rats (there was always a real risk of plague). In trade, action was needed to encourage the wine and lace industries, control food prices, regularise fish auctions (formerly buyers whispered their bids to the auctioneer or *pitkali*, and the fishermen never knew what the final price was, nor even that the highest bid was accepted). Socially, Malta was far behind. Early closing was introduced and hours of work controlled (some employees were working 80 hours a week), third-party insurance made compulsory, hospital accommodation extended and plans made for a full-scale nursing service. A significant item was the ordinance enabling married women to open banking accounts. This caused a tremendous outcry! It was seriously asserted that the measure would undermine family life, and that harassed husbands would have to serve notices on the banks forbidding them to cash their wives' cheques. Charles noted: 'An answer to such nonsense is not difficult and I shall pay little attention to it, but it is an illustration of the sort of difficulties we are up against. In fact 41% of the accounts with the Savings Bank are Bearer accounts, and a large proportion taken out by women: about 2600.' Education was likewise an intractable problem. Even Charles, with his intense interest in the subject, and Dr. Laferla, an outstanding Director of Education, were unable to make much impression here. Over 15,000 children were still without elementary schooling owing to lack of buildings and teachers, and a system of staggered attendance had to be brought in to meet the immediate emergency. Playing fields were also urgently needed.

The social conscience was not of course the sole responsibility of the Government. However, with a few notable exceptions, there was no strong tradition of voluntary service among educated people in Malta, certainly not among the women. This fact made the example set by Madge all the more significant and effective. Thanks to her, new life was put into the Hospital Visiting Committee, whose members made regular inspections of the hospitals, asylums, and lepers' homes. At first it was a matter of receiving the party with bouquets and a polite smile; but this protocol was soon abandoned when the ladies concerned asked to see the refuse bins or the condition of the W.C.s. In some cases there was much to put right —a need for better equipment, modern methods, more beds, or merely new heart to fight a hard battle. Where things could be remedied on the spot, they were—without delay. Where it was a matter of finance or Government sanction, then pressure was brought to bear in the right quarter. In any event the knowledge that these ladies cared and would come back, invigorated not only the staff but the patients themselves, who responded marvellously to the simple tonic of human sympathy. Madge's other main activity was her effort to improve conditions in the orphanages, especially of the girls, who were either true orphans or had come from broken homes. The most effective agency in this campaign was the Girl Guides. It should be said at once, and with disrespect to no one, that nobody was less like a Girl Guide—let alone a chief Girl Guide (even though a figurehead)—than the Governor's wife! But it was the only movement capable of altering the medieval attitude of the nuns in charge, and carried with it the backing of the Church authorities. At one orphanage, where the supervisors were (as always) kindly and well-meaning, Madge none the less found the girls ill-fed, badly taught, and deprived of all healthy recreations except bathing. 'I asked to see the bathing dresses, which turned out to be ridiculous pre-historic gowns, fully pleated from the neck to the ankles. They were positively shocked at my suggestion of an ordinary costume, until I pointed out that their gowns were positively indecent. We compromised by arranging they be cut up into tunics and knickers!' The girls' segregation from the boys was not only absolute but morbid. They were even kept strictly apart in church, by having to sit on opposite sides of the altar. The result was that when a girl went out into the world and 'went wrong', she was far too ashamed to ask help of the only people who could really help her—the good nuns who had brought her up.

Madge was also influential in a quite different direction. Herself a sculptress, and endowed with real feeling for the Renaissance and the Baroque, she decided to rehabilitate some of the State apartments in the Grand Masters' Palace at Valetta. Her colleague in this work—and there could be none better—was Sir Harry Luke whose knowledge of the cultural background of Malta was unrivalled. As a result of their collaboration, the ancient wall-hangings, rotten with age, were replaced with handsome Lyons brocades; new curtains hung; a false ceiling in the famous Tapestry Room removed to reveal the original coffered and painted Renaissance construction above; the entire electric wiring system (then in a dangerous state) renewed; and the ugly Victorian light fittings replaced by wrought-iron replicas of the lanterns of St. Angelo. After several years work, not only were these magnificent apartments saved from disintegration but restored with all their furnishings to their proper dignity, and preserved as part of the historic heritage of Malta. Later, during the 1939 political agitations, Charles noted: 'I hear that one prominent person is saying that Madge wasted a lot of money in doing the redecorations of the Palace, and that she has furnished her office in the most luxurious way. The truth is that by good management she completed the decorations for £400 less than the estimate by the Public Works Department, and that in her office there is a table, two or three chairs, one cupboard, and nothing more.' Happily most of this essential restoration work survived the war, and may be enjoyed today in all its intricate splendour.

Thought was also given to the contemporary cultural traditions of Malta—to the superb crafts of lace-making, inlay marble work, stone masonry, wrought-iron smithing, and book-binding. Moreover, the British Council was encouraged to show that Britain had more to offer than trade and employment. One of the most successful ventures was the visit of the Dublin Gate Theatre, which came to Valetta for two seasons with a repertory of Shakespeare and modern playwrights; likewise the Old Vic whose company made a short tour. Both these companies made an excellent impression.

* * *

In the summer of 1937 Charles and Madge returned to England for their first long spell of leave. Charles took the opportunity of seeing Ormsby Gore at the Colonial Office, to discuss the next step in the restoration of representative government in Malta, as had been promised when the Executive Council was set up in 1936. At that time Ormsby Gore had no clear-cut ideas beyond instituting a Legislative Assembly having a majority of *official* members, with elections for the unofficial members at some unspecified date. So for the time being the matter rested there.

Charles' return to work was delayed by an accident sustained in France, and it was not until the middle of October that he was able to take up the reins again. He then realised that, while he had been away, a significant change had overtaken public opinion in Malta as a whole. It was not merely the extremists who were using self-government as a stick to beat the British with—they could nearly always be discounted—but that this (or something approaching it) now genuinely represented the wishes of the people. Resolutions were being forwarded by professional organisations, members of the Executive Council were being hard pressed, and there were repeated statements and leaders in responsible newspapers, such as *The Times of Malta* owned by the Strickland family, and the *Malta Chronicle* owned by the Bartolo family, both powerful adherents to the British cause.

Charles, therefore, started an immediate and intensive survey of all shades of opinion. At the same time, with the help of Luke and the new Legal Secretary, Sir Edward Jackson (later Lieutenant-Governor, and to whose deep knowledge of constitutional law and other services Malta owes much), he drew up outline proposals for a new constitution. These advocated a far more positive advance, namely a Legislative Assembly but with a majority of *unofficial* or elected members, the elections to take place in 1939. Safeguards as to reserved powers remained as before. To this the Colonial Office replied in February 1938, and the reply came as a shock. It turned down the main point of the proposals (the unofficial majority), and indicated that Malta would have to start again at the bottom of the constitutional ladder. Charles absolutely refused to accept this position. In a further letter he emphasised the change in responsible opinion, and the decline in the power of the extremists (who the Colonial Office feared might dominate an elective assembly) due to the settlement of the language question and the general repulse of Italian influence. He felt so strongly that the Colonial Office was now out of touch with events in Malta that he requested an immediate personal interview: as between himself and Jackson on the one side, and Ormsby Gore and his advisers on the other. This was agreed for mid-March.

Meanwhile a serious complication had arisen, which not only delayed the constitutional decision, but suspended all legislative activity by the Executive Council for several months.

Soon after I returned from leave in October 1937, a case was brought by Lord Strickland against the Collector of Customs, in which the plaintiff urged that the Ordinance of 1936 (introducing the Executive Council as an advisory body to the Governor) was *ultra vires*, and that in consequence a customs duty subsequently enacted was illegal. The judge in the First Hall of the Civil Court rejected the plaintiff's plea. However on March 4th 1938 the Appeal Court quashed the judgment of the inferior Court, and Lord Strickland gained his point.

The Collector of Customs then lodged an appeal to the Judicial Committee of the Privy Council, viz. the House of Lords—an essential move, for had the finding of the Malta Appeal Court stood, it meant that every action of the Government for the past eighteen months would have been deemed illegal. The Malta Appeal Court delivered its judgment a few days before Jackson and I went to the Colonial Office. And although we felt pretty certain that the House of Lords would reverse matters, nevertheless the whole situation was an embarrassment. I also felt it necessary to suspend all legislative measures by the Executive Council while the case was *sub judice*. This was a great nuisance, to put it mildly.

Moreover, I was sure that Lord Strickland, for whom I had the greatest respect, was labouring under the mistaken impression that his action was actually helping to solve the constitutional problem: presumably by forcing the Government's hand. In fact, of course, it had precisely the opposite effect. Neither I nor the Secretary of State was going to submit to pressure of that sort, and it actually weakened my hand when presenting the case for a more liberal constitution for Malta. As anticipated, the House of Lords did in the end allow the Government appeal, but this did not happen until June 30th. Meanwhile Lord Strickland started yet another *ultra vires* case; but this was negatived by the course of events.

At our first conference at the Colonial Office on March 14th, Jackson and I pressed the original proposals. I did not fear an unofficial majority, for it was extremely unlikely that all the elected members would vote against the Government on any really vital measure. Refusal to trust the Maltese would have much worse results. I backed this up with all my previous arguments, and added that the extremist sentiment had been further weakened by the improvement of social relations between the British and the Maltese. I assured the Secretary of State that unless the Maltese demands were met in a liberal spirit, then the support from the steadily increasing moderate opinion would be alienated.

After prolonged discussion, we left the matter over until the second conference four days later. Ormsby Gore then told us that we had made our point, but that he could only agreed to *equal* numbers of official and unofficial members. In reaching this decision he was influenced by the tension with Italy, and the possible deterioration of international relations which might ensue at any moment. Indeed if there was real danger of war in the Mediterranean, then the whole question would have to be shelved. I said that, in that case, the people of Malta would understand and would remain content, if the situation was explained to them.

Jackson and I then returned to Malta feeling that, in the main, we had achieved the object of our visit. We had been deeply impressed by Ormsby Gore and by his willingness to listen to us with a completely open mind. In fact he had virtually reversed the advice given him by his own officials. We were very fortunate to have him as our Minister, and I had been able to establish a close relationship with him since the beginning of my time, mainly by means of personal letters. In these I had felt free to speak my mind without being hampered by official phraseology and etiquette. Two months later he succeeded to the family title as Lord Harlech, and transferred to the House of Lords. I was terribly afraid that all our hard-won progress would now be lost, and that we would have to start all over again. However, I was quite wrong. The new Secretary of State, the Rt. Hon. Malcolm MacDonald, proved just as considerate as his predecessor, and just as deeply interested in the affairs of Malta, as events were soon to show. I continued to write to him personally, as in the past.

Meanwhile the new constitution was being devised in detail, of which the main points were:

(1) A Legislative Assembly (to be known as the Council of Government) of 20 members—10 elected, 2 nominated, 8 official. The Assembly to have a life of 5 years.
(2) Certain powers reserved to the Governor as before.
(3) The exclusion of the language question from any future consideration by the Assembly.
(4) Proportional representation.
(5) The clergy to be excluded from offering themselves as candidates for election, but to have the right to vote.
(6) The language of debate to be English, with permission to use Maltese with an interpreter in cases of necessity.

On July 29th Malcolm MacDonald formally announced the constitution and outlined its main provisions. Ten days later he paid a visit to Malta to test the public reaction for himself. His speech had been quite well received, although there was no lack of criticism, and it was this that he came to assess. Although disappointed that full self-government had not been granted, there was little doubt that most moderate-minded men accepted the new arrangements, and even thought they were the best they could realistically expect. Opposition centred, as expected, in Enrico Mizzi and the extreme Nationalists, while the Archbishop also felt it necessary to make a formal protest against the disqualification of the clergy. As Charles was quick to point out, this disqualification was no disservice to the Church, in that all anti-clerical movements had sprung from resentment of political activity by the clergy, particularly in countries such as Malta, where the clerical population was high. However, he freely admitted that the provision had been clumsily worded—ministers of religion had been lumped together with lunatics and criminals as persons not qualified to stand for election—and this had caused justifiable offence. The draughtsman working in Whitehall can have had little idea of the results of his work. The Governor was made aware of ecclesiastical displeasure when he spoke to the priests at the annual Candlemas ceremony, at which it was customary for him to be presented with a wax candle from every parish. The candles were forthcoming as usual, but the speech was received in dead silence. Later, when there was a possibility of a small tax on property, a Lenten Letter was read out in all churches, in which it was claimed that Christ had intended the Church to be completely free of civil authority.

It was this matter of taxation that generated the most serious opposition. Although distinct from the constitution, the fact that the finances of the island were also being investigated in 1938–9, linked both subjects together and produced a hearty cry of 'No Taxation without Representation'. As everyone outside Malta recognised, the burden of taxation was slight and heavily loaded in favour of the rich. There was no income tax, and only a very low rate of estate duty. An enquiry carried out by Sir Arthur Eborall, a former official of the Inland Revenue, revealed that income tax would be easy to administer, and that even at a low figure would yield £100,000 or more. As the total revenue from taxes amounted to less than one million pounds, this would be a substantial aid. Moreover, it would make possible the remission of an existing tax on wheat and flour which was felt most keenly by the poorest members of the population. The justice of all this was inescapable. But the better-off Maltese did not think so, and criticism grew so strong that Charles feared it might endanger the new constitution. He therefore decided to postpone the whole matter until after the elections, for early consideration by the Council of Government.

Meanwhile he took every opportunity, on public platforms and in private conversations, to air the hottest questions of the day: explaining the intentions of the Government and asking for the co-operation of all fair-minded people. He never ceased to praise the work of the Executive Council as an example of what could be done in public affairs by men of different political opinions, without prejudice to their personal relationship. After some months it became noticeable that the atmosphere in Malta was becoming more settled, and that this was due in large measure to the press. Prominent among the editors was Lord Strickland's daughter, Mabel, who now leads the Progressive Constitutionalists, successors to her father's old party. Her attitude to the problems of government, as expressed in leaders in *The Times of Malta*, contributed much to the moderate temper of the electoral campaign of the summer of 1939.

The Elections finally took place on July 22nd–24th, and resulted in the following distribution of seats: Constitutionalists 6, Nationalists 3, Labour 1. The first meeting of the new Council of Government was held at once, as Charles said 'to get things started and blow off steam'; thereafter all further sessions were postponed until the autumn.

By that time, however, the British Empire was at war, and Malta had reassumed its historic rôle in Mediterranean strategy.

* * *

It is no part of this narrative to discuss the defensive difficulties of Malta, nor recount the preparations made to convert the island into an effective fortress. As commander-in-chief as well as civil Governor, Charles had to bear this vital responsibility in addition to his constitutional and administrative burdens, and it was a ceaseless care. Although the Army contingent had its own field commander, likewise the naval and air forces, his was the overall command. It was his task to co-ordinate all defensive measures, military and civil, and implement them so far as he was able. Thus he never ceased to urge forward the construction of shelters and emplacements, the laying of wire, mines, water mains and cables, the installation of coastal and anti-aircraft artillery, the training of troops and combined exercises, the storage of food and petrol, evacuation plans for the crowded areas of Valetta: above all to demand an adequate garrison adequately equipped. By 1939–40 the island was immensely stronger than when he first came. Its inadequacies (for example, the almost total lack of fighters) were part of the general defensive weakness of the Empire, and arose from the same causes. It did not arise from any lack of effort in Malta itself.

More significant than the purely physical measures was Charles' concern to prepare the Maltese *morally* for war. But here again he came up against the British colonial attitude. In the Army soldiers in the Maltese units (The Royal Malta Artillery and the King's Own Malta Regiment) were paid at lower rates than in British units. Likewise, the Navy offered less pay and inferior employments. Charles was fully aware of the differences in education and living standards, but he did not consider them valid objections to the principle of equal pay and opportunities: the necessary preliminary—to put it at its lowest—to the Maltese making a larger contribution to their own defence. When told that English gunners might object to taking orders from Maltese NCOs, he replied shortly that the sooner they did the better, and 'we had better get rid of that sort of nonsense before it is too late'. The final hurdle was always economy. The Treasury could not afford the increase. This was merely a cloak. 'I have always found it', he wrote, 'more economical to be generous.' It was yet another manifestation of that evil spirit which bedevilled relations between British and Maltese, and which he and Madge had consistently fought since 1936. In an effort to confront the regimental officer with this problem, he composed a paper which was made compulsory reading for all units arriving in Malta. In this he summarised the history of Malta's attachment to the British Empire, described the people, and asked that they be treated with ordinary friendliness and civility. This is printed in full as Appendix C.

All this, and all that has otherwise been related, had its effect: indeed a far deeper effect than was ever realised in 1939. The magnificent loyalty and resilience shown by the Maltese during the war, particularly during the air-raids and near-starvation days of 1941–2, were not merely a matter of native courage, self-interest, and contempt for the enemy. It was something far more positive than that. *The mainspring was a renewed faith in Britain.* For that, the conduct of government and the personality of the Governor in the years 1936–40 were largely responsible.

Since Malta has again been torn by political dissensions, the story must be briefly continued. Although only created in the last days of peace, the Council of Government played a full part in the war. Indeed it worked so well that the leaders of the three political parties privately admitted that it might be the best permanent solution, although in public they had to pretend otherwise. Charles thought so too. After his retirement he urged the Colonial Office to plan ahead and prepare the next constitutional step before the war came to an end. His proposal was an enlarged Council of Government with a heavy preponderance of elected members, and an Executive Council of six ministers acting under the chairmanship of the Governor, who would retain his privileged position.

But events took a different course. Malta's war record reinforced the demand for self-government, and this was finally granted in 1947 in a form recommended by Sir Harold

MacMichael. It provided for a Legislative Assembly of forty members elected for three years, but unlike the 1921 Constitution omitted the Senate or Second Chamber. The Governor is no longer Commander-in-Chief but a civilian appointment,* and his powers are much reduced. In 1955 the Left Wing party came to power under the leadership of Mr. Mintoff, a former Rhodes scholar and an able administrator. He proposed that Malta, while retaining its local autonomy and legislature (with power to legislate on all matters other than defence and external affairs) should be 'integrated' with the United Kingdom, and be represented in the House of Commons by at least three members. An all-party conference recommended the acceptance of this plan, if also accepted by the Maltese people. The referendum that followed in February 1956, however, was inconclusive, and it was decided to hold a second one before the Bill was enacted.

The purpose of 'integration' was to try to solve the intractable employment problem: to offer the Maltese the same privileges and living standards as the British, but which could never be afforded by the island's economy. Negotiations were proceeding on the practical implications of this policy, admittedly unfavourably, when a new complication arose. In April 1957 it was suddenly announced that, owing to strategic changes, Malta would diminish in value as a naval base, and the dockyard employing 13,000 men would be reduced. The principal source of employment therefore was thrown into jeopardy, and naturally enough the Maltese were angered and dismayed. Had this bald announcement been softened by the offer—put out a month later—of generous financial help during the transitional period, the situation might not have deteriorated. As it was Mr. Mintoff, rallying opinion behind him, took up the impossible position of demanding independence, if he could not obtain 'integration' on his own financial terms. From that moment his actions merely added fuel to the fire, culminating in the disorders of April 1958 and his own

* This does not mean that a Service officer may not hold the appointment.

resignation. Thereafter the Governor, who had exercised firmness and tact throughout, was compelled to take over the administration until a new government could be found. In the end the constitution had to be suspended once again.

These events bore an unfortunate resemblance to the past: to the crisis of 1919 which led to self-government in 1921, and to the suspension of the constitution in 1930 and 1932, due in the latter case to Italian influence. None the less the basis of all political dissension in Malta is the same: namely, over-population, which is staggering. In 1931 the census figure was 241,621. In 1957 the estimate was 317,182. This works out on the main island at nearly 3000 people per square mile. Owing to the attitude of the Roman Catholic Church, there is no prospect of limitation by birth control. Hitherto the rate of increase has only been restrained by a high infant mortality (which is declining as living conditions improve) and by emigration, principally to Australia and Britain. The sheer lack of space precludes any normal economic solution—by the extension of agriculture or the development of light industry. The dockyard remains the safety valve, and it is reassuring to hear that it is now to be developed commercially. Whatever the future brings, Malta will always need help, and Britain (to whom the island has been of such immense importance) must continue to provide that help. But political passions and social sensitivity will always accompany over-population. The enormous pressure for jobs permeates every activity, every relationship, every attitude; and produces a highly charged atmosphere, requiring the utmost understanding and forbearance.

* * *

Charles' departure from Malta was sudden and a sad one. His normal term of five years would have expired in 1941, and would probably have been extended in the circumstances of war. Already in 1939 representations were being made to the Colonial Office to prolong his governorship, although he exacted a private promise from Malcolm MacDonald to resist these advances. History shows that extensions often turn into anti-climaxes, and Charles felt that at the end of five years he would have given of his best. None the less, with the outbreak of war, he was naturally anxious to complete his term, and perhaps give help towards the next constitutional change. But all this came to nothing. In April 1940 he had a severe heart attack, collapsed, and endured further complications. He then rallied and was flown home at the end of May, when France was falling. Meanwhile his place was taken by General Dobbie. In the last entry in his journal, he wrote:

> I have found the partings a great trial, probably because I am still pretty weak, but partly too owing to the number of our friends, and the wonderful affection that has been poured on us. We gave our last dinner party on May 24th, our closest friends, and a very cheerful company. I did not have to speak, thank God. I do not think I could have done so without breaking down. I find myself wondering if my life's work is done. With the war going badly, and our army in such a critical position, I feel old and useless.

In England he made a remarkable and apparently a complete recovery, and was soon demanding to be sent back. But even his old friend, Jack Dill, then CIGS, was adamant. There could be no risk of a second collapse, and Charles was 64.

The refusal was borne stoically, but Charles did not pretend that he was not deeply disappointed. It was indeed a hard thing, and a hard moment at which to have to retire. Characteristically, he did not remain inactive for long, but turned his attention to public work: notably the chairmanship of two schools connected with the army. But Malta continued to absorb his mind, and his sadness was assuaged by an affectionate correspondence with Maltese friends, who gave him and Madge a wonderful welcome when they returned for a short visit in 1954.

* * *

A year later he died, at the age of 79, his service done, his days replete with private happiness.

POSTSCRIPT

AT the beginning I declared that my subject was not primarily a chronicle but a theme, not a family but an attitude, common to certain of its members, and expressed by them in different ways during the past 250 years. I have called this liberalism or liberal-mindedness and defined it on page 130 as 'a fearless individualism, tempered by a keen sense of social responsibility and practical humanity, and a genuine belief in democracy as a reasonable and workable system of government, both in Parliament and outside'.

But definitions, without illustration, are rarely satisfactory, and here history provides the full meaning. In the 17th and 18th centuries the emphasis lay in *religious* independence. Unitarians had to keep up a constant fight to preserve their identity, and to campaign against the civil penalties imposed on them for holding their particular beliefs. This religious struggle merged into the *political*. Dissenters as a whole fought as Whigs and Radicals for the abolition of privilege and the reform of Parliament, and the fight continued long after the Act of 1832. Later in the 19th century, when religious and political liberties were no longer in question, middle-class families such as the Bonham-Carters turned to *social* problems; not socialism or class-warfare, which they would not have recognised, but the rights of women, the development of education and nursing, the general improvement of public life; the idea, in brief, of a better society achieved *non-politically*.

In the present century, that idea has been reversed. Social problems *have* to be viewed politically, and the State has entered very closely into the life of its members. The difficulty now is to secure the right relationship between the individual and the society to which he belongs. This is, of course, an eternal question with which we are *all* concerned, owing to the spread of knowledge and the broader distribution of wealth.

Where do liberal-minded people stand in this matter?

Since this is not a political tract, I have no wish to commit myself to a political answer. But one thing is certain. The wheel has turned, and those who value the liberal tradition can no longer turn their backs on politics. Politics have returned to them, and perhaps—to go back further in time—religion will too. Liberty is never certain.

BIBLIOGRAPHY

PART ONE

History of Portsmouth, by William G. Gates.
Extracts from the Records of the City of Portsmouth, by Robert East.
Early Issues of the *Hampshire Chronicle*.
William Smith, M.P. for Norwich. Incomplete, unpublished MS. by Barbara Lady Stephen.
The Unitarians, by Henry Gow (Methuen, 1928).
The Unitarian Movement, by H. McLachlan (Allen & Unwin, 1934).
The Unitarian Contribution to Social Progress in England, by Raymond V. Holt (Allen & Unwin, 1938).
The Passing of the Great Reform Bill, by J. R. M. Butler (Longmans, 1914).
Autobiography of Edward Gibbon, edited by Oliphant Smeaton, M.A. (Everyman, 1948).
Article on 'Buriton', by Arthur Oswald, published in *Country Life* of November 12th, 1948.
Some Account of the History of Petersfield, by E. Arden Minty (John Lane, 1923).
The Village Labourer; 1760–1832, by J. L. and Barbara Hammond (Guild Books, 1948).
The Hambledon Cricket Chronicle, 1772–96, by F. S. Ashley-Cooper (Herbert Jenkins, 1924).
Viscount Althorp, Memoir by Sir Denis Le Marchant, 1876.
English Thought in the Nineteenth Century, by D. C. Somervell (Methuen, 1929).
Julius and Mary Mohl, by M. C. M. Simpson (Kegan Paul, 1887).
Madame Mohl; Her Salon and Her Friends, by Kathleen O'Meara (Bentley, 1885).
Florence Nightingale, by Cecil Woodham-Smith (Constable, 1950).
Florence Nightingale, A Sketch by Rosalind Nash (S.P.C.K., 1937).
Life and Work of Harriet Martineau, by Vera Wheatley (Secker and Warburg, 1957).
The English Village, by Victor Bonham-Carter (Pelican, 1952).

The English Public School, by Vivian Ogilvie (Batsford, 1957).
History of Clifton College; 1860–1934, by O. F. Christie (Arrowsmith, 1935).

PART TWO

The Boer War, by Edgar Holt (Putnam, 1958).
A History of the World War 1914–1918, by B. H. Liddell Hart (Faber, 1934).
Official History of the Great War 1914–18.
Education and the Army, by Lord Gorell (O.U.P., 1921).
GHQ, by 'GSO' (Allan, 1920).
Malta, by Sir Harry Luke (Harrap, 1959).

APPENDIX A

INCOME EARNED FROM THE LAW, BY JOHN BONHAM-CARTER

As a Special Pleader

	£
1815:	80
1816:	192
1817:	234
1818:	over 260

[To these totals must be added an indeterminate sum for pupils' fees.]

As a Barrister

		£–s–d
1819:	Town business	473–11–0
	Circuits, Sessions and Canal cases	276–13–6
		750– 4–6
1820:	Town	540– 4–6
	Circuits etc	339– 3–0
		879– 7–6
1821:	Town	587– 9–6
	Circuits etc	393– 4–6
		980–14–0
1822:	Town	584–17–0
	Circuits etc	392–14–0
		977–11–0

1823:	Town	505–11–0	
	Circuits etc	441–10–6	
		947– 2–0	
1824:	Town	785– 8–0	
	Circuits etc	743–18–6	
		1529– 6–6	
1825:	Town	928–14–6	
	Circuits etc	793– 5–6	
		1722– 0–0	
1826:	Town	927– 3–0	
	Circuits etc	922– 8–6	
		1849–11–6	
1827:	Town	758–17–0	[From Christmas 1826 he gave up attending Sessions, Bail Court, and taking or attending arbitrations as Counsel, with certain exceptions.]
	Circuits etc	724–10–6	
		1483– 7–6	

APPENDIX B

ACCOUNT OF THE 7TH DIVISION IN THE BATTLE OF THE SOMME

BY LT.-COL. CHARLES BONHAM-CARTER, GSO1.

IN the ordinary way the plan for an operation is drawn up by the senior commander in the field, and issued in the form of an order. For the Somme a different system was adopted, at any rate by General Rawlinson, the Army Commander. Divisional commanders were asked what they thought their formations could do, on the understanding that full artillery support would be forthcoming from Corps or Army. On this basis, the Army commander drew up a master plan, allotting to each division frontage, boundaries, and the objectives to be reached at stated times. This was of course a preliminary warning only, subject to modification in detail.

Divisions then made their own plans. I began by studying carefully the preparations for and the whole course of the battle of Loos, and tried to analyse what happened. I also read the training pamphlets on attack issued by GHQ, and based on the general experience of offensives during 1915. As a result I decided first of all that it was essential for assault troops to start their advance not more than 150 yards from the enemy front line; also that reinforcements should get forward under cover. For this, all the preparatory digging was done at night, practically without casualties, by a company of miners, who bored two tunnels towards the enemy close under ground level. The work was so skilfully done that the tunnels were never discovered, although at one place the men actually broke into a German dug-out and had to repair the hole, making it look like fallen earth. Cables were then laid by the signallers, and after the attack was launched the tunnels were uncovered and used as communication trenches.

I also decided that the assault positions should be occupied as *late* as possible. The infantry were therefore kept well back, and I made out a march table giving the exact time for each unit to reach some convenient point on the road, before going up to the assembly position in the front line. This plan also worked well. I and my staff also dealt with every normal and abnormal contingency in regard to traffic, tracks forward through the wire, supplies (water, food and ammunition), reserves, the selection of tactical features to be held against counter-attack, mopping-up, prisoners, and the thousand other things that have to be thought of before a big operation. Most important of course was the artillery plan. This involved the preliminary task of cutting the wire, neutralising enemy fire and positions, and providing a creeping barrage to cover the actual assault. I do not know who first thought of the barrage, but it is my impression that it was used for the first time on a large scale in the Somme battle. Certainly it had many teething troubles, possibly because it was laid on by the field artillery which had never been trained in the technique before the war. Absolute accuracy was essential, and range tables prepared for each gun by means of calibration. This was arrived at by firing through two screens and measuring the velocity of the shell by an electrical recorder. The field gunners, as I say, had never done this before the war, whereas it was the normal procedure of garrison artillery, whose knowledge of scientific gunnery was far superior, and whose methods I had studied when stationed at Portsmouth in 1908. So it happened that at first too many casualties were suffered by our own troops through faulty gun drill or inaccurate calibration. None the less, if well-trained and steadfast, they preferred that danger and to stay within the protection of the barrage as it moved forward over the enemy positions. Another difficulty was to stop the barrage from out-distancing the infantry, especially if the latter got held up. All this vastly improved with experience, but we naturally had many troubles at the beginning.

The infantry finally moved up on the night of June 30th, and the attack was launched early on July 1st. I always regretted I did not witness the march forward. I had however visited every infantry brigade headquarters, and every artillery and infantry unit during the previous two days, and I was dog-tired. I knew, of course, that I should have little rest during the battle. During the night my anxiety that all should go smoothly prevented much sleep, so I did not gain much. I knew for example of certain German machine gun positions that our guns had been trying to destroy, and I feared they had failed. In those days the use of smoke had not been worked out, so we had to depend upon direct bombardment. As it turned out, one of the enemy positions did cause us very heavy loss in the attack.

However, the first day of the battle was pretty successful. The objective was Fricourt village and wood. The plan was for the 21st Division to advance on the west, and for the 7th Division to advance on the east, and to assault the village only after both divisions had got well forward. The 21st failed at first to occupy more than the enemy's front defences, but the 7th made good progress, captured Mametz, and established a flank facing Fricourt village and wood. On the morning of the second day it was found that the Germans had withdrawn, and Fricourt was occupied by the 17th Division, thus closing the gap between the 7th and the 21st. On July 5th the 7th Division was relieved by the 38th (Welsh), and our headquarters returned to Treux. Four days later, Watts was ordered by the corps commander to replace the commander of the 38th. He agreed on condition he could take Maurice Wingfield and myself with him. So up we went to the battle HQ we had just left.

The task given to the 38th Division was to capture Mametz Wood. This was 1200 yards across and rather more from front to back, and covered the left portion of the positions captured by the 7th. We found that attacks had been made by small forces on narrow fronts with heavy artillery support with the idea, I suppose, of saving casualties. In fact 500 men had been lost without any gains at all. Such a policy had, of course, enabled the enemy to concentrate his artillery on the narrow front of the advancing infantry, and prevent them from reaching the wood. I therefore drew up a fresh plan to attack the whole front of the wood, with as good support as could be arranged, and at a meeting with the three brigade commanders and the CRA this plan was accepted. I then handed over to the regular GSO1 of the Division, and stood by as adviser only. The attack was launched next morning and the infantry seized the edge of the wood quickly, but in working through the middle of it they had a bad time. The wood was thick and movement difficult so cohesion was lost. Worse still, artillery of the 21st Division on the left began to fire on German trenches beyond, but some of their shells burst in the trees and caused casualties among the Welshmen. In spite of this the wood was taken, and its capture was essential before any further advance could be made.

On July 11th the 7th Division relieved the 38th to take part in the second offensive of the battle. The plan of the Fourth Army was to attack with two corps towards Bazentin-le-Petit on the left and Delville Wood on the right. The 7th Division was to take Bazentin-le-Grand wood, then part of Bazentin-le-Petit village and cemetery. The Army commander considered that the Germans were sufficiently shaken by the previous fighting to make an immediate attack a feasible proposition; the only alternative being a long preparation which might allow time to strengthen defences and bring up reinforcements. He proved right. The ground in front of the 7th Division rose steadily by about 100 feet for a mile to a plateau about 1000 yards deep, after which there was a slope downhill. The Germans had constructed a wired trench line along the edge of the plateau, but it appeared to be the rearmost defences of their Somme position. Our plan was to put in one brigade to attack the enemy's front line and Bazentin-le-Grand wood, with very heavy artillery support. A second brigade would then pass through and take part of Bazentin-le-Petit village. The third brigade was kept in reserve. We took every precaution we could think of—laid down tapes beforehand, and had parties of engineers and pioneers ready to follow close behind the infantry to prepare strong points in the village against counter-attack.

On July 14th, five minutes before zero hour at 3.30 a.m., there was a terrific bombardment of the enemy position. Directly it lifted the infantry took the forward positions practically without loss, and after an hour advanced to the northern edge of Bazentin-le-Grand wood. Fresh units then passed through, reached Bazentin-le-Petit * and captured the HQ of a Bavarian regiment and 200 men. Work on the strong points started at once, and progressed so well that by the time counter-attacks came in at 8.30 a.m. it was possible to hold nearly all the ground, and re-occupy the village immediately afterwards. We had now achieved our original objective, but well ahead of schedule. Although we knew that the overall plan was fixed and did not contemplate a further advance so quickly, we were desperately keen to exploit the situation. Moreover this had been foreseen. Two days before the attack Watts had gone along to Corps HQ and explained our ideas, suggesting that a division in corps reserve be held ready to renew the advance, together with our own reserve brigade. But the idea was turned down. The corps commander may have thought it unwise to alter the complicated artillery plan, or that our advance might create a dangerous salient. Despite this we considered, when the time came, we could push on unaided. So we brought up the reserve brigade, and at noon or thereabouts asked leave to advance and occupy High Wood. We were again refused on the plea that some cavalry should pass through. Finally permission

* The northern part of Bazentin-le-Petit had already been captured by the 21st Division.

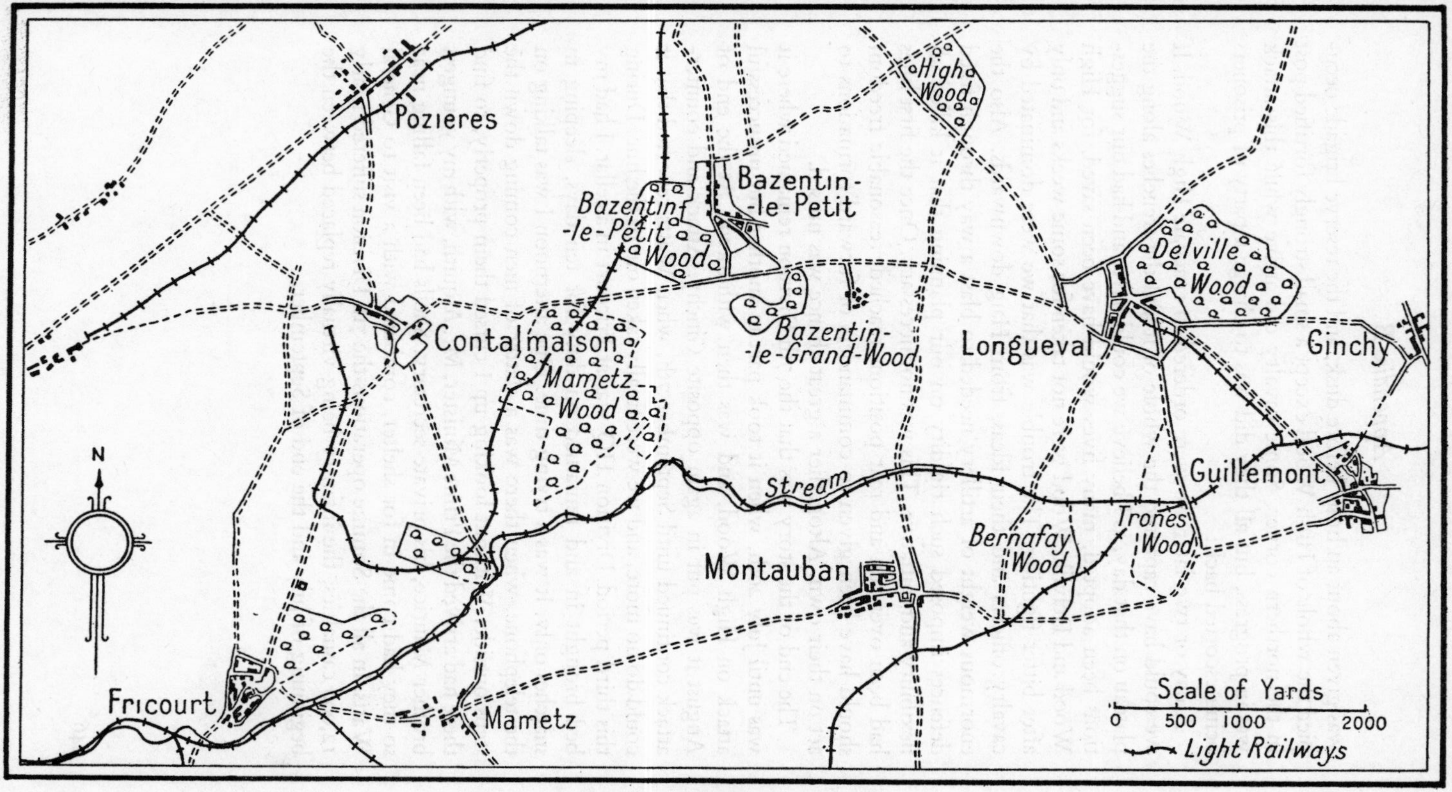

SOMME BATTLE AREA, 1916

was given about an hour before dusk, and the reserve brigade occupied the whole of High Wood except a small strongly fortified post in the northern corner. Some cavalry did arrive while this attack was in progress, but all they did was to charge a party of prisoners being escorted back!

A day or two later we were ordered to evacuate High Wood. If we could have captured the whole of it and the trenches along the plateau on that day, as I believe we could have, and had our suggestions been adopted, many lives would have been saved, for High Wood and Delville Wood were not taken for some weeks and only after bitter fighting. The trouble was that we were dominated by cavalry officers and their ideas, from Haig downwards. Also the enormous weight of artillery needed to blast a way through fixed defences imposed such rigidity on our planning that it killed all flexibility and initiative. This was not necessary. Once the first lines had been over-run and rear positions reached, reasonable freedom should have been given to commanders of forward formations to act on their own. Altogether a great chance was missed.

The end of the story was that the 7th Division remained where it was until July 20th, when it took part in another but unsuccessful attack on High Wood, and was then withdrawn. At the end of August it was put in again opposite Ginchy. Attack and counter-attack continued until September 7th, when Watts reported that it could do no more, and we were finally taken out of the line. During this third period, Division HQ was at Fricourt in a cellar. I had my bed brought in and remained on duty for ten days, sleeping in snatches only. It was a trying time. One afternoon I was talking on the telephone, when there was a clatter of men coming down the steps outside. Without looking up I cursed them properly, to find there had arrived the Prime Minister, Mr. Asquith, with my youngest brother Maurice, his private secretary. Shells had been falling near so they had come in for shelter, combined with a visit to General Watts. In all the Somme operations the 7th Division suffered nearly 12,000 casualties, the infantry being virtually replaced between the beginning of July and the end of September.

APPENDIX C

ADDRESS BY H.E. THE GOVERNOR TO THE OFFICERS OF UNITS ARRIVING IN MALTA

MALTA was in the occupation of the Knights of the Order of St. John from 1530 till 1798. During that time they combined the two duties of the Order, which were firstly to oppose the Turkish Fleet and to suppress the activities of the Barbary pirates from Algiers, Tunis and elsewhere, and secondly to act as Hospitallers. They were far from considerate masters of the Maltese.

On the 12th June, 1798, Napoleon on his way to Egypt captured Malta and turned out the Knights. After spending an active week here tightening his hold on the Island and gathering loot, he left on the 16th June and passed on to Egypt, leaving a garrison in the Island. There he met his first severe check at the battle of the Nile on the 1st August, and lost all his loot at the same time, the 'Orient' sinking with two million pounds worth of valuables from Malta in Aboukir Bay.

Naturally the importance of Malta as a harbour, easily defended, and as an admirable base for ships of war, from which the Mediterranean Sea could be dominated, was realised in England as well as in France, so that when, not long after Napoleon left, the Islanders rose against the French, they received some support, chiefly in the form of moral encouragement, from the British. The French were driven into Valetta and there besieged. Though contributions of arms and food were arranged for by Nelson it was not until February, 1800, that any serious contribution was made by the British to the strength of the besieging force, when 12,000 British troops were landed. Most of the work of the siege, therefore, was carried out by the Maltese themselves. On the 5th September, 1800, the French capitulated and the Island was handed over to the British Commander, Major-General Pigott.

By the Treaty of Amiens, March, 1802, Malta and Gozo were to be restored to the Knights, but they were never handed over as it soon became clear that peace would not last long. In fact, in May,

1803, war broke out once more between England and France. After the end of the Napoleonic wars it was not unnatural that the British Government should be unwilling to take the risk of releasing their hold on the Island. The Islanders themselves were also anxious to retain their new protectors. If you will look at the Latin inscription over the Main Guard in the Palace Square you will see that it says:—'*Magnae et Invictae Britannicae Melitensium Amor et Europae Vox Has Insulas Confirmat. A.D. 1814*', which by very free interpretation means:—'To Great Britain, unsubdued, these islands were entrusted by the powers of Europe at the wish of the Maltese themselves. A.D. 1814'.

I am not going to give any more history because what I have told you already will illustrate to you the two points I wish to make. One is that we British have been responsible for the government of Malta for 137 years, and secondly, that we have never conquered Malta.

The Maltese are a European race, probably of Phoenician origin; their language is Semitic and the root-forms are very like those of Arabic. Their origin is similar to that of the inhabitants of other countries of Southern Europe, who in ages past were overcome by migrations from the East. I was told by a great scholar that he thought the Maltese language was probably as near that spoken by Hannibal as any now existing.

The record of our Government of Malta can scarcely be called one of our greatest achievements. We have regarded Malta as an important Naval base and Fortress in the first place, and have sometimes forgotten that we owed to its people something more than only peace and protection.

In the 19th century it was an accepted principle of all British Governments that there should be as little interference as possible with the private lives and activities of their citizens. They considered it their duty to follow rather than lead public opinion. As a result, in Malta social services became backward. Since then much has been done, but much remains to be done. As an instance, at the present time we are educating only 27,000 out of 44,000 children of school age, and I could mention others.

Our Government of Malta for 137 years has always shown sympathy but it has lacked imagination. Our personal conduct has frequently lacked both.

When I first came here and was trying to learn as much about the Island as I could in a very short time, I sent for a very able Maltese Civil Servant, a man of remarkable attainments and character, and was discussing his race with him, and he said: 'You will often find it difficult to get our true opinions—we all of us suffer from an inferiority complex'. I asked him why, and he said: 'There are two reasons; first, if you ask us to give our opinion on a subject of which Malta gives us little experience we are naturally somewhat diffident; secondly, we are never certain that we are going to be treated with courtesy'.

The Commanding Officer of a Battalion that was here during the time when our differences with Italy were acute, gave me, at my request, his views on the situation in Malta. He wrote:—From the very start I have been tremendously impressed by the charm and friendliness of the Maltese and their loyalty to the King and Empire, but there was a characteristic that at first I did not understand; I now realise that it is diffidence and lack of self-assurance, and I feel convinced that it has been fostered by the attitude of many British people towards the Maltese in the past, and that it is only by the development of the change in this attitude that is being encouraged now and is already showing good results, that the Maltese will become enthusiastically British. A few nights ago it was forcibly brought home to me to what extent this inferiority complex has been caused by us even among the best-born Maltese. A charming Maltese lady unburdened herself to me on the subject and obviously felt that no Maltese were ever treated as equal by the British in Malta. She told me quite openly that not only had she been frequently rebuffed by British, but had actually been insulted.

It is partly the lack of manners by British men and women that contributed to the very serious situation that existed here some two years or more ago. You will remember that in 1935 there was great hostility in the minds of the Italians against us owing to the application of sanctions by the League of Nations; and it became clear that during the preceding few years it had been possible for the Italians to make inroads on the good feeling of the Maltese towards us by propaganda. The mass of the people, probably 99 per cent, or even more, were always loyal, but there was a small group, infinitesimal in numbers but noisy and active, who were definitely pro-Italian politically, and a considerable number of others who were feeling that after all Great Britain was not altogether such a pleasant master and was not worth active support if it entailed discomfort. That situation came about far more as a result of the bad manners of the British than any other reason, and I can assure you that if we had given the Maltese more sympathy and understanding, even from motives of good breeding and courtesy only, the fortress would be stronger from a defensive point of view.

We have every reason to be proud of our race, and while that might rightly give us self-confidence, it should never make us domineering. I can assure you that evil results of rudeness, or even mere thoughtless lack of consideration, by members of the British community, both in their social life and their dealings with shopkeepers, working people and others in similar positions, have been very serious.

Let me give you one small example of what I call thoughtless lack of consideration. It is a common failing of English people to refer to the Maltese as 'Malts'. This term is regarded rightly by the Maltese as contemptuous, and I urge you never to use it. Why hurt unnecessarily the feelings of our fellow-subjects and thereby incidentally do an injury to the Empire?

It is not difficult to suggest reasons for the attitude so often taken up by British Officers of all services, and their wives, in the past. The first cause of all is that most of us are terribly ignorant about Malta and many of us do not trouble to learn. May I urge you therefore, to take an interest in the history of Malta and in the treasures it contains. Much can be learnt from guide books but to those who care to read more deeply Sir Themistocles Zammit's 'Malta' is the best general work, and there are others. Another cause is that we officers have so often adopted in Malta the same attitude towards its people that we do in other colonies and military stations. In practically all other colonies the inhabitants are coloured and non-Christian, so that social intercourse with them is often difficult and sometimes impossible. It is worth remembering, however, that in India our lack of manners did much to foster and strengthen the political agitations of past years. Some of the most violent anti-British agitators in India took the first step in their careers as such owing to some slight or rudeness by British officers. Zaghlul Pasha in Egypt began his political career as pro-British and as the friend of Cromer.

In Malta no such excuse can be urged. Malta is, for all practical purposes, the only colony in the British Empire in which the inhabitants are European, for one quarter of the people of Cyprus are Turkish; the inhabitants of Gibraltar are Spaniards, but their position in relation to us is somewhat different; and the Falkland Islands are unimportant as having a population of only 2500. There are no others.

As regards language, Maltese is the ordinary tongue of all classes, but the educated classes, with practically no exceptions, now also speak English. There is, therefore, now no difficulty of language in social intercourse.

When you meet the Maltese you will find them to be friendly and easy to get on with. I urge you to take every opportunity to make friends with them. Naturally you will not get a great number of opportunities of meeting them to start with, but a good many will call on your mess—and among the officers of the Royal Malta Artillery and of the King's Own Malta Regiment, which is a Territorial unit, you will meet many very pleasant men and keen soldiers.

It is of enormous importance to the Empire that Malta should never be in danger of capture by an enemy.

If we were to fail to hold Malta, our position on the Suez Canal and in Egypt would be precarious, we should probably lose the Sudan and have to withdraw from Palestine, if it were possible. I am convinced that a failure to hold Malta would mean the end of the British Empire.

If all the Maltese were British in feeling, not only from self-interest but also from devotion to British institutions and affection for the British people, as indeed a great number are, one danger would be removed permanently. There would be no fear of the spread of Italian influence in the Island and Italian propaganda would lose all power.

The Maltese would soon become aggressively British if our Government and those of the Dominions were to treat them exactly in the same way as we treat each other, in fact, as in every way our equals, and if friendships between ourselves and them were more common.

So I urge you all (including your wives) to guard your tongues and watch your manners and to let us make some amends now and repair the evil which our predecessors in Malta have wrought by a racial exclusiveness that did much harm. If you do so, you will find, I am sure, that your advances are met more than half-way, you will make pleasant friends and acquaintances, and you will be doing a service of great value to the Empire. I can assure you that there is no people more responsive to friendliness than the Maltese.

CHARLES BONHAM-CARTER

1936

INDEX

This is a selective index. Entries serve as a guide to further subjects and personalities described in the text.

Index

Index

PRINTED BY R. & R. CLARK, LTD., EDINBURGH